POPE PIUS XII LIB., ST. JOSEPH

3 2528 01325

Hammering Swords into Ploughshares

Essays in Honor of
Archbishop
Mpilo Desmond Tutu

EDITED BY BUTI TLHAGALE
AND ITUMELENG MOSALA

WILLIAM B. EERDMANS PUBLISHING COMPANY
GRAND RAPIDS, MICHIGAN

AFRICA WORLD PRESS, INC.
TRENTON, NEW JERSEY

Copyright © 1986 The Desmond Tutu Theology Series Committee
First published 1986 by Skotaville Publishers, Johannesburg

This edition jointly published 1987 through special arrangement with Skotaville
by Wm. B. Eerdmans Publishing Co.,
255 Jefferson Ave. S.E., Grand Rapids, Mich. 49503
and Africa World Press, Inc.,
P.O. Box 1892, Trenton, N.J. 08608

All rights reserved
Printed in the United States of America

Library of Congress Cataloging-in-Publication Data

Hammering swords into ploughshares.

    1. Tutu, Desmond.   2. Peace — Religious aspects —
Christianity.   3. South Africa — Race relations.
4. South Africa — Church history.   I. Tutu, Desmond.
II. Tlhagale, B. (Buti) III. Mosala, I. (Itumeleng)
BX5700.6.Z8T8745   1987   276.8′082   87-5242

Eerdmans ISBN 0-8028-0269-9
Africa World ISBN 0-86543-054-3

Acknowledgements

The Editors and Publishers gratefully acknowledge the contribution by individuals and organizations who helped in various ways when this book was researched, collated and published. A word of thanks goes especially to Ms Enid Siwisa for typing the final draft of the manuscript and the Black Theology Project under whose auspices this book was compiled.

Some of the articles were first presented on the rostrum for community organizations or theological journals and appear in this book with kind permission.

Contributors

Millard W. Arnold: African-American lawyer.

Allan Boesak: Moderator of the NG Mission Church.

David Bosch: Professor of Theology, University of South Africa.

James H. Cone: Charles H. Briggs Professor of Systematic Theology at Union Theological Seminary, New York.

John W. de Gruchy: Professor of Religious Studies, University of Cape Town.

Sheena Duncan: Senior official of Black Sash, a human rights pressure group.

Siqibo Dwane: Bishop of the Order of Ethiopia.

Bonganjalo Goba: Senior lecturer in Theology, University of South Africa.

Shun Govender: Secretary General of the Belydende Kring.

T.S.N. Gqubule: Principal, John Wesley College, Federal Seminary, Pietermaritzburg.

John Lamola: Co-ordinator of Theology in a church correspondence college.

Essy Letsoalo: Field researcher in the rural areas of the Northern Transvaal.

Simon Maimela: Professor of Theology, University of South Africa.

Sophie Mazibuko: Director, Dependents Conference, South African Council of Churches.

K.E.M. Mgojo: Theology lecturer and President of the Federal Seminary.

Mmutlanyane Stanley Mogoba: Secretary General of the Methodist Church of Southern Africa.

Itumeleng Mosala: Lecturer in Old Testament and Black Theology, University of Cape Town.

Mokgethi Motlhabi: Director of the Educational Opportunities Council.

Cecil Mzingisi Ngcokovane: Theology lecturer at the Federal Seminary.

Albert Nolan: Catholic priest and official of the Institute for Contextual Theology.

Lebamang Sebidi: Director of Adult Education at the Funda Centre, Soweto.

Gabriel M. Setiloane: Assistant Professor of Religious Studies, University of Cape Town.

Buti Tlhagale: Catholic priest and liaison officer at the Educational Opportunities Council.

Charles Villa-Vicencio: Professor of Religious Studies, University of Cape Town.

Benjamin Witbooi: Theology lecturer at the Federal Seminary.

Paulus Zulu: Research Analyst, Industrial Relations, University of Natal.

Preface

This collection of essays in honour of Archbishop Desmond Mpilo Tutu takes its title from what must be one of the most revolutionary, even socialist, texts of the Bible : "They will beat their swords into ploughshares, their spears into pruning knives ... Each man shall sit under his vine, under his own fig tree; And no one will be terrorised ..." (Micah 4:3,4).

It is an appropriate title, both to Archbishop Desmond Tutu and to the contributions which his fellow Christians and theologians have written in honour of him. *Hammering Swords into Ploughshares* seeks to defend and explain the dignity and ministry of a much maligned person. For a man who has been so maligned as to be identified with those who collude with acts of terrorism it was necessary for a group of self-respecting fellow Christians to come together to defend and explain his real stance that *Swords must be beaten into ploughshares.* Thus the support which Desmond Tutu received for being chosen Nobel Peace Prize winner, and that is expressed again in many of the articles in this book, is eloquent testimony to his real stance in matters of peace and justice.

Hammering Swords into Ploughshares, nevertheless, seeks to defend and explain the dignity and ministry of a perennially misconstrued person. In a world in which ideological forces vie for dominance, and in which struggles are easily hijacked for opposite purposes to the original, it was necessary to explain Tutu's position that peace is not a passive spiritual condition, the absence of conflict (to use a tired phrase). In fact, contrary to middle-class liberal distortions of peace, *Hammering Swords into Ploughshares* seeks to reaffirm Tutu's stance in agreement with Herbert Marcuse's perceptive words that:

> "In terms of historical function, there is a difference between revolutionary and reactionary violence, between violence practised by the oppressed and by the oppressors. In terms of ethics, both forms of violence are inhuman and evil — but since when is history made in accordance with ethical standards? To start applying them at the point where the oppressed rebel against oppressors, the have-nots against the haves is serving the cause of actual violence by weakening the protest against it".[1]

It is this understanding in Tutu's stance in the disinvestment/divestment debate which his liberal exegetes have almost deliberately ignored. For them swords that are used to kill the oppressed must be proliferated because prior to being used in this way they offer the oppressed jobs! Talk about convoluted logic! But no, when it comes from the privileged classes it is not convoluted logic, it is "hard-nosed Realism"!!

Hammering Swords into Ploughshares, in the spirit of Tutu's ministry, sees the call for peace as not simply a call to lay down arms, irrespective of whether one is speaking of the liberation movements or the government forces. The call to peace is more and deeper than that. It can only be properly understood in terms of a transformation of Swords into Ploughshares, Spears into Pruning Knives. To translate this into modern parlance, the call to peace is empty unless it means a transformation of both AK-47's and Casspirs and tear-gas canisters into Houses, into Clothing, into Food, into Medicine, into Transport, and into *free* productive activities; into a state of complete absence of fear. In point of fact, *real peace* is not possible unless it is understood in basic biblical terms: "Each man shall sit under his vine, under his own fig-tree; And no one will be terrorised".

Hammering Swords into Ploughshares is also a challenge to Archbishop Desmond Tutu in terms of his ministry shifting locale to the area of South Africa where KTC and Crossroads serve as constant distraction from the apparent peace which the City of Cape Town and its environs exude, especially for those who have the wherewithal to enjoy it. Can swords be turned into ploughshares in these parts?

In biblical hermeneutical terms, *Hammering Swords into Ploughshares* is a call to the biblical roots, understood as an attempt to connect with the struggles of the poor and the oppressed in the Bible without simplistically taking the entire Bible to be on the side of the poor and the oppressed. But equally, *Hammering Swords into Ploughshares* is a call to the Black roots, as many of the articles attest; it is a call to a recovery of the trajectory of Black struggle as an important discursive weapon in theological practice against oppressive structures.

In short, *Hammering Swords into Ploughshares* is a fitting tribute to a son of the soil, *(mwan' envu)* whose life and ministry are dedicated to the liberation of the oppressed and exploited.

ITUMELENG JERRY MOSALA
University of Cape Town August 1986

Reference Note

1. Herbert Marcuse "Repressive Tolerance", *Critical Sociology* (ed) Paul Connerton, Penguin Books, Hammondsworth, (1976) pp. 315f.

Contents

Contents (continued)

Contents (continued)

Part 1

Personal Tributes

CHARLES VILLA-VICENCIO

Archbishop Desmond Tutu: From Oslo to Cape Town

South Africa has never treated its Nobel Prize winners very well, but then has not had much practice. The only other South African recipient of such a prize was Albert Luthuli, President of the banned African National Congress, who said "I am in Congress precisely because I am a Christian." He was banned in 1959 and received the Peace Prize for 1960.[1] Obviously one of South Africa's greatest sons, his award was greeted with derision by the government, scorn by many white South Africans, and jubilation by most black South Africans. Archbishop Tutu's award has been greeted in the land of his birth in a slightly different way. This time there was an official silence from the government, although some mutterings about a "political award" have been heard. Yet, even the staunchly pro-government newspaper *Die Vaderland,* thought that while "the man says things that stick in one's claw and send blood rushing to one's head ... formal congratulations by the State for one of its citizens who had gained international recognition decidedly would have been in order".[2] But South Africa is a strange and divided society. Even those who are supposedly "on the Archbishop's side", have responded with reservation. Dr. Alan Paton, for example, seems to feel that the Peace Prize should go to someone whose concern is to feed the hungry and not one who calls for economic pressure which "could put a man out of a job and make his family go hungry so that some high moral principle could be upheld."[3] Someone else concluded his contribution to a discussion on the award with the resigned comment: "Well he's certainly not Mother Theresa." To which yet another responded, "Thank God for that." The retort intended no disrespect for Mother Theresa, but rather recognition that it would take a different kind of initiative to bring peace, feed the hungry and institute social justice in South Africa.

Scarcely having learned to live with a home-grown Peace Prize laureate, South Africans were asked to take a futher quantum leap. The turbulent priest became the first black Anglican Archbishop of Cape Town. The elective assembly of the Diocese of Cape Town, meeting at Diocesan College, Rondebosch, gathered amidst weeks of speculation whether anyone could be elected ahead of Bishop Tutu. Newspapers weighed and assessed every aspect of this man's career and character: He had rescued a supposed police informer from the wrath of a lynch mob, he had lashed out at blacks for killing fellow-blacks, he had said that South African blacks would welcome invading Russians as liberators, and he called on the international community to apply punitive sanctions immediately against South Africa. State controlled radio and television services castigated the man, and did their best to create a gross caricature of all that he stood for. Despite this the election process moved quickly. There was a two-thirds majority on the first ballot in favour of Bishop Tutu in both the houses of clergy and laity, and the Synod of Bishops approved the choice unanimously.[4]

The Rt Rev Kenneth Oram, who presided over the elections as Dean of the Province of South Africa, assured the press gathered outside of the Diocesan College that the assembly had been "fully aware of what they were doing". The Dean of Cape Town, Ted King, was "delighted". Alan Paton would rather have had someone else but hoped "the new Archbishop would do well", while Louis Nel, the Deputy Minister of Information said that he trusted that "his eminence would assist in the socio-economic development of all people in South Africa which is *of necessity dependent on economic growth*". In welcoming the Bishop's election, the Archbishop of Canterbury, Dr Robert Runcie, said he is "a spiritual leader of the kind that South Africa needs at this moment". And Bishop Tutu? "I am overwhelmed and deeply shattered by the sense of responsibility that God, through the Church, is placing on my shoulders". Then, more pensively, he continued: "I suppose some people will not exactly be enamoured by my election... If they are angry with me they must not be angry with God".

Heads of Churches in South Africa have in the past often stood amidst controversy, and Anglican Archbishops have been no exception. The first Anglican bishop of Cape Town, Robert Gray arrived in 1848 — and the fledgling Church of the Province of South Africa was soon thrown almost immediately into controversy with Gray charging his erstwhile friend Bishop Colenso of Natal with heresy.[5] A century later in 1948 the ruling National Party came to power in South Africa, and in that same year, Geoffrey Clayton was elected Archbishop of Cape Town. Close on a decade later (1957) he would stand in confrontation with Dr Hendrik Verwoerd, the then Minister of Native Affairs, whose Native Laws Amendment Bill would make it virtually impossible for black people to worship in churches located in so-called white areas. Clayton wrote to the Minister stating: "... we feel bound to state that if the Bill were to become a law in its present form we should ourselves be unable to obey it or to counsel our clergy and people to do so". Clayton took Ambrose Reeves, the Bishop of Johannesburg aside and said, "Reeves, I don't want to go to prison. I'm an old man. I don't want to end my days in prison, but I'll go if I have to".

That was Ash Wednesday. The next day Clayton was dead.[6] He was succeeded by Joost de Blank in October of that same year. These were politically intense times and de Blank resisted the State on every issue. He provoked, cajoled, confronted and charmed his adversaries.[7]

There have also been less charismatic Anglican leaders, but clearly Desmond Tutu stands firmly in the tradition of Gray, Clayton and de Blank. Said a senior Anglican cleric recently: "He is of the same kidney as de Blank — in political posture as well as lifestyle. Bishopscourt is already being prepared!"

Desmond Tutu lives life boldy. He celebrates what is good with a certain exuberance. He fights what is wrong, and he ministers often controversially, to all people. He has always done this. The conferring of the Peace Prize, and more recently his election as Archbishop, incited each of these tendencies. His enthronement promises to be the biggest and most colourful event seen in Cape Town for years. He has dismissed President Reagan's speech on South Africa as "nauseating". "The West", rejects sanctions, and "for my part, can go to hell." Yet, not without severe criticism from the black community, he has met with P W Botha "for frank talks". This, he argues, is all part of what it means to be a minister of the church of Jesus Christ.

Archbishop Tutu is a man of peace, and it is here that the controversy begins.

Allan Boesak reminded the Vancouver Assembly of the WCC that "peace is never simply the absence of war, it is the active presence of justice...one cannot use the issue of peace to escape from the unresolved issue of injustice, poverty, hunger and racism."

If we do, then we will make of our concern for peace an ideology of oppression which in the end will be used to justify injustice".[8] It is this affirmation for peace — *shalom,* the active, positive exaltation of justice and social harmony, which Bishop Tutu has come to symbolize. He is an ethical realist, and knows that it will take moral, political and economic pressure to reverse the tide of injustice and black exploitation in this country. He has recognized with Reinhold Niebuhr that peace and justice will come "only by setting the power of the exploited against the exploiters",[9] and with Martin Luther King that "evil must be attacked by a counteracting persistence, by the day to day assault on the battering rams of injustice".[10]

The Nobel Prize awards committee has consistently recognized these kinds of peacemakers, as well as the saintly figures of this world, like Mother Theresa.

Archbishop Tutu's award is an honourable tradition. It includes names like those of Albert Luthuli, Martin Luther King and Lech Walesa. The institutional church has, in turn, often rejected those of its sons and daughters who have used the very teaching on which they have been raised to challenge and disturb society. Desmond Tutu has disturbed both churches and society, but his church has now made him the contemporary representative of an honourable tradition of "fighters for God". To recognize Archbishop Tutu as standing within this tradition is not to affirm him in a hagiographic way. To affirm those who have gone before us is to recognize that others, like the Archbishop, in all their human ambiguity, stand tall within that tradition. In so doing we are content to know that we follow precisely in the *amasiko* of the African people, as we affirm our fathers and our mothers in the faith.

A Curriculum Vitae

In his own unique way the Archbishop entertained, and needled, the recent Eloff Commission, appointed by the government to investigate the activities of the South African Council of Churches, by explaining, with a touch of irony, how his father Zachariah, a school headmaster and a somewhat proud Fingo, inexplicably married Aletha Matlhare, a Motswana woman, who washed clothes for a white family. Is he Xhosa or Motswana? He soon, together with his two sisters, learned to speak Xhosa and Tswana as well as English and Afrikaans. His roots are inherently African. He can be no other. He is intensely South African, and yet when he shows his "travel document" to an international audience, it declares the nationality of the Archbishop as "indeterminable at present". Such are the tragic complexities of South Africa's bantustan policy.

The rest reads much like an impressive CV of any other internationally acclaimed person,while the record of his early schooling carries the scars of segregated "Bantu" education.

• Born, 7 October 1931 in Klerksdorp in the Transvaal.
• Married Leah Nomalizo Shenxane, a school teacher, and former student of his father.
• The Tutu's have four children: Trevor Thamsanqa, Theresa Thandeka, Naomi Nontombi, and Mpho Andrea.
• He attended and matriculated at the Johannesburg Bantu High School, Western Native Township, 1945-50.
• Teacher's Diploma from Pretoria Bantu College, 1951-53.
• A correspondence BA degree from the University of South Africa, 1954-58.
• Taught at Johannesburg Bantu High School, and then at Munsieville High School in Krugersdorp, 1955-58.
• Licentiate in Theology at St Peter's Theological College, Rosettenville, Johannesburg, 1958-60.
• Ordained deacon, 1960.
• Ordained priest, 1961.
• Student at Kings College, University of London, and part-time curate at St Alban's, living in Golders Green, London, 1962-65.
• BD Hons, and M.Th. (London), and part-time curate at St Mary's Blechingley, in Surrey.
• Lectured at the Federal Theological Seminary, Alice, Cape Province, and Anglican chaplain to Fort Hare University, 1967-69.
• Lecturer in the Department of Theology, University of Botswana, Lesotho and Swaziland, in Roma, Lesotho, 1970-72.
• Associate Director, Theological Education Fund of the WCC, based in Bromley, Kent, 1972-75.
• Anglican Dean of Johannesburg, 1975-76.
• Bishop of Lesotho, 1976-78.
• General Secretary, SACC, 1978-85.
• Nobel Peace Prize laureate 1984.
• Bishop of Johannesburg 1985.
• The Order of Jamaica 1986.
• Archbishop of Cape Town 1986.

The conferences he has attended are too numerous to mention here, and lists of lectures, speeches and sermons delivered around the world would fill many pages. It is at this point that the CV throws off its mundane character, and when it begins to address the topic of awards, it becomes almost unique. Fellow of Kings College, London, ten honorary doctorates, a designated member of numerous international societies, the recipient of several international awards and medals, and Nobel Peace Prize laureate for 1984. Yet there is a strange and yet predictable irony about this list of acclamations — not one honorary doctorate from a South African university, and when the diocese of Johannesburg met shortly after it was announced that he would receive the Peace Prize, it was not able to give him the clear majority required to be elected Bishop of Johannesburg. It required a meeting of the Synod of Bishops to elect him. But, eighteen months later, his election as Archbishop was quite clear and decisive.

But who is the Archbishop?

A record of accolades and snubs does not ultimately enable one to identify the person of Desmond Tutu. Indeed human identity is simply too complex to be understood at all, but these are some of the facets of the Archbishop's character which stand out in bold relief:

He is a strong person in his own right. On receiving the news, while on sabbatical in New York, that he had been named Peace Prize laureate, he responded by saying, "the prize is for all of those engaged in the struggle at home". In a sense he is a product of that struggle but he is also a person in his own right, who has bravely taken risks, boldly paid the price of resistance, and courageously declared his priorities in life. But perhaps what stands out most clearly in his person is the mix of dignity and commonality, which characterizes his person. He carries all the pomp, ceremony and lavishness associated with high church episcopacy with aplomb, distinction and even a sense of regality. Yet he is also a man of the people, a simple parish priest and a son of the soil of Africa. He can talk with all the solemnity and precision of an ecclesiastical teacher of things divine, and laugh, joke and taunt with all the eloquence of the Soweto and Johannesburg streets. He is a man for all occasions. He can speak to alienated black youth, to the most pious evangelicals, to white nationalist Afrikaners, and to the secular business fraternity. So talented is he in "becoming all things to all men", in order to "save some", that it has been asked whether his own credibility was not at stake. Never aloof, or given to the kind of ideological purity which locks him into a ghetto of moralistic purity, he manages to make his point in that way which cuts to the quick. Yet this he does with an

ineluctable humour, and in a disarming manner.
He is a personable man, ready to make a phone call or write a note
or send flowers at the right moment. He can speak to the highest in
the land as an equal. "I am writing to you as one human person to
another human person, gloriously created in the image of the selfsame God, redeemed by the selfsame Son of God" he once wrote to
the irate and intractable Prime Minister of the time, John Vos-
ter.[11] He is a great leveller, reminding his oppressors that they will
end up as the "flotsam and jetsam of history because the liberation
God of the Exodus is always on the side of the underdog.[12] He
can be unguardedly honest. He, on an occasion with provocation,
told a meeting of ecclesiastical leaders gathered from around the
African continent that there were presently more violations of human rights in parts of Africa than there were in the much maligned
colonial days. "This," he said, "you cannot allow to continue for
the sake of Africa, and for the sake of those of us who continue in
captivity in the south. It militates against our struggle." On
another occasion, the assembly of the WCC meeting in Vancouver,
struggled to formulate its response to the Soviet invasion of
Afghanistan in the face of the cautious response of the Russian
Orthodox Church. He said sternly to the South Africans with
whom he was sitting, "An unequivocal stand by this will certainly
make our stand easier at home!" Then more graciously, he later
conceded that each church was to determine its own style of prophetic ministry. To which a Geneva bureaucrat responded that
"the WCC can only support the stance taken by member churches
and local churches in their witness. We dare go no further." When
one looks at the far less equivocal stance of the WCC assembly on
South Africa, one knows that this was testimony to the witness of
the SACC under the leadership of the Bishop in South Africa.

He is a profoundly religious person. The Archbishop is profoundly
religious in a way that most Protestants, and certainly those within
the free-church tradition, cannot understand. He is a man of prayer,
meditations and fasting. An SACC staff retreat has often included
several days of silence, and when those non-conforming participants
felt constrained to break their silence in an enclave of talk and re-
freshments, the Archbishop would suitably reprimand them, but also
benignly tolerate his less "ascetic" brothers and sisters.

He carries with him a deep sense of spiritual assurance. At times he
will withdraw to be alone, or say mass, and then announce "God's
declared purpose" for the church in South Africa. It is this, at times
magisterial sense of conviction, which earned the response of a delegate

at an SACC consultation on racism at St Peter's Conference Centre at
Hammanskraal, "You put me at a disadvantage Father, I would dare to
argue with you but not with God". Such resolution comes to him from
thought, debate, political analysis and consultation, but never without
prayer and meditation. It is the latter which makes him both confident
and also dogmatic at times. Yet he has an enormous sense of grace,
which encompasses his enemies as well as his friends.

He will go to the second mile, consult with the Prime Minister,
when counselled not to, and "try again" when everyone has given
up trying. Yet there comes a moment when he will simply dig in
his heels and compromise no further. Former Prime Minister Vos-
ter discovered this when the Archbishop terminated his talks with
the government several years ago. The Minister of Law and Order
experienced another side of the Archbishop's resolve when he told
him: "Mr Minister, we must remind you that you are not God.
You are just a man. One day your name shall merely be a faint
scribble on the pages of history while the name of Jesus Christ, the
Lord of the Church, shall live forever."[13]

This certainty and audacity, which tempers while it sustains his
affirmation of grace, is firmly grounded in an all-embracing theology of history. An academic in his own right, he has debated with
the most articulate scholars around and never compromised his
sense of God's hand being operative in history. In the heady and
radical sixties, as death of God theology was sweeping South Africans universities, he had addressed the students of Rhodes University, availing himself to all the arguments of the philosophical and
theological tradition to affirm the God of history who he saw to be
operative in the affairs of the land. Liberal white students, well
versed in the jargon and word games of the day listened in silence,
and ultimately responded with silence. Desmond Tutu's scholarly
paper was beyond their ability to understand.

It is also his depth of religious belief which has given him courage to stride in where others have feared to tread. The worst thing
that can happen to us, he often says, is for them to kill us. This he
can handle because "Death" he insist, "is not the worst thing that
could happen to a Christian."[14]

He is an activist. Christians have repeated it by rote over the years:
faith without works is dead. Nobody can accuse the Archbishop of
lacking spirituality and faith, but neither can the critics of the church,
who accuse Christians of using their religion to escape the world, find
any evidence for such a claim in the life of Desmond Tutu. Whenever
there is action, protest, unrest, police violence, forced removals,

strikes or student boycotts, he is engaged and concerned. At times his participation could be described as reckless. He has met banned African National Congress delegates in Europe, and while some judged it prudent for him to keep this secret, he returned home to announce the success of his talks with them. He has made no secret of his support for the general aims of this organization, while stating that at the present time he could not support all their methods.

His participation has also been provocative. He has a natural propensity to take the debate to his opponents. This is nowhere clearer than in the parallels he draws between the black struggle for human dignity and political rights, and the struggle waged earlier this century by the Afrikaners for the same ends. The masterliness of the art of debate in this regard was perhaps nowhere better seen than in his submission to the Eloff Commission:

> The aim of the church is to bring about social justice. Justice must be done to the poor and oppressed and if the present system does not serve this purpose, the public conscience must be roused to demand another. If the church does not exert itself for justice in society, and together with the help she can offer, also be prepared to serve as the champion for the cause of the poor, others will do it. The poor have the right to say: I do not ask for your charity, but I ask to be given an opportunity to live a life of human dignity.[15]

It all sounds so much like what the SACC was being accused of by the Eloff Commission. This, to quote from the report of the Commission, was that the Council was involved in "political, social and economic issues". Yet, as the Archbishop pointed out, those were not his words but those of Rev. C.D. Brink, spoken to the Afrikaner Volkskongres, in promoting the cause of the Afrikaner poor during the depression of the nineteen thirties.

Peace Prize Laureate and Archbishop

In December Archbishop Desmond Mpilo Tutu received the Nobel Peace Prize for 1984. The previous year which constituted the focal point of the selection process for the peace prize winner, was not significantly or qualitatively different from former years: The Eloff Commission, which was in existence for more than two years, heard the bulk of its evidence that filled eighty-two volumes during 1983, and finally published its report in February 1984. The main charge of the Commission was that the SACC is undermining the political and economic structure of the South African state. This commission eventually gave to the SACC, and the struggle of oppressed people in South Africa, a measure of visibility and exposure that could not have been bought with millions of rands of advertising. Then, when the WCC General Assembly met in Vancouver the South African government again provided the infrastructure for Tutu's exposure. He was at first denied a passport to travel and then after extensive representations and the usual bureaucratic bungling he was given a "travel document", enabling him to attend the assembly. This, however, meant he arrived late, after other dignitaries and many others who fight the good fight for human and political rights in places of oppression around the world. He received a hero's welcome, with the eyes of the media on him alone. Now, this man who has come to be recognized by the entire world as among South Africa's greatest sons, is not only the chief pastor of the Anglican Church in this country — but possibly the best known cleric to be found anywhere.

It is, however, important to end this comment where it began. Archbishop Tutu is also a person in his own right, not only the symbol of a greater struggle, or a world-wide movement for peace and justice. His recognition is therefore one which warrants acclaim for him in his own right. In his own right he stands in the *amasiko* of Africa. It is, however, also important to reflect on the thoughts of Robert Mangaliso Sobukwe, the banned Pan Africanist Congress leader, influential as he was in the Archbishop's life, who mused as he lay dying from cancer in Groote Schuur Hospital: "...we must cling to the message and not the person — and this is a message of faith, of hope, and of glory. Don't forget, also of glory." Archbishop Tutu is ultimately a preacher and as such the bearer of a message.

REFERENCE NOTES
1. Albert Luthuli, *Let My People Go* (London: Collins, 1962).
2. Harold Pakendorf in *Die Vaderland*, October 1984.
3. Alan Paton in the *Sunday Times* October 21, 1984.
4. The *Cape Times,* April 15, 1986. Other quotations on Archbishop Tutu's election are from newspaper reports during this time.
5. Jeff Guy, *The Heretic: A study of the Life of John William Colenso, 1814-1883.* (Johannesburg: Ravan Press, 1983).
6. Alan Paton, *Apartheid and the Archbishop: The Life and times of Geoffrey Clayton* (Cape Town: David Philip, 1973), p. 286.
7. Victor C Paine, *The Confrontation Between the Archbishop of Cape Town Joost de Blank and the South African Government on Racial Policies (1957-1963)* An M.A. Thesis submitted to the Department of Religious Studies, University of Cape Town, 1978.
8. Allan Boesak, "Jesus Christ the Life of the World," *Journal of Theology for South Africa,* No. 45, Dec 1985, pp. 48-54.

9. Reinhold Niebuhr, *The Contribution of Religion to Social Work*. (New York: Columbia University, 1932), p. 82.
10. John J Ansbro, *Martin Luther King Jnr: The Making of a Mind* (Maryknoll Orbis Books, 1984), p. 160.
11. Desmond M Tutu, *Hope and Suffering* (Johannesburg: Skotaville Publishers, 1983), p. 1.
12. Buti Tlhagale, "Introduction", *Ibid*. p. XII.
13. Quoted in Allan Boesak, "Jesus Christ the Light of the World", *Journal of Theology for Southern Africa*.
14. Tutu, *Hope and Suffering*, p. 13.
15. Archbishop Tutu's submission to the Eloff Commission of Inquiry into the South African Council of Churches, 1982.

SOPHIE MAZIBUKO

Archbishop Tutu — The Man

He joined the staff of the South African Council of Churches (SACC) in 1978 as its first black General Secretary following the Reverend John Thorne who took office six months before but had to resign the post due to ill-health.

His first few months were self-informative — finding out who his colleagues were, their backgrounds and where they were then, spiritually and socially. To do this, he introduced times of introspection and praying, times of sorting out relationships, times of establishing relationships with God and fellow Christians, times of planning and evaluating for oneself into the SACC during a staff retreat held over four days at a quiet spot in one of Johannesburg's less elite suburbs.

This retreat was the beginning of a long, meaningful and appreciated leadership of Desmond Mpilo Tutu. He penetrated the lives of some fifty staff members who fondly called him Baba (Father). I am referring to a cross-section of people — Africans, so-called coloureds, whites and Indians. Under his leadership, colour was unknown and not recognized. Staff changes were not common and when they did occur, people realized that they had joined a different organization and not the ogre some people in this country had painted it.

Baba was a warm and sensitive person — all staff problems were his own and he knew what to say when. He was like a well from which all drank to quench thirst, he was a symbol of hope, determination and preparedness.

In 1982 the South African government instituted an enquiry into the financial affairs and workings of the SACC. Throughout this hectic and trying period, this prophet was the only one who kept staff members sane and sober, controlled and logical. As a result, no one ever resigned from work despite an uncertain and doubtful future.

In the midst of all the uncertainty regarding the future and the possible closure of the SACC, his concern and love spurred the staff on and injected enthusiasm into all. His wit and humour brought life into SACC staff members throughout his seven years of service. Some of his jokes, daily life and public appearances are well known to many Christians in this country, and they characterize Baba at all times.

Instances when he has been very angry and hurt to the point of crying are common. This shows his sensitivity to issues whether they affect him personally or not, it is an indication of his humanity.

He is Xhosa — should carry a Transkeian passport, he has no vote, no permanent residence in the urban area, he is the Archbishop of Cape Town. How ludicrous! When does he stop being black and start being a colourless Archbishop? These are but some of the things be must face even though it may not be easy. So much for reform and the status quo!

Earlier on, I mentioned his concern, warmth and sensitivity to people's problems. May I now cite an example. One staff member, an innate baptized Afrikaner, who never touched black hands, and was very adhering to white desires and aspirations, principles and relationships with blacks, had a problem, viz;

— Working with the SACC.
— Under a black boss.
— Having to be touched/kissed by a black person now and again (leaving or arriving in South Africa).
— Having to share personal (monetary) problems with a black boss.
— Having to share emotional problems with a black boss.
— Having to accept the fact that a black has made it "over a white".
— Having to be subordinate to a black. This particular person is today a changed person because he has proved that there is no black person/ogre; but that we are all created in His image and love. An instance which persuaded his thinking is of one occasion when he was lonely and forlorn and needed someone to relate to. Archbishop Tutu came to his rescue and demon-

strated God's love to him by being practically involved in rendering material assistance to his family in need.

Also when Tutu arrived back from overseas after a strenuous three months' tour, he had just learned that he was winner of the highest and most important prize in history — the Nobel Peace Prize for 1984.

Hundreds of people awaited his return and among them — an elderly white woman who, like most of us, had had several emotionally draining experiences. On sight, he wanted to know how she had coped with her problems during the few months of his absence! (Not implying that he would help — but just expressing concern). The lady was overwhelmed and to this day, she understands more than any other person (black or white) what it is to belong and to be wanted.

Now, to come to the day to day happenings in our lives at the SACC offices, first at Diakonia House and subsequently at Khotso House (The House of Peace) in the heart of metropolitan Johannesburg.

The man called Mpilo brought a new dimension into the lives of the inhabitants of Khotso House. Over the years the tenants of this building have shared common fellowship, fun, love, aspirations, expectations, friendships and sorrow and have developed to be a community undivided in goals and intent.

The normal day at Khotso House starts with morning prayers conducted by a group of four members from the Khotso House Community. By the way, the Khotso House Community consists of:

First floor	— EOC: Educational Opportunities Council
	CCAWUSA: Commercial and Catering Allied Workers Union of South Africa and Black Sash.
Second floor	— CPSA: Head offices for the Church of the Province of South Africa.
	IMP: Inter Church Media Programmes
	DWEP: Domestic Workers Employees Project.
Third Floor	— SACC; Administration and Finances.
Fourth floor	— FELCSA, ELCSA and SACC Youth Project.
Fifth floor	— SACC — Justice and Society — Bursaries Section, Dependents Conference, Justice and Reconciliation.

| | Justice and Development — Inter Church Aid, Home and Family Life and Womens Desk. |
| Sixth floor | — UDF: United Democratic Front, Annex — cleaners. |

Despite all this — and the extent and number of people — Baba knew them all, even the house staff (cleaning and security). He would make a fuss about their birthdays, family anniversaries, deaths, births, achievements, sorrows, illnesses and successes and all that attributed and enhanced family life.

Baba was loved by all — he was the pivot of all happenings at Diakonia and Khotso House.

Now, on a person to person attribute, he is very emotional, he cries and laughs easily. I recall many instances at morning prayers when he broke down, but I will not forget how he wept after the invasion of Maseru in Lesotho by the South African Defence Force (SADF), and also at the funeral of Father Rakale and Brother Norwood.

Instances which were God's will or man's will — often made him cry with sorrow and concern.

In Khotso House:
• What did the death of a family member mean:
  (i) Contributions from staff towards the expenses that family incurs.
  (ii) Actual attendance at such occasions and personal condolences.
• What did marriages and engagements mean to him?
  (i) Attendance and contribution towards a party.
  (ii) Special prayers and celebrations.
• What did wedding celebrations mean to him?
  (i) A special word by the General Secretary.
  (ii) Celebrations and feasts — with contributions from staff.
• What did the release of colleagues from detention or prison mean to him?
  (i) Special mention and word of concern from Khotso House.
  (ii) Prayer and identification.
  (iii) Even time off in case of staff members.
• What did personal staff expenses mean to him, for example, school expenses or legal expenses?
  (i) All these meant personal involvement and a way of solving them by providing the means of payment through appeals to donor partners and through the General Secretary's discretionary fund.

Baba is a straight forward and upright person. In fact his wife warned us from the start that if you do not want anything repeated — do not say it to him. In Xhosa we say — *Ukhatywe lihashi esifubeni* (he was kicked in the chest by a horse). He himself would chuckle and say, "Tell me — I won't repeat it," knowing very well that he would. This man has no grudges — no ill-feelings, no envy, no hate, no malice. In the seven years we have realised that we had a solid being — a father, a friend, a true Christian, and still a man not appreciated in his own country. Some of us who had the opportunity of going to Oslo for the Nobel Peace Prize celebrations had a first-hand experience of sharing his glory. We felt what it is to work and be associated with a great person. Everywhere we went, a red carpet was unfolded — even the captain of a plane said: "I am delighted to have you on board and for people to realise that it is not an everyday thing for us to have a Nobel Prize winner with us, in fact they don't grow on trees".

To some of us, seeing him sign so many autographs everywhere he went was an eye-opener! From our part of the world we have never seen a black being asked for an autograph by a white! We've never been in an airport VIP lounge — be waited upon, have someone collect our tickets, take them through customs, check luggage in — whilst we sit and chat! All this through Baba! So much for shared glory.

I need to mention that Baba has all the points I mentioned but that as much as he enjoyed laughing he also *wanted to be loved,* to be *appreciated,* to be *given warmth* in return. Very often staff members of the Khotso House community 'had their share' of him when he left on or arrived back from a trip. This was demonstrated by the exchange of friendly kisses with the womenfolk in the building and hugs for the menfolk.

In his very caring manner, concern and outgoing personality, he would in a very special way remember little things like a joke he shared where and when and with whom — he has an elephant's memory! As for names, he never mixes people's names and events.

His hates and dislikes:

- Baba abhors gossip and unfounded stories and would say so. On many occasions he has spoken very strongly against those who label others informers and would say people should never allow hatred and distrust to be sown among them. He even encouraged people to love even those believed to be informers. He loves peace and talks peace and lives peacefully.
- Baba dislikes lateness. Late coming prompted him to write memo

after memo to the staff of SACC. His day starts at 4.00am and
ends long after normal working hours. In the seven years at
SACC he has proved to all that there is no 'African time'. The
few instances when he lost his cool were instances of not being
punctual. He would notice anyone absent and late and would expect an explanation from the person.

• He dislikes people talking of a 'thou' instead of thousand, (even
  when phoned in Norway from South Africa). He would rub it in
  that slang is not acceptable.

• He hates the use of derogatory labels, for example, Coolie, Kaffir
  etc.

His likes and favourites: Food: fat cakes, marshmallows, dried fruits,
especially dates and nuts; lime or orange juice, Yogi Sip.

Characteristic habits:
Prayer and retreat, lunch hour nap, laughter, loves being loved, commitment, appropriate dress, singing (folk and classics) and dancing.

The Meaning of Prayer:
When Baba joined the SACC participation in morning devotions
was optional and obligatory. Over the years, through personal example, he has demonstrated to many of us that prayer should form
an integral part of our lives — that prayer is our means of com-
municating with God, that prayer gives meaning to life, that prayer
takes care of all problems said and unsaid.

This versatile man (both boss and friend to all) whose humble
beginnings are traced to a township to the west of Johannesburg,
has not grown pompous from all the fame he is showered with. He
remembers his roots, he remembers who he is, where he comes
from. Often he talks of his parents and in particular his mother
who was a washerwoman earning 25c per week from which she
paid for his schooling and upkeep!

We give thanks to God for Baba and his life and wish him all
Gods blessings.

SIQIBO DWANE

Archbishop Desmond Tutu — A Personal Tribute

Since 1967, when our paths crossed for the first time, I have had the privilege to walk in some of Archbishop Desmond's footsteps at King's College London, at St Peter's College in the Federal Theological Seminary at Alice, and in the ecumenical movement where I stood in for him at meetings of Faith and Order when travel restrictions prevented him from going abroad. I arrived at King's College in 1967 and discovered that he had not only left behind a magnificent academic record, but that he was also remembered with much affection by the Dean of the College and members of the faculty. In those days it was regarded either as a mark of foolhardiness or of academic distinction to read both Greek and Hebrew. For Archbishop Desmond it was a case of the latter, which is borne out by the fact that he finished with an upper second class in the BD honours list. As a rather bewildered first year student, I found it awesome to step into his shoes, and the expectation expressed from time to time, that I would have to live up to his reputation, daunted me. But I too held him in high esteem, and endeavoured not to destroy the trust that he had won for us overseas students.

When he returned to South Africa and joined the staff of the Federal Seminary in 1967, he immediately set out to teach his students how to approach theology in the black South African context. As shown by his early articles published in theological journals, he himself was at that stage reflecting upon such issues as the world view, and on how the ancestral realm impinges upon the lives of loving descendants. Up until then, for the greater part of this century, black people hadn't had the courage to talk openly about the beliefs and practices connected with their ancestry. So he

was one of the first people to take the lid off the pot, and, in a
sense, the 1985 'Forum' on African Christianity is the culmination
of a process which he and a few others here in Southern Africa
had set in motion.

For Archbishop Desmond Tutu the emergence of African theology wasn't going to mean a sentimental nostalgic trip to the African's past, but a discovery of his roots, so as to be able to stand
firm in the present. He wrote in one article that Black and African
theology were not 'antagonists' but 'soul-mates'. Both were concerned with the 'decolonization' of the African Soul. Some of the
students who had sat at his feet in the Seminary remembered with
much gratitude how Archbishop Desmond had inspired them to
investigate what is entailed in being human and African, and to
apply their findings to their situation of rootlessness and deprivation.
In other words, his teaching was geared to the upliftment of the
underprivileged and the down-trodden. Desmond is an academic of
no mean repute, but he is not an inhabitant of the ivory tower. He
has never been known to indulge in the pursuit of recondite and
high-faluting ideas either for selfish enjoyment, or in an attempt to
impress lesser mortals with his learning.

For him knowledge is for the common good, and he has consistently used his share of it for building up other people.

Perhaps it is true to say that Desmond gained recognition as an
indefatigable defender of human rights while he was Dean of
Johannesburg, yet his concern for people has been a constant feature
of his ministry. Two examples might illustrate this: While he was
Chaplain to staff and students of Fort Hare University an ugly confrontation between students and the University's administration
took place in 1968. As Chaplain he felt bound to express solidarity
with the students in their powerlessness. This gave him the opportunity to witness at close range the brutality of the state against unarmed students. He was touched very deeply by what he saw and
literally shed tears. Another example which illustrates his care for
people is that of his ministry as an assistant in the parish of Blet-
chingley, on the outskirts of London. I met his former rector in a
procession on some big occasion, and he urged me to come and
visit his parish "for Desmond's sake". So my family spent a lovely
week-end there meeting people who remembered the Tutu family
with much affection and gratitude for their ministry. Apparently
Desmond used to haul the rector out of his study every fortnight
or so, put him on the back of his motorbike, and speed with him
to some quiet spot where they would spend the day together reflecting and praying. At that stage Desmond was quite fleshy and

Father Brownrigg tall and hefty. It must have been quite a spectacle to watch the two men as they sped on their buzzing two-wheel transport! But the ride was fun, and the ministry made a deep impression on the rector. One of the parishioners told me how good Desmond was at noticing who was not at the Eucharist on Sunday. She was startled when it was her turn to be noticed and asked to account for her absence! In a society in which people are not accountable to each other, but are schooled in the art of defending their privacy and minding their own business, one's next door neighbour could die and go unnoticed. But not so in the church, and the priest who cares for the flock takes the trouble to know them so as to notice when one of them is missing.

Desmond's concern for people is the obverse side of his experience of God as incredible generosity. He speaks of Him as the God who gives Himself in a total way and holds nothing back. When it touches the human heart, His amazing generosity moves human beings such as St Paul or St Francis of Assisi to acts of heroic and incalculable surrender to Him. Desmond's courageous stand against the powers of darkness reveals the extent of his surrender to his God.

Love is not an ideal, but a relationship between Father, Son, and the believer. Those who know God burn with zeal for his righteousness and the well-being of His people.

MMUTLANYANE STANLEY MOGOBA

From Munsieville to Oslo

I am privileged to have known Archbishop Desmond Mpilo Tutu personally and for a considerable time.

His life is an epic which could be called "From the dusty roads of Sophiatown or Munsieville to the Red Carpet in Oslo." His story epitomizes a miracle.

Frail in health, it was the achievement of medical science that the tuberculosis he contracted responded to treatment. Twice he had to miss out on important examinations — Standard 6 and Junior Certificate — because he had to be hospitalized. His teachers realized his intellectual acumen and promoted him to the next class, where he became a top scholar.

I met Desmond for the first time at the Pretoria Bantu Normal College — a post-matric teacher training college. This college was the result of a policy devised by the architects of apartheid. "Bantus" had to be separated and in their schools the culture of their people had to be preserved and promoted. Thus our dormitories and classrooms were grass-thatched *rondavels*. We only obtained a few rectangular classrooms after our biology tutor had complained that the rondavels did not have adequate light for microscopes.

It was in one of these rondavel dormitories that we spent some time together. I can still recall a day when Desmond had a visitor, Father Trevor Huddleston. This tall white monk sat on Desmond's bed and we all marvelled at this. A white man visiting a black youth like Desmond and being quite at home on a bed in a rondavel.

It must be said in Father Huddleston's favour that he was possibly one of the earliest prophets to discover and to affirm that Desmond would become a great leader. One of the visits by Father Huddleston is described in his book *Naught for Your Comfort.* Father Huddleston had given us a brilliant address entitled: "In the beginning God......" After that address our principal invited the speaker to the house for tea. The speaker together with the African priest who had accompanied him, Father Tsebe of the Pretoria diocese, were served with tea in the lounge and in the study. Father Huddleston said he wondered if the two teas had come from the same teapot.

I must add that the relationship between Desmond and Father Huddleston was pastoral rather than "political". Desmond at that time did not show any political inclination of a party political nature or of being a career politician.

Desmond has always had great humour and a near explosive laughter. He always poked fun at his big nose and none of us escaped similar or appropriate treatment. At the college he was popular with all of us. Even those who today, because of their jobs or political stances, may seem to be poles apart are still fond of him as a friend and former colleague. I must digress a little and share a typical school story. One of our teachers whose English was very fragmentary and who translated literally from Afrikaans to English (for example, "students, you must remember me to show you a diagram ...") made one of these cracks in class. We all suppressed ourselves. Someone kicked Desmond from under the table and he exploded. He was sent out of class for a few days.

Desmond was one of the best students, particularly in English. Our English lecturer forbade most of us from using long words but Desmond and a student called Kaiser Harvey were given the licence to use any word they wished to. Some of us had come from schools manned by multi-racial staff and were taught English by English men and women, but these two good students came from black schools, Madibane and Orlando High Schools. Actually, when we first came to the college, we were told that Desmond was disappointed because he had missed a distinction in English — he obtained a "B" symbol. In those days to obtain a "B" or a distinction from the Joint Matriculation Board was like a dream in the black schools. We who came from the mainline English Church Schools had much difficulty obtaining "D", "E" or "F" symbols.

All in all, Desmond was a brilliant student with a unique intellect. We used to study and revise together. He had a photographic mind which once it recalled a few things on a page, could see the rest of

the page, the previous as well as the following page.
So we became friends and one week-end he invited me to go
home with him. It was my first visit to the West Rand.
We went to Munsieville, the African township of Krugersdorp, and I met his
parents and sisters. Here was a simple home, even frugal and I was
received very warmly. His father was an urbanized Xhosa (Fingo).
As a teacher himself, he was interested in us and amused us with
his many insights. His mother spoke Xhosa and Sotho. This was a
typical African family which gave birth to a son who became truly
African. Up to today, Desmond speaks Sotho and Nguni languages
with amazing facility and there is no sign of any ethnicity about
him. I always remark that the architects of ethnic apartheid came
on the scene too late. They could have wrought more havoc and
destroyed our nationhood beyond a point of recovery, but today
many families are made of parents from both the main language
streams and besides, language in the metropolitan areas is not such
a divisive factor. It is only now that it is being whipped up to give
credence to the "multi-nationalism" of our present day government.

Even at college, his leadership qualities were already clearly evident. He was elected to the Students' Representative Council. I
was again privileged to share with him intimately in matters of student leadership. I must hasten to add that the student scene in
those days was a far cry from what it is today.

At the end of three years we parted. He returned to the Rand to
teach and I was posted to the Northern Transvaal. A few years
thereafter we heard rumours that Desmond had responded to a
Call to the Ministry. Many of his former friends were disappointed
in him. Why did he not remain as an English teacher and later become a professor of English. Some of us felt that perhaps Father
Huddleston had had a hand in this. Little did we know that some
of us, after taking a circuitous route, would also heed a call from
God which would cause us to leave our fishing nets and follow the
"Fisher of Men".

As fate would have it, I nearly became his student at the Federal
Theological Seminary but he had left a few months before I
arrived to take up a post at Roma University in Lesotho.

His stay in Lesotho was brief. He began his career as a "World
Ecumenic" when he became Director of the Theological Education
Fund of the World Council of Churches. This was a post which
took him throughout the entire Christendom and enabled him to
make contact with many scholars and theological institutions. I
have attended a few World Conferences and personally experi-

enced how widely-known and esteemed he is. It was at this time
that he started featuring in important conferences on African and
Black Theologies.
The call of the soil became louder and irresistible. He was
appointed Dean of Johannesburg. This gave us an opportunity to
meet him more frequently. The situation in the country was gradually deteriorating.
Meanwhile the Lesotho See became vacant and he was appointed
Bishop of Lesotho. I remarked earlier about his broad national
sentiments which crossed the borders of tribalism or ethnicity. If
ever the architects of tribal *laagers* were proved wrong, it was certainly in Desmond's career. The days of John Rees at the South
African Council of Churches came to an end. A search for a suc-
cessor began. Some friends asked me to consider this appointment.
I did and was even interviewed. The selection panel decided on
Rev John Thorne of the United Congregational Church. His term
of office, however, lasted for only a few months. The Fathers of
the Council appointed Desmond who had a very difficult decision
to make. He agreed to come back to Johannesburg to occupy the
hot seat that had become hotter since the 1976 Soweto crisis.
Desmond is very deeply spiritual. All those who had come to
know him closely, come to appreciate that all his thoughts and
actions are rooted in a very deep spirituality. I remember travelling
with him to a very difficult meeting in Pretoria. At the end of the
meeting we had to rush to Jan Smuts Airport to enable me to
catch a plane to Durban. I stopped to chat to a few friends, and
then had to start looking for him. I eventually found him in the
back seat of his car saying his evening office. This was not just a
habitual routine, but a search for spiritual replenishment after an
exacting meeting. Another time I also travelled with him and we
had to start from his home to catch an early flight to Pietersburg.
We had to be at an early morning Mass in spite of the morning
traffic through which we had to find our way to Jan Smuts Airport.
Many more examples could be cited. At the South African Council
of Churches' offices, he put down the stamp of his spirituality by
starting and inspiring daily services which have now become such a
prominent feature of Khotso House.
The Eloff Commission of Enquiry into the South African Council of Churches will go down in the history of our land as a tragic
act which nevertheless saw the integrity of Desmond shine through
all the mud that was slung at the Council. I have said elsewhere
that he had become a World Ecumenic. During his term of office
as General Secretary of the South African Council of Churches, his

fame and stature rose and, the Church and other leaders showed this very clearly when they came to our land to give what vindication was possible or at the very least to manifest Christian presence and support.

My evidence before this commission was focussed mainly on what could be called the "Black point of View". It was a real privilege to be able to testify what Desmond meant to the blacks in particular, and that some of the "sins" he and the South African Council of Churches were supposed to have committed, like radicalizing theology, were corporate sins and that most of the black churchmen were equally guilty of the same "crime". I brought as evidence my own speeches and writings since at least 1970. This evidence, like that of others seemed to have been ignored. On the whole the Eloff Commission was a big boomerang.

I now address myself briefly to a question that has often been put or insinuated. Is Desmond really a man of peace?

It would be the easiest or safest thing in the world for him to be quiet like most of us church leaders. No. He finds this difficult in the Name of God. Problems which are brought to the offices of the South African Council of Churches and people who knock at their door daily, bring extraordinary pressure on the Council and its leadership. Sheer integrity and a sense of Christian vocation would compel one to become or to fulfil the role of a prophet.

He has repeatedly warned that there is going to be trouble in this country and that sheer love for the people and country, compelled him to shout like the prophets of old. For this he was blamed for inciting violence.

He called for sanctions and boycotts, not because he gloated at the thought of this country's economy crumbling but, as he has often repeated, because he does not believe in violence and wishes to advocate non-violent means which would effectively save this country from what appears to be an unavoidable cataclysm. For this some whites in the country accused him of unpatriotic and almost treasonable behaviour. What most of them want is non-violent "non-change".

He pleaded with the Dutch Reformed Churches to return to the Christian fellowship of the South African Council of Churches and to join in finding a Christian solution to our problems. I was present at a Conference in the St Peter's Centre, Hammanskraal, where he read his correspondence with these churches and their negative and unsympathetic responses. The black delegates were very angry with Desmond for going a second and third mile by pleading with these churches to come closer to other churches in the interests of the whole Church of God and this country. I was one of those who defended his stand, but nothing came out of extending his hand of Christian love. Some people today, particularly after apartheid has been declared a heresy, will not easily recall that gesture of love and friendship. When the black universities went through crises, I was privileged to be in the delegation he led to Fort Hare and the University of the North. The visit to the University of Zululand was cancelled on the eve of the appointed date when the University advised us that all meetings in the Empangeni District had just been banned. The visit to Zululand was arranged at very short notice. Desmond had a very busy schedule and was due to leave for overseas. He agreed to drop everything and come to Zululand. At the other two universities we had difficult meetings with principals, staff (mostly Deans) and student leaders. He led us very ably at these difficult negotiations, although again these efforts did not seem to bear much fruit in the short term.

Disturbances in our schools have had many casualties. Many young people will not see the dawn of freedom because they gave their lives that others may gain or enjoy freedom. One of these was Miss Emma Sathekge from Atteridgeville, Pretoria. Her death nearly plunged the country into another Soweto 1976. The Executive Committee of the South African Council of Churches felt that an urgent meeting with the Government should be arranged. This was immediately after the publication of the Eloff Commission's Report so that there was no love lost between the Government and the South African Council of Churches. Yet Christian commitment demanded that something be done. It fell into the lap of Desmond to arrange this meeting. The then Minister of Education and Training, Mr Barend du Plessis, agreed to meet Desmond on the very next day in Durban. I was again privileged to accompany him. It was a tough meeting with "brutally frank" exchanges made (to use the phrase that was bandied around at that meeting). As a result of this meeting, Desmond was asked to try and mediate in the Atteridgeville crises. Again I accompanied him and what a meeting it turned out to be. We were spiritually bruised to witness the black community turning upon itself and threatening to destroy itself. Luckily some compromise was reached and some assurances given that Miss Sathekge would be given a fitting and respectable funeral with the community and nation doing their best to comfort the family. She was given a heroic funeral. Of course, the problems in the community did not disappear. They continued in some form or other throughout that year and in the year that followed.

One had to be at that meeting to appreciate how much that compromise was a miracle by God through the reconciling service of His servant.

I have described this meeting in some detail because I am certain that many people, particularly the whites, are oblivious of the real situation in our black townships, and hence they condemn anyone who is a spokesman or an interpreter of what is going on. Some misguided people even go to the extent of labelling such a person an agitator.

Let me make a passing reference to the role he has tried to play in reconciling the United Democratic Front and the National Forum. A daunting task and unfinished business. His role, as always, was to point out a South Africa that is greater than all of us and to warn about the dangers facing us all.

Desmond, through interventions like the ones described above and for being a mouthpiece of the suffering majorities of our land, has virtually become a household name. I have seen young children with bright eyes and innocent smiles, recognise him in some of the areas we went to, and crowd around to see him. I was travelling in a train in Europe when I met some black youths who, I suspected, came from Africa, even Southern Africa. It turned out that they had come from Namibia. They came close to me and, in the typically African way, began a conversation. When they realized I came from South Africa, their faces froze with fear and suspicion. One asked me if I knew Desmond and I said, "Yes, very well; actually I have been sent by him to the Conference I am going to attend." You should have seen the transformation in them. They now trusted me or could risk to converse with me. They had never met Desmond in person but they respected and loved him. So he is not only a household name in South Africa but even in the remote parts of Europe.

In 1984, an International Conference on Religion and Peace was held in Nairobi. Desmond was the one invited to give the key-note address and I was one of the ten South African delegates to the Conference. He spoke as usual on Human Rights, Apartheid and Peace. He was given a standing ovation by an audience of nearly a thousand people including about six-hundred delegates from all over the world representing all the major faiths in the world — Christian, Muslim, Hindu, Sikh, Jain, Zoroastrian, Buddhist, Jewish, Shintoist — to mention but a few. One Kenyan spoke to me about Desmond's courage, particularly when he addressed himself critically to African Independent States on the thorny question of genuine human rights and freedom. The Kenyan said that that was unheard of, even in independent Africa!

I have mentioned these personal observations to try to show what assessment the ordinary man and woman has on the life, work and witness of the man, Tutu.

Internationally he has been honoured by ten universities. He was awarded the gold medal in New York and the Africa-America Institute very generously made it possible for me to return from Washington to attend the ceremony. It was a real privilege of a life-time to be present on that occasion to hear and see what the world outside South Africa thinks of him.

All these took place before he was awarded the Nobel Peace Prize. A colleague of Desmond's at the South African Council of Churches, Mrs Sophie Mazibuko, described to me her personal experiences of this occasion. Those of us who were not present, should not miss the eye-witness account of those who actually walked on the red carpet in Oslo. What a life! What a man!

From the dusty township roads of South Africa to the red carpet in Oslo. God be praised!

Part 2

Theological Tributes

T.S.N. GQUBULE

They Hate Him Without a Cause

I was sitting at the airport in Durban waiting for my flight to Cape Town. I had my clerical collar on. Next to me was a white lady whose age I guessed to be about sixty. She said to me:

"You are a Father aren't you?"

"Yes, I am," I said.

"You know Bishop Desmond Tutu?" she continued.

"Yes, very well," I said.

"He is looking for trouble, isn't he?" She went on.

"No, I don't think so. Why do you say that?" I asked.

"Well, the government thinks he is looking for trouble," she said.

"There is a world of difference between what the government thinks and reality," I remarked.

The conversation continued until my flight was called and I had to go. The little of the conversation that I have given above shows that the attitude of many white people towards Desmond Tutu may not be that of positive hatred, but is strongly determined by what they believe the government thinks of him, and this they get from the media, the press and the South African Broadcasting Corporation — radio and television.

The good lady told me that she was a good Anglican, but she did not like clergymen who messed with politics. I did not ask her about clergymen who give theological support for apartheid, or those who lead prayers when Blood River is celebrated, or those who messed with the Broederbond, or those who, like the late Dr D Malan and Dr A Treurnicht, leave their parishes and go full-time into politics.

Reasons for animosity towards Tutu seem to include the following: That he is **Mixing Religion With Politics:** This seems to be a matter of convenience and it depends on the kind of politics the person is pursuing. If, like Bishop Abel Muzorewa, one pursues politics that do not threaten the *status quo*, then one is acceptable. If the New Constitution of South Africa has a long "religious Preamble", that shows how Christian we are and it is not mixing up religion with politics. If in the course of a political address President P W Botha quotes Romans 13, that is not mixing religion with politics. "Our boys" are fighting and dying "on the border" and our ministers should not only pray for them but should also go to the border and minister to them. That is not politics, but pastoral work. No, these people are not interested in keeping religion pure from political contamination. They do not want anybody who, in their view, is "stirring the pot of trouble". They ought to know that the Judaeo-Christian religion knows nothing about a dichotomy between the spiritual and the material, the sacred and the secular. The prophet Nathan told the Israelite King David: "Thou art the man." The prophet Isaiah told the King of Israel in his day that he ought not to form a political alliance with Egypt. John the Baptist told Herod that it was immoral for him to take his brother Phillip's wife. It is not just a matter of quoting passages like these: it is a matter of understanding that the religion of Israel emphasized that God is controller of all history and that the destinies of all nations lie within the hollow of his hands. The Christian religion teaches that God is Lord of the whole of life and the Lord of all Creation. There is no sphere of life such as politics, economics, education which is not under his Lordship. So the prophet condemns the traders roundly when they cheated the consumers. They regarded it as part of their duty to God to do so.

There is a dangerous heresy in South Africa today that separates spiritual from material things, that separates religious beliefs from social, economic, political, cultural and educational issues of our country. We have been told that ministers should keep out of politics, stick to the pulpit and leave politics to politicians. I submit that it is our Christian duty to insist that our rulers who call themselves "Christian" should have something of the mind of Christ — His justice, His compassion, His love and His mercy. To condemn Tutu because he believes in a Gospel that permeates the whole of life is to condemn him because he practices and enforces the religion of the Bible.

His Opposition to Apartheid:
I can almost hear a white "Liberal" saying: "I am also against

apartheid". Then I remember Steve Biko saying that blacks must realize that not every opponent of apartheid is an ally. Very few if any whites would go as far as Tutu goes in his opposition to apartheid. Every white benefits to a greater or lesser degree from apartheid. To give an obvious example, every white child will go to a white school where the facilities are incomparably superior to any that may be found in a black school. So whether he likes it or not he benefits from the system. Voting on the New Constitution showed that about 66% of the voters favour apartheid. This, as I have said, is not surprizing as apartheid is advantageous to whites whether they like it or not. It entrenches white privilege, white control of the running of the affairs of this country with a control of its politics, its economy, its social structure etc.

Because of all this, whites who speak against apartheid are too ready to accept little tinkerings with apartheid as indicating more changes to come. They are not at the receiving end of apartheid and, therefore, are more inclined to say: "Half a loaf is better than no bread at all". Like most Africans Desmond Tutu is not interested in a re-arrangement of the apartheid furniture, but in a complete dismantling and scrapping of the whole thing. It does not help to call apartheid sweet names. "Apartheid is as vicious, as evil, as unchristian and as immoral as Nazism". There should be no compromise with it. Tutu and the rest of us are not interested in making apartheid more palatable, but in ridding this beautiful land of ours of the deadly scourge of apartheid. For those whites who believe merely in the amelioration of apartheid, Tutu's insistence on the total scrapping of apartheid seems unreasonable. They would expect us to be grateful for some of the crumbs of apartheid that fall from the master's table at his behest.

Tutu's church, and other churches in this country, have declared apartheid a heresy. It is, therefore, reasonable to expect every Christian to act daily as one who believes that apartheid is a heresy. One cannot be a Christian and still believe in apartheid. No aspect of apartheid is acceptable. Apartheid with its residential segregation, its segregated schools and toilets, its differentiated and inferior education, its mass removals of people and influx control, its deliberate impoverishment of black people, its killing of children and dumping people in relocation areas, its robbing of millions of people of their citizenship in the land of their birth and its whole gamut of unspeakable evils, must be scoured away.

So Tutu is right: We will accept nothing but a complete dismantling of apartheid. In his own words:

"We want to dismantle apartheid and the perpetrators of

apartheid don't like that at all. They could hardly regard us as
blue-eyed boys because the privilege they enjoy as a result of
apartheid is threatened. And so we have the total onslaught of
the apartheid machinery turned against us. We are concerned
to work for a new kind of South Africa, a non-racial, truly
democratic and more just society by reasonably peaceful
means."

Since many whites are opposed to this they hate the proponent
of this view.

At the heart of the South African problem is the arrogance of
the rulers of this country who abrogate to themselves alone the
right to decide how this country is to be run and what is good for
everybody in this country.

The Disinvestment Issue:
Whites hate Tutu more than mentioned above because they believe
that he advocates disinvestment which is a threat to their economy
and a direct hit on the pockets of the wealthy and big business. Yet
Tutu himself says:

"Note well, that in fact I have not yet asked for economic sanctions against apartheid. I have consistently spoken of pressure —
diplomatic, political, but above all economic which need not yet
be sanctions."

At his enthronement as Bishop of Johannesburg Tutu said that
he will call for disinvestment in two years' time if nothing is done
to dismantle apartheid. So for him the call for disinvestment aims
at the elimination of apartheid. If apartheid is done away with in
any other way then there would be no need for disinvestment.

In an interview filed in 1984 he expressed himself as follows:
"I have said and most of us have said, speaking to Christians
and members of other faiths that:

• They need to bring to bear their spiritual energy on our
  situation. For Christians that means prayer that God will
  change the hearts of all of us so that we realize that we
  belong one to another.

• They must be as well-informed about what is happening in
  South Africa as possible to counteract the government's
  campaign of disinformation which is designed to say that
  things are changing for the better when in fact things are
  getting worse day by day.

• They should help create the kind of moral climate in their
  countries which would make it as impossible for governments to collaborate with the perpetrators of apartheid as

it would be with Stalin or Hitler.

- They try to exert pressure on South Africa — political, diplomatic and above all economic pressure, which would be persuasive pressure, to say to the South African government that they are prepared to invest in the Republic of South Africa provided certain conditions are met. If these conditions are not met then let the pressure become punitive — then let sanctions be applied."

There is a lot of dishonesty in the disinvestment debate. First, there are those who argue that sanctions against South Africa will not work. They have not worked in the past. They did not work against Rhodesia. Then I ask: Why are they worried about the growing disinvestment campaign?

Why should they spend over a million rands to mount an anti-disinvestment campaign in the United States? And Tutu asks: "Why is it that the United States up to this day applies trade sanctions against Cuba?"

Secondly there is the dishonest and hypocritical argument that disinvestment would hit mostly those it is intended to help, namely, Africans. They are worried about the growing disinvestment campaign, not because they are now suddenly concerned about the welfare of the poor, starving black fellow, but because of what it will mean to their wealth. Long before the black fellow who is already starving in the Valley of a Thousand Hills starves the financiers will be hardest hit on their pockets where it matters most. To quote Tutu again:

"When did whites suddenly become so altruistic? Have they not benefitted from massive black suffering in the form of migratory labour and cheap labour for many years? Why should they suddenly worry whether blacks suffer or not? Have not more than two million been uprooted and dumped as rubbish in unviable poverty-stricken and drought-stricken Bantustan resettlement camps; are they not still the victims of the pass laws, have they not been raped of their South African citizenship?

If these people really had the welfare of the African at heart they would:

Mount a campaign throughout the country to persuade the government to stop forced removals of people immediately;

Protest against the denationalization of Africans which robs them of their South African citizenship;

Protest against the continuation of an inferior, segregated and discriminatory system of education and replace it with a non-racial, non-discriminatory, unitary system of education that would be common to all.

Plead with the government to scrap influx control regulations so as to enable all the people of this land to have freedom of movement and sell their labour at the best available markets throughout the country.

Plead with the government to scrap apartheid which has caused and continues to cause untold suffering to the Black people of this country, and replace it with a free, non-racial society.

The Tutu I know:
My contention here is that many, many white South Africans do not know Desmond. All they know of him is the ogre presented to them by the media and many of them have accepted the media picture of him uncritically. In 1984 I spent about ten days in the home of a nice, cultured, well-educated, young Christian couple. The young man switched on the television. It was announced that Bishop Desmond Tutu had been chosen to receive the Nobel Peace Prize for 1984. The young man said: "Oh, no!"

He did not know Desmond. He had never met him, but from the South African media he knew that he was not the man to receive the Prize. In a recent survey it was revealed that three-quarters of the white population of the country believe that Tutu should not have received the Nobel Peace Prize and that he should not have been appointed Bishop of Johannesburg. I have read some letters in the press written by whites saying that he is not a Christian!

The Rev Arthur Lewis, who says he is an Anglican priest, says: "In a few years Bishop Tutu will probably be no more than a forgotten demagogue. In the meantime, we urge all South African Christians to pray for the *conversion* of the Bishop."

This is an incredibly cruel, arrogant, self-righteous and unchristian statement.

I was with Desmond Tutu in Oslo, Norway, when he received the Nobel Peace Prize. I was with him when he met and was honoured by the highest government authorities in both Norway and Sweden. As we moved from one reception to another in both countries I could not avoid the thought that in his own country this man did not receive even the courtesy of a congratulation from the government. Even "liberal" institutions like universities in this country have not given him the honour he deserves. In stark contrast to all this the world community has heaped upon him one honour upon another. World institutions of higher learning have conferred the following honours on him:

- The Fellowship of King's College (FKC) from his own University of London;
- D Div (GTS) in New York;
- LLD (Kent) United Kingdom;
- LLD (Harvard) U S A;
- D S Th (Columbia) U S A;
- DHL (St Paul's) U S A;
- LLD (Claremont) U S A;
- D S Th (Dickinson) U S A;
- DD (Aberdeen) Scotland;
- DHL (Howard) U S A;
- Prix d'Athene;
- Nobel Peace Prize.

If the good lady at the Durban Airport had given me a chance I would have told her something of the Tutu I know which is far different from the ogre of the South African media.

I met Desmond Tutu for the first time in December, 1961, at a conference of theological students at Wilgespruit. I was introduced to him and was told that he was due to go to King's College, London, the following year, for further studies in theology. He was one of that rare breed of Africans at that time who went to study theology after obtaining a University degree. He had received a B A degree from the University of South Africa by candle light before proceeding to St Peter's College, Rosettenville, Johannesburg, to train for the Anglican priesthood. He obtained the Hons B D and the M Th degrees of London University. On his return to South Africa, in 1967, he joined the teaching staff of the Federal Theological Seminary. I had been the only black member of the teaching staff of that institution since its inception in the early sixties. Now we were two. Desmond left the Federal Theological Seminary at the beginning of 1970 to take up a lectureship in theology at the University of Botswana, Lesotho and Swaziland. After two years at the university he was appointed Associate Director of the Theological Education Fund (TEF) of the World Council of Churches in Bromley, Kent, United Kingdom and was responsible for all of Sub-Sahara Africa. In this capacity in a period of three and a half years he travelled extensively in several countries in North America, Europe, Asia and had personal experience of life and conditions in every African country South of the Sahara. He himself says:

"I have seen a great deal and experienced much that I would

like to see in South Africa. I have seen the harmony in Scandinavian countries and the poverty of India. I have seen the violence and repression of Amin's Uganda. I have been in Ethiopia just before the overthrow of Emperor Haile Selassie and the terrible aftermath of the Biafran war and the toll it took on human relationships and on the material resources of a great country. I have been shattered at what I saw in Belfast, hearing of young girls who battered a sectarian enemy of their age to death by beating her brains out with bricks and then going to a pub to celebrate without the slightest remorse.

I was detained at Kampala airport by Amin's security police, who held up my plane as they went through my papers some of which contained a report which was highly critical of the regime and by God's mercy the police missed it. I was searched at Salisbury airport by Ian Smith's security men, one of whom, on reading a Black Theology paper I was preparing screeched that that was not theology but politics. I attended the Salvation Today Conference in Thailand and experienced the exhilaration of belonging to the variegated Church of God."

I lived in Desmond's own house in the South East of London. I remember driving through the streets of London at midnight with his wife, Leah. I walked into his TEF office in Bromley. His secretary told me that Tutu was the greatest fund-raiser TEF had ever had.

Early in 1975 we were attending a conference of theological teachers at St Peter's College, Rosettenville. During the tea-break Desmond told me that, "out of the blue", the then bishop of Johannesburg had asked him to become Dean of Johannesburg. He wished to know what my advice would be on the matter. My wife and I had already gone through the agony of having to pull our children out of the excellent British system of education to the appalling iniquity of Bantu Education, from a life of free thought and free association in Britain to the dehumanizing indignities of an apartheid society. Could we advise the Tutu's to do the same? We did. So he came back to be Dean of Johannesburg for all too brief a time because in August 1976 he was elected Bishop of Lesotho and went to live in Maseru.

All that I have written thus far is completely unknown to the vast majority of whites in South Africa. They know Tutu as the General Secretary of the South African Council of Churches. They do not know that he got to that position only in 1978. They have combined their hatred for the South African Council of Churches, about which they know very little, with their hatred for its General Secretary about whom they know even less. They say he has caused "untold damage to his country" when actually he loves this country passionately. Unfortunately many whites make no distinction between opposition to South Africa as such and opposition to apartheid. That is because even those who oppose apartheid are not prepared to do so *actively* and *completely* because they benefit from it... Tutu, like most of us, hates apartheid like poison. The world does not hate South Africa as such. But the whole world abhors apartheid. If, for whatever reason, white South Africa clings to apartheid then white South Africa will sink to the abyss clinging to apartheid. Drop apartheid and we would join the world community of nations today, with no sports boycotts, no arms embargoes, no threats of disinvestment.

Finally Desmond Tutu is no ogre, black devil with horns and a long tail. He is a man of peace who richly deserves the Nobel Peace Prize; he is a reconciler, a task in which he is engaged daily; he is a preacher and a pastor as his flock in Johannesburg soon realized; he is a man of deep compassion from whose eyes tears flow readily. Out of this compassion he tells the following story which he says has been "seared" into his memory:

"I shall never forget my visit to Zweledinga, a resettlement camp near Queenstown where I met this little girl coming out of a shack in which she lived with her widowed mother and sister. I asked her:

'Does your mother receive a pension, or grant or something?'

'No', she replied.

'Then what do you do for food?'

Then she said, 'We borrow food.'

'Have you ever returned any of the food you borrowed?'

'No,' she replied.

'What do you do when you can't borrow food?'

'We drink water to fill our stomachs.'"

Desmond Tutu gives his own credo as follows:

"I believe in a democratic, non-racial society and so I believe in majority rule, not black majority rule, but majority rule. I believe in adult suffrage, for that, we were told, is an unalterable feature of true democracy. I believe in a common citizenship for all South Africans in an unbalkanized South Africa."

SIMON MAIMELA

Archbishop Desmond Mpilo Tutu A Revolutionary Political Priest or Man of Peace?

The choice of the title for this paper is deliberate, and has largely been dictated by an acute awarenes that not everyone in South Africa was pleased by the announcement that Bishop Desmond Tutu has been voted the winner of the 1984 Nobel Peace Prize, as can be judged by the hostile outbursts especially from the South African Broadcasting Corporation news media, and also from a number of newspapers in the country which seriously question the claim that Archbishop Tutu is a man of peace. [1] In my view, the title of this paper sums up appropriately the contradictory perceptions which different people in South Africa have of Archbishop Tutu's role. The objective is, therefore, to explore those contradictory perceptions and to assess the extent to which they are a true reflection of what this man of God is all about, and to ask what the award of the Nobel Peace Prize is trying to say to us about him.

Theology and Politics
What makes Archbishop Tutu so controversial and appear revolutionary in the eyes of many white South Africans is because he dared to declare apartheid the most vicious and evil system since Nazism, and to commit his ministry to the dismantling of apartheid so as to bring about a new South Africa which is more just, more

equitable for all its citizens. [2] It is a commitment which has put
him at the centre of political storm, because he is viewed by the
white establishment as having failed to neatly separate religion and
politics so as to confine his ministry to the proper business of the
church, namely, the spiritual sphere.

In other words, the controversy surrounding Archbishop Tutu's
public statements on the socio-political nature of South Africa has
to do with the age-old problem as to whether there is any relation
between religion and politics, which often arises in countries where
there is no official "State" Church, and where the separation
between church and state is often invoked. Here ministers of religion are encouraged and expected to stick to religion and leave the
realm of politics to the so-called political authorities. In consequence, the extent to which political issues raise theological questions and vice versa is never reflected upon and clarified. This is
because people often operate with a mistaken assumption of con-
fining the meaning of "politics" to "party politics" and "casting of
votes" in which case the church *qua* church is expected to take a
"neutral" stance so as not to alienate or divide its constituents by
giving the impression that it favours one party over and against
another. It is this confusion which has led some to conclude that
Archbishop Tutu is a "political priest", a subversive at best
because of his public utterances on the evils of apartheid. [3]

However, it should be pointed out that politics need not be understood in this narrow sense of "party politics" and, therefore,
theologians and church leaders need not and should not remain
without words in the political situations in which they find themselves. Whether we admit it or not, political exercise involves the
people of God and of necessity therefore has theological dimensions.

It is against this background that we have to understand Archbishop Tutu's insistence that he is not a "political" leader even
though his actions and utterances have direct political implications.
His concern with secular things such as politics and economics,
rent, education, resettlement, influx control, etc., arises out of his
relationship with and acknowledgement of God as the Creator of
and Lord over human life in all its aspects, be they socio-political
or economic. Indeed for Archbishop Tutu, it is impossible for a
Christian to be non-political because that would imply that there is
"a substantial part of human life in which God's writ does not
run". [4] According to him, such a view creates an unacceptable
dualism between the spiritual and material, and implies that there
is another Lord who is in charge of the political sphere than God

the Father of our Lord Jesus Christ. Indeed, to invoke the separation between religion and politics in order to uphold this dualism is to suggest that human beings somehow belong to the powers that be, that is, they are at the mercy of political authorities who can do what they please with them without fear of rebuke from God through the prophetic ministry of the Church. It would further mean that as Creator, God is totally indifferent to what happens to and among human beings and how they treat one another. Significantly, however, the witness of the Church throughout the ages has denied the possibility that God is indifferent to what human beings do to themselves and to the life entrusted to them, because everyone of them must account for their actions before their Creator. For this reason, what happens to and with human beings makes the difference as to whether they are under the dominion of some demon or the Lordship of True God, One who does and can demonstrate that he/she is the Creator who authorises human life by coming to its defence. The cash value of this claim is that the problems of politics and theology are not as separable as it is often assumed by those who advise priests to stick to religion and not meddle in politics.

In view of the inseparability of religion and politics, we have to appreciate Archbishop Tutu's refusal to apologize for being "political", when he condemns apartheid as an unjust, wholly immoral, and unchristian political system which must be dismantled and replaced by a more just, humane political order. Archbishop Tutu feels constrained to resist the evils of apartheid because he believes that the God he worships is one who:

"Cares enormously about children in resettlement camps, who must drink water to fill their stomachs because there is no food; he cares about shivering women at Nyanga whose flimsy plastic shelters are being destroyed by police; He cares that the influx control system together with Bantunization are destroying black family life not accidentally but by deliberate government policy; He cares that people die mysteriously in detention; He cares that something horrible is happening in this country when a man will often mow down his family before turning the gun on himself; He cares that life seems so dirt cheap." [5].

It is because God cares so much about the life the Creator has made that God is not useless and irrelevant to human struggles for political freedom, but is worthy of praise and worship. In consequence, Archbishop Tutu believes that he cannot be the disciple of such a caring God and remain aloof from socio-political involvement. For he is conscious of the fact that in their interactions with one another, human beings, by virtue of being social beings, are of necessity political beings whose actions have both political dimensions and involve moral responsibility before God and their fellows. [6]

Incarnational Theology as the Basis of Christian Involvement in Socio-political Issues

In order to fully appreciate Archbishop Tutu's rejection of a neat separation between religion and politics, it is important that we should examine his theological motivations. Archbishop Tutu is a thorough-going incarnational theologian who is persuaded that the dichotomies or dualisms which are popular in the minds of some people, who demand the separation of religion from politics, have to be fought and overcome on the basis of the Christian tradition and of Scripture. Both teach that, in becoming a real human being of flesh and blood in Jesus Christ, God took the whole of human life seriously, thus demonstrating that God is the Lord of all life: spiritual and secular, sacred and profane, material and spiritual. For in the Jesus-event God declared that the material has the potential of gloriously being shot through and through with the spiritual so as to share God's own glory. That is, the incarnation declared in no uncertain terms that this unlikely material, this human body so frail and so impotent, has the potential of bearing the weight of divine glory and of being suffused with the divine light so that it is translucent. [7] Yes, by taking to the divine self the material nature of the creature, God united the human nature with the divine nature, and in so doing bridged the gulf that existed between the spiritual and material aspects of reality. [8] In Tutu's view, the Christian doctrine of incarnation was a very revolutionary teaching in the ancient world, which was noted for its dualistic teaching between evil and good, spirit and matter, sacred and profane. For it declares that those dualisms are abrogated by the Wholly Other God who became man in Jesus Christ.

Drawing important implications from the Christian doctrine of incarnation, Archbishop Tutu points out that Christians can no longer afford the luxury of compartmentalizing life so that they may think that religion should keep to its boundaries and not impinge on the things beyond its ken and competence. That is, religion should have no right to interfere with things political, and should keep to the sanctuary in a well-ordered society and not keep straying out of its bounds into the socio-political sphere. [9] For the God Christians worship, though transcendent, wholly other than finite creatures, is also one who is not a cosmic absentee landlord but one in whom we live, move and have our being. Therefore our God is the Lord of all life in the political as well as the religious sphere.

In the light of this thoroughgoing incarnational theology, Archbishop Tutu is fully persuaded that as a follower of Christ he has no other way of establishing and working for the Kingdom of God, the Kingdom of peace, of justice, of compassion, of love, and reconciliation than by following in the footsteps of Jesus Christ, carrying his own Cross and standing side by side with those who are casualties of man's inhumanity to man, in the form of the most vicious political system of apartheid which treats God's people as if they were rubbish which could be shoved from one place to another. [10] But precisely this way of following Jesus leads him to no other position than that which forces him to take active interest in the earthly, secular things such as politics and economics, detentions without trial, pass laws and migratory labour, etc., because "Jesus would not permit him" the luxury of dwelling in spiritual ghettos unrelated and unconcerned with real life issues. [11] For as Jesus says, in as much as we do or do not do something for our fellows who are the least of his brethren, we did or did not unto Him (Matt 25:31-40). To sum up: Archbishop Tutu has developed and works with a thoroughgoing incarnational theology which makes it impossible for him to be a non-political Christian leader, and therefore to be a dualist who neatly separates religion from politics. For God in Christ has demonstrated a keen interest in socio-political issues because the so-called secular sphere also falls under the divine Lordship of the Christian God. This leads to our next point.

Christ-Event as a Declaration of Divine Preferential Option for the Poor and the Oppressed

As an avowed black theologian of liberation and a thoroughgoing incarnationalist, Archbishop Tutu places a high premium on the fact that in becoming human in Jesus, God, the King of Kings, was not born in the sumptuous palaces of kings. Rather the Almighty and transcendent God chose to empty the Godhood of divine power and glory in order to take on the nature of a slave. God came down from his/her throne and chose to be born by poor parents, to live and to die as a poor and oppressed human being so as to give the oppressed poor and the downtrodden new life and hope. In doing so our Creator in Jesus Christ chose to identify the Divine Being with and to share human suffering and pain so that God might win freedom and life in its fullness for humanity. This, as Archbishop Tutu points out with insight, is what lies at the core of the lowly birth of Jesus in a stable manger, because there was no room in the inn for God-incarnate. He further notes that Jesus was numbered among those who are rejected by society. He came unto His own and His own received Him not, just as those sleeping under bridges and at railway stations, dying of exposure because of the bitter cold. It was not the high and mighty who were the first to receive the good news of His birth. It was humble rustic shepherds who did not count for much in the world's reckoning of these things. No, the Kings wanted to liquidate Him and so He joined the long line of those who have been refugees from their own lands because of injustice and oppression — the Vietnamese boat people, the Cambodians, the Haitians, the Afghans, the Ethiopians, the Namibians — the woeful catalogue is endless.

"Christ has been there in His complete identification with us at our lowest points. As Hebrews put it "He was like unto us in all things, sin excepted". He *ekenosend* Himself. He emptied Himself quite deliberately, stripping Himself of all divine glory, identifying with us to the ultimate, taking on the form of a slave and becoming obedient even unto death, yea the death horrible and horrifying of the Cross, being numbered with the transgressors. Paul boldly declares that He who knew no sin, was made sin for us so that we could acquire His righteousness, He who was right was made poor for our sakes so that we would become rich through His poverty. Identification and exchange. Just too intoxicating." [12]

The background to this long quotation is that oft-misunderstood but controversial claim by liberation theologians that in Jesus, God has in fact revealed the Divine Self as the One who takes the side of the oppressed, the excluded, the outcasts, the despised. Archbishop Tutu puts it eloquently in this way:

"In the process of saving the world, of establishing His Kingdom, God, our God demonstrated that He was no neutral God, but a thoroughly biased God who was forever taking the side of the oppressed, of the weak, of the exploited, of the hungry and homeless, of the refugees, of the scum of society ... So my dear friends we celebrate, worship and adore our God, the biased God, He who is not neutral, the God who always takes sides." [13]

Archbishop Tutu is persuaded that this motif of God's preferential option for the poor and the oppressed runs through the Bible like a red thread. It is discernible most clearly in the Exodus event in which God took the side of the oppressed Israelites against the oppressive Pharoah and his underlings, when God comprehensively supported this somewhat unattractive and bickering lot, not because they deserved to be sided with or because they deserved to be delivered. No, the issue was not that a particular people were sinless, loveable and therefore deliverable or redeemable. Rather the issue was the concrete evil of oppression, injustice and suffering to which the enslaved and exploited Israelites were subjected. It is in an encounter with those manifestations of evil that God cannot help or but feel constrained to come out on the side of the poor, the oppressed and the downtrodden. [14]

Agreeing with his fellow liberation theologians Miques-Bonino and Cone, among others, Archbishop Tutu believes that this divine partiality in defence of the interests of the poor and the underdogs is made known also by the fact that Jesus identified himself in the manner of His birth, His life and death with the marginalized. [15] As a consequence, he was numbered among those who were rejected by society. Archbishop Tutu believes this is the point that St John is making when he declares that "He came to his own and his own received him not" (John 1:11).

According to Tutu, it is by this complete identification with the downtrodden at their lowest point that Christ upset the powers that be. For by his preferential option for the poor, he

"deliberately chose as his friends, not the Bishops' and Canons' and Deans' company — No, His companions were the sinners, the prostitutes, the traitors, the scum of society; the sick who desperately needed a physician and knew it. The others thought they were whole. He was the good shepherd who risked the lives of ninety-nine perfectly good and well behaved sheep to go out and look for the smelly troublesome old ram and when He found it, placed it on His shoulder and went and had a party with His friends to celebrate the find." [17]

In view of this biblical evidence of God's preferential option for the poor and oppressed, Archbishop Tutu is persuaded that, "in a situation of injustice and oppression it is impossible" for the disciples of the God we worship "to remain neutral. To be neutral is already to have taken an option to support the unjust *status quo*". [18]

The impossibility of neutrality here lies in the fact that in a situation of oppression and dehumanization one is confronted with a conflict between life and death embodied in a conflict between the oppressor and opressed, a conflict between the powerful and the powerless. In such a conflict a believer, taking his/her cue from the biblical God who is not neutral but always takes the side of the weak, of the exploited, of the hungry, and of the powerless in society, is forced to be for life against death, for the oppressed against the oppressor, for the poor and powerless against the rich and powerful. It is this attempt to understand society from the point of view of the poor, of the little ones, and the oppressed blacks, that informs and influences Archbishop Tutu's actions. They express themselves in a particular concern for the widow, the orphan and the stranger, because they represent those who are marginalized, pushed to the periphery, the voiceless ones without power and influence. (Deut. 24: 6-22). [19] Similarly, this understanding of God's preferential option for the poor and powerless has guided the South African Council of Churches' programme designed to carry out what under the then Bishop Tutu's leadership is believed to be:

"Christ's work of compassion and love; feeding the hungry, providing blankets for the aged against the bitter cold winter, providing clean water supply in the rural areas and giving health education and building creches and day care centres and giving scholarships to enable thousands of children to get secondary and tertiary education, looking after the families of political prisoners, and supplying legal defence for those appearing in political cases as well as supporting self-help community development programmes." [20]

Indeed as Father Davies rightly points out, it is because Archbishop Tutu believes that God expects his people to opt for the poor in any situation of injustice and suffering that he tries to embody God's compassion in his life and actions by letting his heart go out:

"To the suffering, the afflicted, the oppressed and poor — but again, it is not only the political or social level — it is the personal concern shown to an individual in distress. His compassion for individuals makes him accessible to all who want to see him, with seemingly tireless energy." [21]

It should be noted that this insistence on the preferential option for the oppressed and marginalized, to which Archbishop Tutu and other black theologians have committed themselves and their activities, is one which is not based on mere human compassion for the underdogs. Rather, as we have already pointed out, it is based on what they believe is biblical revelation. For, according to black theologians, God has already taken the side of the oppressed, the outcasts and the despised, when God elected to liberate the Jews from Egyptian bondage. God confirmed this preferential option by calling and sending the Hebrew prophets to denounce injustices and exploitation perpetrated by the powerful against the powerless widows and orphans. It was brought to new heights in the coming of Jesus who, as a poor and oppressed man of sorrows, suffered and was crucified as the rejected outcast. In opting for the poor, God declared that the Divine Self is not prepared to put up with the social situations in which the poor and the powerless are oppressed and humiliated. Consequently, black theologians, such as Archbishop Tutu, argue that, just as God liberated Israel not only from spiritual sin and guilt but also fom oppressive socio-political and economic deprivation, God will again liberate the oppressed black people not only from their personal sins and guilt but also from historical structures of evil, exploitation and oppression, embodied in the apartheid system.

Archbishop Tutu, like most black theologians, is fully aware that his advocacy of God's preferential option for the poor, sounds relentless and harsh to those who are well-placed and are privileged in our society. Indeed, many among them will argue that God is a neutral God who does not have favourites but loves everyone equally, be they masters or slaves. Archbishop Tutu is quick to remind them that even though such a theological proposition is attractive because it agrees with our sense of fairness and equity, the fact of the matter is that that proposition is not supported by biblical evidence. It does not uphold the view that the Egyptians under Pharaoh were convinced that God dealt with them in a neutral way, when God devastated their land with all those plagues so as to deliver a rabble of slaves. Or would Egyptians agree that God was neutral in the manner that they were dealt with at the Red Sea — because God in fact took sides, by supporting the oppressed Hebrew slaves.[22]

In view of this overwhelming evidence that God does take sides in order to bring freedom to the oppressed, Archbishop Tutu believes that Christians have no other option but do likewise. For, as he rightly observes, in the final analysis the Christian concern for:

"The hungry, the oppressed, the exploited, has got everything to do with our faith, our religion, our commitment to God, for we worship an extraordinary God who says that in order for your worship of me to be authentic, in order for your love of me to be true, I cannot allow you to remain in a spiritual ghetto. Your love for me, your worship of me, are authenticated and expressed by our love and your service of your fellows."[23]

Unfortunately, as Archbishop Tutu himself notes, this Christian attempt to opt for the poor, the widow, the orphan, the powerless and marginalized in obedience to our God who also intervenes on their side, is one which is not often appreciated by the powers that be, because they construe such activities as being subversive.[24] Archbishop Tutu retorts by reminding the authorities that it is not he who is revolutionary and subversive but the Bible itself is, as a revolutionary book, written out of the situation of oppression, by the oppressed and for the oppressed. It is the Bible that should be blamed for proclaiming the biased God who forever takes the side of the oppressed and for inviting us to take its message seriously by following in the footsteps of this "biased" God; thereby threatening the security of those who rule unjustly and are tyrants.[25] Therefore, rather than retreat from activities that show God's bias in favour of the poor and defenceless, for fear of incurring the wrath of the powers that be, Archbishop Tutu believes that he has no option here but rather obey God than man, "whatever the cost". [26] For as Tutu does not tire of reminding us, if the Church follows in the footsteps of Jesus and, as a consequence, opts for the suffering, homeless and voteless, thus descending into the vale of human need so as to speak on behalf of the downtrodden, it must of necessity suffer and even die, because "suffering for the sake of Christ and for the Gospel's sake is an inescapable part of being a disciple".[27]

Rejection of the Apartheid System as a Theological Necessity
In the light of Archbishop Tutu's thoroughgoing incarnational theology which leads him to affirm God's preferential option for and bias on behalf of the oppressed and defenceless, it is logical for him to draw important conclusions from this divine intervention. The Christian God is one who cares enormously about human oppression and is prepared to confront and destroy social systems that perpetrate injustice, and violate the dignity and the humanity of God's people. It is as a result of his firm belief that every person is important before God because each and everyone bears the image of God and is the temple of the Holy Spirit. Archbishop Tutu feels himself constrained to denounce the system of apartheid, which, in his view, treats people as if they are a set of statistics to be juggled around, uproots and dumps bearers of God's image as if they were dirt, and creates misery and suffering by its systematic destruction of family life through the influx control laws, etc.[28]

Furthermore, beside the fact that the apartheid system is objectionable on theological grounds, it also denies that every human being is created and is endowed with a unique and infinite value as bearer of God's image, because it proclaims that it is some biological characteristic which makes any person valuable. [29] Therefore, on the basis of his theological critique of the South African social order, Archbishop Tutu believes that apartheid should be rejected and dismantled. It is a heretical teaching which is in conflict with the Christian faith and practice. For, as Tutu correctly observes, the central Christian teaching is that Christ's work on the cross has accomplished reconciliation, that God in Christ came to restore human brotherhood and sisterhood which sin had destroyed.[30] On the contrary,

"Apartheid quite deliberately denies and repudiates this central act of Jesus and says we are made for separateness, for disunity, for enmity, for alienation, which we have shown to be the fruits of sin. For this reason alone apartheid is totally unchristian and unbiblical for it denies not just a peripheral matter but a central truth of the Christian faith."[31]

Confident that there are sufficient grounds for the claims of apartheid to be evaluated and refuted on the basis of biblical evidence, Archbishop Tutu has often issued a challenge to the supporters of the *status quo* to prove to him that this evil and immoral social system is not at variance with the biblical message. Archbishop Tutu goes on to assure his detractors that the day they can convince him that apartheid is biblical he is prepared to burn his Bible and stop being a Christian, because he wants no part in a faith that would sanction the social system which is as "totally evil, unbiblical and unchristian" as apartheid, Nazism and Communism are.[33]

Satisfied that apartheid can be condemned on theological grounds, Archbishop Tutu is often annoyed by the accusation that his attacks on that social system and his encouragement of civil disobedience against unjust apartheid laws do not stem from theological, biblical convictions but from political or ideological motivations. In response to these allegations, Archbishop Tutu eloquently retorts:

"It is not politics that impels us to speak up against the vicious and iniquitous policy of forced population removals... It is not a political philosophy that makes us declare apartheid to be wholly immoral, unbiblical, evil and unchristian ... It is not politics that makes us say that Bantu Education is designed to be inferior and an abomination, a system intended to turn blacks into perpetual serfs no matter how much money is being spent on it; it is not politics that compels us to condemn the migratory labour system which forces married men to live unnatural lives for eleven months of the year in single-sex hostels, helping to destroy black family life, not accidentally but by the deliberate policy of a government that declares itself to be Christian; it is not politics that says we cannot remain silent when such a government dumps God's children in arid poverty-stricken bantustan homelands making them starve, not accidentally but by deliberate government policy. No my friends, no South Africa, we are constrained by the imperatives of the Gospel of Jesus Christ. Until my dying day I will continue to castigate apartheid as evil and immoral in an absolute sense."[34]

To be sure, the issues about which he and the SACC are concerned, as they point out and denounce the evils of apartheid, may be thoroughly political, thoroughly mundane. But because these were the same issues with which Christ himself was concerned in his earthly ministry to the underdogs, Archbishop Tutu is persuaded that they should also constitute the agenda of Christian witness and action in solidarity with the poor and oppressed. For what matters is not the verbal polemics about the separation of religion from politics, but the Christian involvement in "God's mission and purpose" whose goal is "to bring about wholeness, justice, good health, righteousness, peace and harmony and reconciliation".[35] For if the Bible itself is as revolutionary as it appears to be against all tyranny, Christians cannot afford to be less revolutionary if their activities are to see all God's people free from all that enslaves them, and from all that makes them less than what the Creator had intended them to be.[36]

Away with the Apartheid System

Having concluded that the evil system of apartheid is unacceptable on theological grounds by virtue of its treatment of God's people as if they were a means and not an end, thereby proving to be inconsistent with the gospel of Jesus Christ, Archbishop Tutu is finally pushed to draw important consequences from that theological stance. Among others, he is persuaded that because God is mortally opposed to all evil, suffering and oppression, injustice and exploitation, Christians have no other option than to condemn apartheid roundly as part of their prophetic ministry.[36] Also, the Church must take concrete steps to demonstrate that it stands "side by side with those who are casualties of man's inhumanity to man" even if this should mean Christians have to suffer at the hands of those who uphold the apartheid system.[37] Furthermore, seeing that we are here concerned with an evil social system, Christians must commit themselves to a radical dismantling and eventual destruction of that system, so that they may create a new society — one which is truly democratic and just. This will be a new society in which people of different races, colours, cultures and sexes will come together into a fellowship that transcends all differences, and in which the diversity of the human family will be regarded as a source of enrichment rather than of separation and division. [38] This commitment to the dismantling of apartheid and replacing it with a new order has been a consistent message of Archbishop Tutu since 1981. He stated categorically that he is prepared to use the resources of the SACC and his own resources towards working for fundamental change in South Africa through peaceful means. He even expressed his intention of joining forces with the government in bringing about the dismantling of apartheid and replacing it with a social system that is more humane, just and equitable to all South Africans. [39]

That commitment towards a peaceful dismantling of apartheid was restated in even stronger terms at the 1984 SACC Annual Conference, where Archbishop Tutu reminded his audience that it is God's justice, peace and reconciliation which requires them to be agents of the destruction of the South African social order because it is evil and unchristian. For, in his view, the way in which South Africa is currently ordered politically, socially and economically, is not only morally indefensible, but also guarantees its destruction through disintegration into the chaos of lawlessness, violence and revolution. [40]

In order to counteract that possibility which is too ghastly to contemplate, Archbishop Tutu believes that the apartheid system must be done away with. This is the only way towards the realization of true peace and reconciliation based on justice and security for all. To be sure, this calls for a costly peace because it calls for the death of the existing social order, but true peace and reconciliation are always costly as demonstrated by our reconciliation with God which cost God the life of Jesus. [41]

It is against this background of a commitment to the dismantling of apartheid that Archbishop Tutu's support for conscientious objectors has to be understood. For in agreement with the SACC Resolution of Hammanskraal in 1974,[42] Archbishop Tutu believes that our South African social system is basically unjust, immoral and utterly indefensive and therefore constitutes institutionalized violence against the oppressed, powerless and exploited black majority. Therefore, any activity that aims at defending and supporting, rather than destroying it, constitutes an involvement in what is immoral and unjust. For that reason, Archbishop Tutu has found it necessary to call upon the Churches to declare that any war to defend apartheid is unjust, one in which Christians cannot

be engaged without violating their consciences. [43] It is in the same
vein that Archbishop Tutu has often been heard to say that if the
Cubans or the Russians, for whom he holds no brief, were to
attack and threaten to destroy the present vicious and evil system
of apartheid, very few blacks would lift a finger to defend South
Africa, because almost anything would, to them, appear preferable
to what is embodied in the present system. [44] Also, it is against the
background of the indefensibility of the apartheid system that
Archbishop Tutu feels perfectly justified by labelling the blacks
who serve in the Defence Force as "traitors to the cause of liberation" because for him "South Africa as it is presently ordered is
not worth fighting for and certainly not worth dying for". [45] On the
contrary, it must be dismantled and done away with and replaced
by something better.

Is Archbishop Tutu a man of peace?

We have almost come full cycle trying to explore reasons why Archbishop Tutu is perceived as an obstructive and implacable foe of the
apartheid system — all arising out of his belief that it is an immoral
and unjust system that cannot be reconciled with Christian faith, and
also out of his conviction that he is called by God to be God's fellow
worker in the dismantling of that system. His objective is to transform the "ills and ugliness, the hatreds and animosities of our society,
its despair and sorrow, its anguish embodied in the cry of the hungry,
the homeless and the powerless unto God's Kingdom of justice,
wholeness, laughter, joy, and reconciliation." [46] In carrying out his
declared intentions of creating a new, non-racial, just and peaceful
South Africa, by dismantling apartheid, the question is whether Archbishop Tutu has acted in a manner that is contrary to the peaceful
resolution of South African woes?

In trying to answer the question, one will have to concede and
agree with Archbishop Tutu that it all depends from which perspective one looks at what he does. For, as he points out in his 1984 General Secretary's Report, the activities of the SACC and his own look
different to those who benefit from the *status quo* than to those who
suffer under it. Accordingly, while most whites consider him subversive and obstructive to peaceful evolutionary change because of the
confrontational stance he has adopted towards the South African
regime, "virtually all the blacks would say the SACC has helped us
keep body and soul together, the SACC has given us hope, the SACC
has helped us to get an education. The SACC has helped us believe in
a God who cares about injustice, about unemployment, about hunger, about harsh laws, about vicious forced population removals." [47]

With regard to those who portray him as a subversive political priest, as a revolutionary anti-white extremist, Archbishop Tutu reminds them that, because of his strong commitment to reconciliation between blacks and whites based on justice, he has earned the wrath of young black radicals who regard him as soft, and delaying liberation through his contacts with whites. He goes further to remind his accusers of his fervent commitment towards negotiation, dialogue and peaceful dismantling of the apartheid system by pointing out that:

He was the one who initiated dialogue between the government and the churches in order to mutually find peaceful ways of resolving our conflict-ridden situation. He did this despite the provocations and vilifications from the supporters of the government after his passport was withdrawn.

He has been building bridges between whites and blacks as can be seen in his dialogue with the Afrikaans students at their university campuses.

He even shared platforms with SABRA and the Broederbond at the University of Pretoria.[48]

He offered his offices to serve as mediator in helping to resolve a labour strike in Cape Town.

He once intervened to try to save the life of a policeman at the funeral of Mr Mxenge in King William's Town.

He tried to stop stone throwing at Regina Mundi, Soweto, on June 16, 1983.

He was one of the few who sent a telegram appealing to President René of Seychelles to release white mercenaries who were condemned to death for an abortive coup because of his strong opposition to capital punishment.

He struggled to bring peace to black university campuses.

He worked tirelessly to try to resolve the intractable school boycots throughout South Africa.

He continues to maintain contacts with the ANC whose aim — to work for a truly democratic and non-racial South Africa — he supports, though he holds no brief for their methods. These contacts are meant to build future bridges with these liberation movements hoping that at an opportune time he might "persuade them to come to the negotiating table" with the South African government so that both blacks and whites may jointly find ways to resolve our conflict situation.[49]

An objective look at all these activities in which Archbishop Tutu is involved, does not seem to lead us to the conclusion that he is a revolutionary, non-peaceful political priest. Taken individually or jointly those activities seem rather geared towards creating a climate in which a peaceful resolution of South African racial problems could be effected. It was therefore in recognition of Tutu's reconciliatory role that the Norwegian Nobel Committee characterized him as a "unifying leader figure in the campaign to resolve the problem of apartheid in South Africa" when it awarded him the prestigious international Nobel Peace Prize on October 16, 1984. Furthermore, the award of the Peace Prize wanted to underscore in no uncertain terms the fact that Archbishop Tutu is a man committed to peaceful fundamental changes in South Africa, contributing thereby the promotion of brotherhood and sisterhood between our racially torn people. In according Archbishop Tutu this honour, the Nobel Committee was saying to all of us that the negative perceptions that are held by some whites and pro-government news media, to the effect that Tutu is a subversive, anti-white, obstructive revolutionary priest, are unfounded in the light of what this man of God has been going and saying over the years as General Secretary of the South African Council of Churches. This is also the view held by the majority of voiceless blacks on whose behalf Tutu speaks as he tries to work for justice, peace and reconciliation in South Africa.

But it is precisely through his political involvement and pronouncement against the evils of apartheid that Archbishop Tutu has projected himself to the world as a man of peace and won the admiration of all those who pray and work for fundamental peaceful change. At the same time, those same activities have earned Archbishop Tutu the label of a "political priest". It is a label for which he does not apologize, especially because he is being called "political priest" by virtue of the fact he refuses to believe that apartheid is a just, moral and Christian socio-political system. For those who accuse him of being a "political priest", Tutu asks very revealing and penetrating questions, when he says:

"Is it not interesting just how often people and churches are accused of mixing religion with politics? Almost always whenever they condemn a particular social political dispensation as being unjust. If the South African Council of Churches were to say now, that it thought apartheid was not so bad, I am as certain as anything that we would not be finding ourselves where we are today. Why is it not being political for a religious body or a religious leader to praise a social political dispensation?"[50]

Because the label "political priest" is virtually vacuous and can mean anything that its users want it to mean, Archbishop Tutu seems destined to remain controversial and "political" in his prophetic witness against the apartheid system which he wants to dismantle. For Archbishop Tutu is a man who has fully accepted the fact that, if

Christians are truly to live and act according to the imperatives of the Gospel of Jesus Christ, they cannot with integrity remain aloof from socio-political involvement. For as he rightly reminds us: "Our relationship with God demands and is authenticated by our relationship with our fellow human beings. The Kingdom of God is not a nebulous platonic "ideal state" in the hereafter. It is, as Jesus said, among us, and its signs are tangible, this worldly effects ---- when demons are exorcised; when the hungry are fed and the naked clothed; when the lepers are cleansed and the lame made to walk again, the deaf to hear and the blind to see; when sins are forgiven and the dead are raised to life again. When all are exposed for what they are and evil is overcome by good; when oppression and exploitation are resisted, even at the cost of freedom and life itself, then we have a real foretaste of Heaven.[51]

Archbishop Tutu's refusal to remain aloof from socio-political involvement in obedience to the imperatives of the gospel and to speak out against the evils of oppression and domination of the powerless by the powers that be, appears to have stamped him, for better or worse, as a "political priest" in the minds of some South Africans. Fortunately for him, there have been others before him who have suffered a similar fate. Archbishop Tutu, to be precise, stands in the tradition of some of the greatest missionary figures who refused to separate socio-economic issues and political repression of black South Africans by colonial rulers from evangelism. Here one could recall such Christian giants such as Vanderkemp and Philip who, in assuming the mantle of being the voice of the oppressed and voiceless, were not looked upon with favour by the colonists in the Cape Colony, who saw them as "political priests" bent on mixing religion with politics. Also, one may recall the efforts of Archbishop Colenso on behalf of justice for some of the Zulu chiefs that earned him the wrath and enmity of whites in Natal.

In the recent past, one may recall the prophetic witness of Geoffrey Clayton, Colin Winter, Denis Hurley, and others against the evils of apartheid. All these religious leaders appropriated in one way or another the prophetic tradition of Vanderkemp and Philip who refused to accept the belief that the Gospel of Jesus Christ has little or nothing to do with a repressive socio-political system.[52]

Archbishop Tutu has to be understood against this prophetic tradition of noble church leaders who worked relentlessly to overcome evil with good, to try to create social conditions that will make justice, peace and freedom the common property of all South Africans regardless of race, colour or creed. For it is only when such a situation is obtained that one could ever hope of bringing about true reconciliation among our racially divided communities. Towards that end Archbishop Tutu has not spared any effort or opportunity in what he says and does, even if this should earn him the undeserved label of being a "political priest". But that he is a man of peace, committed to peaceful transformation of our tragic socio-political conditions, his actions bear ample testimony, the testimony also accepted by the international community which has awarded Archbishop Tutu the well-deserved Nobel Peace Prize. For our part, there seems to be no reason why we cannot agree with that judgment, namely: that Archbishop Tutu is a man of peace.

REFERENCE NOTES
1. Cf. *Ecunews,* Vol.8, December 1984, pp 8-10, in which sampling of Newspapers is printed.
2. Bishop D. Tutu, *General Secretary's Report to the Annual National Conference,* 1981, p.2. Hereafter referred to simply as *General Secretary's Report* plus date. Unless stated otherwise, the reports cited here are unpublished.
3. *Ecunews,* Vol. 8, December 1984, pp 8-10. Also see, Bishop Tutu, *Hope and Suffering,* Johannesburg: Skotaville Publishers, 1983, pp. 136, 141. Referred to hereafter as *Hope and Suffering.*
4. *Hope and Suffering,* p. 136
5. *General Secretary's Report,* 1982, p.5 . Also see his *Hope and Suffering,* p. 125
6. For further discussion about theology and politics see my "Theology and Politics in South Africa" in *The Chicago Theological Seminary Register,* Vol. LXIX, no.2, Spring 1979, pp. 11-25
7. *General Secretary's Report,* 1981, p.2
8. *General Secretary's Report,* 1982, p.1
9. *General Secretary's Report,* 1981, p.1
10. *General Secretary's Report,* 1982, p.2
11. *General Secretary's Report,* 1982, p.4
12. *General Secretary's Report,* 1984, p.5
13. Ibid., p.3
14. Ibid., p.4
15. Ibid., p.4
16. Ibid., pp. 4-5
17. Ibid., p.5
18. Ibid., p.6
19. Ibid., pp. 3-4
20. Ibid., p.8
21. Cf *Ecunews* p. 15
22. *General Secretary's Report,* 1984, pp. 3-4
23. *Ecunews,* p. 15. Also see, *General Secretary's Report,* 1982, pp. 4-5
24. *General Secretary's Report,* 1984, p.8
25. *Hope and Suffering,* p. 141
26. Ibid., p.19
27. *General Secretary's Report,* 1981, p.11
28. *Hope and Suffering,* p. 135. Also see, *General Secretary's Report,* 1982, p.12
29. *Hope and Suffering,* p. 133
30. Ibid., p. 133; Also see, *General Secretary's Report,* 1981, p. 11

31. *Hope and Suffering*, p.133
32. *General Secretary's Report*, 1982, p.12
33. *General Secretary's Report*, 1984, pp. 25-26
34. *Hope and Suffering*, p.141
35. Ibid., p.141
36. Ibid., p.141
37. *General Secretary's Report*, 1982, pp.2, 6
38. Ibid., p.2
39. *General Secretary's Report*, 1984, p.36
40. *General Secretary's Report*, 1981, p.9
41. *General Secretary's Report*, 1984, pp. 34-35
42. Ibid., p.36
43. The full text is reproduced in the *Report of the Commission of Inquiry into the South African Council of Churches*, Pretoria: Government Printer, 1983, pp. 188-190. Referred to hereafter as *Eloff Commission's Report*.
44. *General Secretary's Report*, 1984, pp. 15-16
45. *General Secretary's Report*, 1982, p.8
46. *Eloff Commission's Report*, p. 197
47. *General Secretary's Report*, 1984, pp. 36-37
48. Ibid., pp. 27-29. Also see, *General Secretary's Report*, 1981, p.9
49. *General Secretary's Report*, 1981, p.9
50. *General Secretary's Report*, 1984, pp.
51. *Hope and Suffering*, p.136
52. Bishop Tutu, "God's Strength in Human Weakness" in *Your Kingdom Come: Papers and Resolutions* of the *12th National Conference of the SACC, Hammanskraal 1980*, Nash, M (ed), Johannesburg: SACC, 1980, p. 14
53. For a detailed and perceptive analysis of the debate on the interaction between religion and politics, the reader is referred to Adrian Hastings "Mission, Church and State in Southern Africa" delivered at the International Association for Mission Studies, University of Zimbabwe, January 8-14, 1984.

(a)   A concern to develop a biblical theology of liberation.
(b)   A call for the church to be a community of liberation.

A Concern for a Biblical Theology of Liberation
Archbishop Tutu is basically a biblical theologian. By this I want
to suggest that the foundations of his theological hermeneutic are
grounded in the liberating message of the Bible. To illustrate this
point let me quote from one of his statements:
 "Where there is injustice, exploitation and oppression then the
 Bible and the God of the Bible are subversive of such a situation. Our God, unlike the pagan nature gods, is no God sanc-
 tifying the *status quo*. He is a God of surprises, uprooting the
 powerful and unjust to establish His Kingdom. We see it in
 the entire history of Israel."[2]
Archbishop Tutu makes numerous references to the Bible as
part of the development of his theological hermeneutics. Unfortunately this biblical hermeneutics thrust in his theology is not developed in the form of a theological treatise — but merely as a crucial
ingredient in his theology. I want to show why this theological concern is crucial to the way we do theology in the South African
context.

The Place of the Bible in Black Theological Reflection
Since the inception of Black Theology in the late sixties many
essays have been published on the task of Black Theology. In most
of these essays reference is made to the significance of the Bible in
black theological reflection, however, without spellingout how this
should be done. I must confess I am not a biblical theologian, but
as a theological ethicist I have an obligation to respond to the challenge of the authority of the Bible. But apart from that I believe
most of our theological categories would lose their meaning if they
lack a biblical basis which evolved out of the faith of the early
Christian community.

There is renewed interest in the study of the Bible particularly
using methods from the Social Sciences. More biblical scholars are
turning to Sociology and Sociology of Knowledge in their attempt
to unravel the early social world of both the Old and the New
Testaments. I believe this is a very important development which
hopefully will shed new insights on the significance of the Bible for
theology and preaching. This will also enable us to appreciate why
certain Biblical themes have attracted the attention of particularly
those who engage in the theology of liberation, especially the
theme of the Exodus. As the scope of this essay does not permit
me to examine these new developments, I will focus my attention

on one aspect, that is, viewing scripture as a liberating word and then use it as a basis for understanding the place of the Bible in black theological reflection.

One of the prevailing misconceptions about the theology of liberation is that this kind of theology is inspired purely by radical ideologies such as nationalism and Marxism, and not the Bible. We need to examine this misconception in order to put the record straight. What we must recognize is that one of the central themes of the Bible is liberation/salvation. What theology of liberation has succeeded to impress on our minds is that the God of the Bible is the God of liberation. Daniel Migliore in his book *Called to Freedom* makes the following observation:

"Liberation theology finds the centre of Scripture in its story of God's liberating activity. In the Old Testament God's saving action is focussed in the Exodus, the liberation of a people from political, cultural and religious bondage. By this event God has become known as the liberating God. 'I am the Lord your God, who brought you out of the land of Egypt, out of the house of bondage'" (Ex. 20:2).

Because of this basic theological thrust Migliore has suggested that the Bible should be interpreted (a) historically, (b) theocentrically, and (c) contextually.

Let us examine what he means by these three categories. (a) To interpret the Bible historically plays an important role in theology, or preaching for that matter, in that it compels the exegete to take seriously the particularity of God's actions. This approach enables us to appreciate the liberating acts of God in history. But more than this consideration, it enables us to appreciate the problems and the limitations of the early Christian community.

We come to understand the possibilities that remained as a challenge to that community. As Migliore states, "To interpret the Bible historically is to see in its narratives not only memories of past events but promises of new possibilities."[4] The point which Migliore emphasizes is that in studying the past of God's liberating activity, we are challenged to understand its implications for the present. But further, this approach enables us to link our present struggle with that of the early Christian community.

I believe Archbishop Tutu, as a biblical theologian, has been very conscious of this principle in his work. He displays a very strong consciousness that the God of the Bible acts within human history. That God sides concretely with the wretched of the earth within the historical context of their struggle. For Archbishop Tutu the incarnation is a historical event that signals God's determination to liberate humanity from oppression and dehumanization. The God of the Bible acts in history to liberate humanity, this is the message of the ministry of Jesus Christ. In one of his important sermons delivered at Steve Biko's funeral he made the following statement:

"Yes, the God Jesus came to proclaim He was no neutral sitter on the fence. He took the side of the oppressed, the poor, the exploited, not because they were holier or morally better than their oppressors.

No, He was on their side simply and solely because they were oppressed. Yes, this was the good news Jesus came to proclaim — that God was the liberator, the one who set free the oppressed and the poor and exploited. He set them free from all that would make them less than he wanted them to be, fully human persons as free as Jesus Christ showed Himself to be. And so all the mighty works which Jesus performed, healing the sick, opening the eyes of the blind, forgiving the sins of all sinners, were to set them free so that they could enjoy the glorious liberty of the children of God. And His followers believed He would restore the Kingdom again to Israel. He would set them free from being ruled by the Romans and give them back their political independence."[5]

For Archbishop Tutu God is involved in the struggle of the oppressed. God takes sides within a specific historical context. This principle is important for it compels whoever reads the Bible to contextualize.

The other important point which Migliore makes is that the Bible should be interpreted theocentrically. This principle, I believe, is so central to our theological hermeneutic that without it, it becomes impossible to engage in any meaningful biblical exegesis. Migliore makes the following observation about this:

Scripture must be interpreted theocentrically; however, the meaning of "God" is radically redefined in the biblical story of liberation.

The central actor in the biblical drama is God. Scripture witnesses to the reality of God, to the purpose of God, to the kingdom of God. The content of the biblical story is God's faithfulness in acts of judgment and mercy, in the covenant with the people of Israel and in the history of Jesus. The biblical narrative has many aspects, but in the midst of the many aspects is the central theme: the mystery of the faithful God who takes up the cause of justice, freedom, and peace on behalf of the creation oppressed by sin and misery. Scripture witnesses on the promise of God even in the midst of judgment. It declares God's benevolence toward us even in the depth of our sin: "While we were yet sinners Christ died for us" (Rom. 5:8). Scripture proclaims the decisive ratification of all God's promises in the resurrection of the crucified Jesus. "For all the promises of God find their Yes in him" (II Cor. 1:20). [6]

Reading his articles or listening to Archbishop Tutu one gets an interesting insight about how his theology is centred on the notion of God. For Archbishop Tutu God is alive and involved in the struggle of the oppressed. It is thus the God of liberation of the exodus who is the source of his prophetic piety. God is not just an idea but becomes the vision the embodiment of a real liberating presence in the world. In one of his sermons Archbishop Tutu made the following observation:

"So let us remind ourselves again and again just what kind of God our God is. He is always there. He has always been there. So don't despair. No matter how long it may take or seem to be. He is there. He hears, He cares and will act. We must not doubt that He will take our side and that He will rescue us and lead us out of bondage, out of our slavery, out of our poverty, out of our suffering. He will make us His own people to worship Him and He is almighty. Nothing will eventually stop Him." [7]

This vision of a God who takes sides is so real for Archbishop Tutu, God is not neutral for in Jesus Christ He identifies with the poor and the oppressed. This theocentric approach, I believe, is reflected in most theologies of liberation. Liberation theologians are so conscious of this God who liberates the wretched of the earth. I believe this principle is a pivot on which our hermeneutic is based for without this profound consciousness of a God who is involved in the struggles of humanity, there would be no theology or theologies of liberation.

The other important principle that Migliore mentions in his book is that the Bible must be interpreted contextually. He makes the following observation about this:

"Scripture must be interpreted contextually; however, the context of our interpretation must be increasingly open to and inclusive of the yearnings of the whole creation to be free.

The context of our interpretation of Scripture will always include and will frequently begin with our now personal awareness of captivity and yearning for freedom and new life: with our own anxiety, guilt, frustration, alienation, loneliness and despair.[8]

I believe that Archbishop Tutu has been very faithful to this principle. For in his sermons and speeches he interprets the Bible contextually. For him the Bible is so relevant to every situation of life. The word of God addresses the South African situation. It is the word that unravels the contradictions and the evils of the political system of apartheid. Speaking about the church he makes the following statement:

"The church in South Africa must be a prophetic church which cries out 'thus saith the Lord' speaking up against injustice and violence, against oppression and exploitation, against all that dehumanizes God's children and makes them less than what God intended them to be. The Church of God in this context must show forth the features of the Lord and Master who tied a towel around His waist to wash the feet of His disciples."[9]

This concern with the present contest of oppression and suffering is reflected in his theological vision. As he attempts to interpret the word of God contextually, he at the same time proclaims its promise for liberation in the here and now. Through Archbishop Tutu, God speaks so powerfully to the South African situation. It is this commitment that has earned Archbishop Tutu both enemies and friends.

So what we see in this brief analysis is the development of a biblical vision that addresses itself to the current political struggle of the oppressed. The Word of God addresses itself to the plight of the poor and the oppressed. It is not only the word but the word made flesh in the liberating ministry of Jesus Christ. What we see in Archbishop Tutu's theological vision is the development of an incarnational approach in which God's concern becomes alive through the commitment of those who serve God in the world today. In this, Archbishop Tutu succeeds to make the Bible relevant to the struggle of authentic human liberation. I believe Archbishop Tutu must be given credit for this, for the Bible has been silent for a very long time in our struggle for liberation within the South African context. My real concern, however, is with the black Christian community in responding to this challenge which Archbishop Tutu has presented before us. The question before the black Christian community is, how do we keep this biblical vision alive in our churches? For without this dynamic biblical vision we will lose our theological mandate to be involved in the struggle for liberation but also we will betray the purpose and goal of our mission as the people of God. Archbishop Tutu has been very conscious of this challenge and it is my hope that as black theologians we will continue to search for a biblical theology of liberation which addresses itself to our situation.

A Call For the Church to be a Community of Liberation

In his work as the General Secretary of the South African Council of Churches, Archbishop Tutu succeeded in making the Christian aware of the churches' role in the struggle for liberation. His preaching and speeches have demonstrated the need for the churches to be involved in the struggle for liberation and perhaps this is one aspect that has made him extremely unpopular with those who support the *status quo*. It will be very interesting to observe how this concern will be viewed by members of his diocese as the new Archbishop of Cape Town.

When we examine particularly his speeches and sermons there is a theological motif that runs through and becomes a central hermeneutical principle. This theological motif is God's radical concern for the world fully realized in the coming of Jesus Christ as the Messiah. There is a sense in which — Jesus' Ministry is the continuation of this radical concern for the world. Those who are members of the Body of Christ participate also in this radical concern for the world. Archbishop Tutu's ecclesiology is shaped by the doctrine of God in its many facets. It is an ecclesiology which seeks to demonstrate God's care and love for the world and particularly the wretched of the earth. In one of his sermons he makes the following statement:

"We must witness by service to others, by being their servants in all sorts of ways. In our country, South Africa, the church must be there in the poverty and squalor, to bring the love and compassion of God amongst the sick, the hungry, the lepers, the disabled and the naked. We must proclaim that in a country of injustice and oppression where blacks receive inferior education, are forced to live in match box houses, cannot move freely from place to place, and have to leave their wives and families behind when they want to work in town — we must declare that this is God's world. He is on the side of the oppressed, of the poor, of the despised. We must say these things even if they make us suffer. It is not politics. It is the Gospel of Jesus Christ, the liberator who will set us free."

As members of the Christian community we have no choice but to participate in the process of liberation. We have no choice but to challenge the forces of oppression and dehumanization. But one remarkable aspect of this involvement, is that God has already taken sides. God is on the side of the oppressed and this is part of the message of the Gospel of liberation. Even in the ministry of Jesus Christ, we see this identification with the poor and the oppressed.

Archbishop Tutu, more than any other black theologian, has challenged the Christian community to participate in this process of liberation and reconciliation. It is because of this vision that the SACC assumed a very important role in the South African situation — a role that resulted in the Eloff Commission. I believe this vision about the task and mission of the church comes at a very critical time when many young blacks are beginning to question the role of the church in our country. Although many of our young blacks are suspicious of the church, they hear a new challenge coming from Archbishop Tutu's vision about the church.

I believe that when the church responds courageously to that vision, there will be hope for Christianity in this country. It is when the church becomes involved in the struggle for authentic liberation — that will challenge many to begin to take the Gospel seriously.

But the vision of the church as a community of liberation raises a number of complex and difficult issues. For example, how does the church, as a divided community, participate effectively in the process of liberation? For as we know the church in this country is divided on many levels. The church is divided on racial as well as ideological lines. It is also divided on theological lines as well as on a class basis. These divisions are found virtually in all our Christian communities. This problem of division within the churches raises both theological as well sociological problems. The theological problem has to do with our understanding of the nature and mission of the church. The sociological problems have to do with how social forces and structures of society influence the nature of Christian fellowship or presence in the world today.

Because of the urgency of this assignment I cannot address myself adequately to all these problems. However, one observation we have to make, is that apartheid has not just divided the South African society but it has sadly fragmented the Christian community as a whole.

The church represents both a theological phenomenon as well as a concrete organizational entity. These two aspects of the church are inseparable. They influence each other either positively or negatively. One of the problems that has plagued our theological vision for a long time is the failure of the church to relate the two aspects within the context of the South African political realities.

The church has and continues to present a truncated theological vision of the church as something totally separate from the world. The church is seen as an institution from which we escape the sinful realities of this world. This vision of the church defines salvation as an escape from the demonic world. This is a common view in any of our churches.

Because of this rather strange view of the church, many Christians, both black and white, have failed to grasp the challenge of their responsibility in changing the world. Evangelization has meant drifting away from the realities of this world. I believe such a view is a product of a truncated theological vision that has dominated and continues to dominate our thinking about the church today. And as long as this theological vision prevails, the church will continue to be irrelevant to the struggle for liberation that is going on at the moment.

But if we respond to the challenge Archbishop Tutu presents of the church as the expression and promise of God's radical concern for the marginalized and oppressed of society, there is hope. I believe the church, as the embodiment of this radical concern of God fully realized in Jesus Christ, offers us a number of possibilities. First we become aware that the vision takes expression in real concrete forms, when Christians begin to challenge the oppressive powers of this world. When they demand that justice should become a crucial ingredient of the ordering society. In other words Christian consciousness expresses itself in actions that demand justice. This view of the church is in keeping with the biblical understanding of God's involvement in the world. For the God of the Bible is one who demands justice. The God of the Bible expresses love in a concrete way, one which leads to the wilderness experience in the Old Testament and the crucifixion in the New Testament.

Secondly, if we take the theological vision of the church as the community of liberation, we become aware of our structural involvement in society. The awareness of our political entanglements in economic as well as political institutions that are oppressive, leads to a new understanding of our faith and witness as form of protest. But protest without action is futile. For Jesus Christ, His ministry of protest against the religious and political establishments of the day led to the cross. We also, as members of the church in South Africa, have no other option but to become a living symbol of protest accompanied by actions and critical involvement in the struggle for liberation.

Archbishop Tutu as a theologian represents so vividly this symbol of Christian protest within South Africa. But for him it is protest motivated by a deep commitment to the biblical faith accompanied by a passion for peace and justice. This is the challenge that he presents and portrays in his ministry to the church in South Africa. May we all learn and be inspired by his example — *Amandla Awethu!*

REFERENCE NOTES

1. Tutu, *Hope and Suffering* p.26-27
2. Ibid p.141
3. D. Migliore *Called to Freedom,* p.32
4. Ibid p.35
5. Op. cit, p.13
6. Migliore, *Called to freedom*, p.36
7. Tutu, *Hope and Suffering*, p.77
8. Migliore, p.38
9. Tutu, *Hope and Suffering*, pp.109-110
10. Tutu, *A Voice Crying in the Wilderness*, (1982), pp.31-32

Part 3

African Theology, Morality in African Tradition and Social Ethics in South Africa

GABRIEL M. SETILOANE

Salvation and
the Secular

Writing his contribution to the Festschrift, *Essays for G.C. Seligman* (Kegan Paul, Routledge, etc. London 1934) Isaac Schapera in the essay "Oral Sorcery Among the Tswana" deals with the phenomenon called *Kgaba* or *Lehutso*. What is striking about this practice is that the "sorcerer", so-called by social anthropological definition, does not employ any material to effect his/her intentions. All he/she needs is to utter a word *"O tla bona"* — "You will see". The only physical activity accompanying might be the "pointing of the forefinger at the victim", which could also be done without a word being uttered:

> The material factor is entirely lacking. The most potent factor is the feeling of malevolence against a person by someone else. The latter makes use of no *"ditlhare"*, he utters no spells, he performs no special rites, nor does he have to observe any taboos or other special usages. All the necessary ingredients of magic are lacking. The only thing necessary for him to have is a bitter heart against his enemy. (Schapera, 1934, p 296).

Schapera expresses a sense of disgust at witnessing an injustice when, in the appropriate traditional court, where normally *boloi* (sorcery) is regarded as a very serious offence, the *Moloi* (sorcerer) in this case is treated as if he/she were the offended party while the victim who has suffered all the ill-effects is judged to be the guilty and offending party. *Kgaba* occurs mainly among close relations, and is often inflicted by older people who are hurt and disadvantaged by the behaviour of some younger, proud, and powerful member of the community. When it happens outside the family community it is called *Lehutso* (an evil wish). Even then it does not need any material factor. All it needs to be activated is a strong sense of injustice committed, or a grudge felt by the "sorcerer". When the court considers the plaint of the victim it also considers the circumstances which have caused such a situation to arise. The judgment often (and this is what surprised poor Schapera!) is that the victim is liable for damages — a sheep, a goat or a beast — which he pays to the "sorcerer". Thereafter he also has to bear the cost of a "peace-feast" in the name or in honour of the "sorcerer" to ensure that his/her "heart is returned to its proper abode". In other words the ritual healing is done to the "sorcerer" and not the victim of sorcery and, even worse, by the victim.

For those who may not know, the idea of the "peace-feast", is that every time blood is shed in ritual slaughter and the community comes together, the ancestors — *Badimo,* participate — their presence in the community is intensified. They are always present of course, but this time it is as if they preside over this feast of reconciliation, as they do over all important communal occasions. Ultimate healing comes when the "sorcerer" (heart returned to its proper place) utters a blessing (a reversal of the *Kgaba* or *Lehutso*) to the victim: *"Badimo B'eno ba go roballe"* — "May your ancestors rest at peace for you".

Explanation of the principle involved
The dynamics of what actually is seen happening in this and similar cases is usually revealed through divination by a *Ngaka:* the offended party, at wit's end, invokes the assistance and intervention of the ancestors against the victim, by brooding over the hurt, uttering the words *"O tla bona"* or just pointing a finger. The effect of this is a diminution of ancestral (Divine) protection and goodwill over the victim, resulting in making his/her *Seriti-Isithunzi* light, and him/her prone to misfortune, illness and lack of control of affairs. *Kgaba,* therefore, is a very effective weapon in the hands of the old, the weak and powerless against the thoughtlessness, arrogance, and overbearing ways of their more powerful neighbours. The mere going about with "a heart out of place", broken and heavy, of a defenceless, powerless member of the community as a result of someone's heartlessness and thoughtlessness (sometimes even if it is not on purpose or calculated) is enough to invoke the wrath of the "guardians of the morality of the community" (the ancestors). As Schapera found out then, no court on earth is able to alter the situation.

W C Willoughby, a very celebrated missionary among these people at the beginning of this century, relates how he witnessed

an attempt by some chief's councillor to influence him so that, by
his action and decision, the course of justice would miscarry, and a
poor man made to suffer wrongly. The chief remonstrated: "How
dare you make me do that? I shall not do it! Else, how shall I look
my fathers (ancestors) in the face?" (Willoughy: *The Soul of the
Bantu,* SCM, London, 1928).
This is understanding the community at its deepest. The idea is
that the so-called "secular order" is made up of more elements
than that which is physically observable. The Ancestors — *Badimo*
(according to my study "The People of Divinity" or God if you
will, and therefore a means or form in which Divinity [God] is
made available to physical natural existence, like in the "Christian
concept of the Holy Spirit!") as "vital participants" (V Mulago: *Un
Visage Africain du Christianisne,* Paris, 1965) in the community
and guardians of its morality are continually watchful of any injustice and thoughtless behaviour which is apt to disturb its harmony
and peace. But, perhaps even more important, it is the interests of
the old, the powerless and the poor which seem to be most under
this divine protection. Several expressions in the everyday life and
language bear this out. Let us look at only two:
Ntwa ya Khutsana e lowa ke ditshoswane (an orphan's cause/case is
taken up by ants). This is said in consolation to or by one who has
received short-shrift at the hands of authority, court, or someone who
wields power. Said by the recipient of such unjust treatment, it is in
fact a pronouncement of *Kgaba/Lehutso,* Schapera's "Oral Sorcery"
on the guilty party. It is an appeal to the unseen guardians of morality
— *Badimo* — to come to one's assistance, a cry to heaven for
vengeance.
Modidi ke Moloi, translates: "A poor man (i.e. who has nothing of
his own) is a sorcerer". Therefore the underlying purpose of Sotho-
Tswana community life is to ensure that there are none totally destitute. Unfortunately we cannot go into that now. *Modidi ke moloi* is
often said by the rich, the powerful and successful, to remind themselves of the lot of the poor. Perhaps it is this principle which lays the
charge at the door of African society that it discourages entre-
preneurship which excessively increases the gap between the successful man and his fellows. Success, in order to be permanent and
lasting, must be shared with the less fortunate. There is a ritual which
is common among all the African people of this land, educated or
not, Christians or non-Christians alike. Euphemistically it is called
Umzebenzi-Tirelo — A service (i.e. to the ancestors). In Sotho-
Tswana it is called *Pha Badimo.* To this feast or party, celebrated
after some success, or just thankfulness that "we are alive" and called

"A feast gift to the ancestors", all and sundry come to eat and drink freely, even non-relatives. It is literally free food and drinks on the house. The understanding is that as the poor and erstwhile hungry, now well-fed and fully drunk, wend their way to their homes, or as they dance in drunken joy at the feast, expressing their thanks to the one who gave the party, they are in fact pronouncing a blessing on him or her, imploring *Badimo's* favour on his behalf.

The very opposite of *Lehutso*. The tight-fisted stingy rich forfeit this blessing, but instead earn the envy *(Lehutso)* of his/her poor neighbours. This envy of the rich by the poor can lead to their downfall and must be guarded against. That is why *"Modidi ke moloi"*. The underlying principle is that everyone who has, whatever it is, power, position or authority, riches or success, holds whatever he/she has only at the approval and blessing of his/her poor destitute communal fellows. *Pha Badimo,* therefore, is a manner of self-protection, an insurance against the sorcery of the poor and powerless — *Kgaba, Lehutso.* To keep their success the rich must be on constant guard to keep them happy and kindly disposed. In this way the successful and fortunate in this life are drawn out of the snare of avarice and selfishness to having concern for the less fortunate, the old, the poor, the orphans, widows, etc.

Two very significant points stand out in this world-view, and both make nonsense of Western presuppositions, even when they attempt to be religious:
a)   In reality there is no such thing as the "secular" being separate and apart from the "sacred". Divinity, through the participation of *Badimo* is shod through with the totality of existence. Even at its best Christian ethics of society do not in my view reach this depth of insight. I have looked at John Wesley rather seriously and still believe that he goes further than most in an attempt to relate the Divine-Human experience (Salvation) to the community (society). His declared goal "to spread Scriptural holiness throughout the land" was to be achieved through individuals who had gone through the experience of "conversion", and graduated by "regeneration" into some life of "Christian perfection",
... When I am all renewed,
When I in Christ am formed again,
And witness, from all sin set free,
All things are possible to me. (MHB 548)
Seen from an African perspective Christianity at best advocates "Salvation in the secular order" only as a by-product, not the main, of the individual's experience and attainment of "Salvation". As in his own teaching, John Wesley pitched this goal of Christian perfection

so high that he made it almost unattainable — I have no quarrel with him there — and it would be almost impossible to have enough "saved" and "born again" people in a community, it means the "Secular Order" remains perpetually damned. In spite of his "concern" for society, and despite the fact that he never really did agree with Luther's teaching on the Two Realms, John Wesley could never reach a Christian position which "confronted" the very pillars of secular authority, however much he might have agreed that it was unredeemed.

The African position, I believe, is much more incisive. It says all aspects of life (its totality) are spheres of Divine activity in all its intensity — and one ignores this at one's own risk. Old Samuel Broadbent did not know what a fluke he had made when standing between my great grand ancestor's Chief Sehunello of BaRolong, he challenged him: "There is a King of Kings, Modima, to whom all people and kings must give account; human life is at his disposal only". He thought he had won a Christian victory: "This reference to the Supreme authority appeared to strike him with a degree of awe, and he withdrew...". He withdrew because it struck familiar cords within his so-called "heathen" African chest, viz: That there is a Power — Divinity — at work in community life — all community, human, animal and vegetable, which does not brook the upsetting of order.

b) *Salvation,* therefore, is when peace, order and happiness are maintained in the community. This way all live and let others live. A disturbance of this harmony in life is a threat to the well-being of the whole, and therefore calls for the punitive intervention of Divinity. Thus in *Kgaba/Lehutso* the offender *(moloi)* is the one who flouts the norms of social behaviour, disturbing its equanimity, peace and harmony. Why the traditional court could not find against the one whom Schapera identified as the "Oral Sorcerer" is because this person is in fact on the side of harmony which promotes the survival of all and therefore the good and perpetuation of the community.

We need to admit here that the concept Salvation, in as far as it implies a prior situation of a fallen-ness or built-in depravity (original sin), is foreign to African thought and worldview. If ever the term Salvation were to come to mind as we are using it here, it would be expressed by an understanding of harmony within and between the elements that make up the community, and that would mean people, animals, vegetation and nature generally. This lies behind that classic example of what has been described as Animism of African belief viz: an African tribesman praying to the tree before he chops it! Even the hunter must, through a ritual performed by putting his hand on his prey, or a conversation with its *"Seriti"* explain why he has to disturb

the harmony of nature in this manner, go through the process of restoring the peace. That is why every mishap or unusual tragic happening must be accounted for by consulting "those who know" —
Bo-Reaitse: The *Ngaka.* The norm is a situation of coolness —
Lotsididi, we say in Setswana. The word is used ritually at the end of
the funeral service of a member of the community, after that passing
has been duly registered in the appropriate court *(kgotla)* comprising
both the seen and unseen by an official announcement. It is a disrup-
tion of the order and peace in the community of nature. This
announcement is called *Tatolo.* At the end of what is an obituary of
the deceased, the announcer cries, or rather prays *"A go nne
Lotsididi"* — May coolness come over us. The congregation then
responds: *Ee Lotsididi:* "Indeed, may there be coolness": — Let the
placid harmony of the community of nature be restored, and the
scorching sun, feverish death and human avarice stop causing disrup-
tion and suffering. For in African understanding, nature is essentially
good.

To summarize therefore, African understanding of the secular
order is that of community composed of the seen elements (human
and vegetable) as well as the unseen. I rather prefer to use the terms
seen and unseen than "living" and "un-living" or even Mbiti's "living
dead". For the concept of *"Seriti"* is not restricted to life nor to
people. Divinity *(Bo-Modimo,* comprising *Modimo* and *Badimo* is
not detached or outside the entity of the community; instead it is present, manifesting itself in the energy dynamism that generates the
very life of the community and maintains its morality and wholeness
through *Badimo* — the ancestors, as they participate in it imparting
to everybody, every moment, and every day the *mysterium tremendum et fascinans:* holiness. There is no "sacred" apart from the "secular". The ideal for all is harmony, peace — *Lotsididi* where the unity
of all the elements is maintained within the totality, each carrying on
with its functions of justice, fairness, fully conscious of inter-depen-
dency and that no part is greater than the whole. For life is a totality
and salvation is when it is kept so.

Application of the principles
But enough of this Western attempt at fathoming the mysteries of
African thought and theorizing over it as Westerners like to do.
Let us settle down to some good old African divination. Employ-
ing the insights expressed so far, let us attempt a diagnosis of our
South African community today, African-style. Let us throw the
bones:-
For ages now the Africans have been convinced that the policies
of the white people in this land are contrary to Divine intentions,

and not calculated to bring about peace, harmony and coolness — *Lotsididi*. Our history is a catalogue of repeated inroads into the being of people by the physically powerful whites. With equal persistence the victims have registered the objection. The recorder of history, being Western, has missed a very important point viz: that the African struggle all the way from Nxele (Makana) through Nongqawuse, the formation of the ANC, which follows very closely on the rise of Ethiopianism in the churches, Bullhoek, etc, is essentially a religious inspired struggle. Still the flouting of the norms of life in community have continued from generation to generation. Not a decade has passed without some major step — called Act of Parliament taken, to disrupt the lives of the people : 1910, 1913, 1924, 1936, 1948 when this obviously anti-will-of-God attitude towards life-together-in-community was declared and espoused as the principle and way of life, backed by all the courts of the land, with the first application, thereof in 1954, through the Bantu Education Act.

Seriously, how many times have the powerless, defenceless Africans gone to bed with aching hearts, because of injustice and inhumanity they can do nothing about: removal from ancient homes and ancestral shrines, cutting them off and making non-humans of them (for what person is a person without his ancestors?). How many mothers, wives and children have shed a tear in despair because some father, son or husand has been rendered impotent as breadwinner and maintainer of the family! What humiliation and sense of emasculation have many an African man felt, rendered so by the order of the day. I remember some time in the sixties, in this very city (Pietermaritzburg) an old devout man of God, to me as a young man in the trade, a true Eli, a High Priest of God and keeper of His Shrine, the Rev W Gcabashe. He was called before the white chairman of the district and given a good dressing down because, we the younger impatient lot had canvassed and voted for him to become chairman of the district. How could a responsible man like himself allow his name to be misused in that manner by these young radicals, whose calling into the work of the ministry is even doubtful? *"Wa thini ke wena, Baba?"* "How did you respond to all this?" I asked. *"Bengi zo thini Setiloane, mtwan' am?"* Then he added in Zulu: "The sweat of a dog gets lost in its fur". One who is a dog does not show anger, he goes to bed with an aching heart, and a heaving chest. Many Africans have been asking themselves: Does it really mean that our fathers had it all wrong, that evil prospers over good, and wrong and inhumanity wins the day? We have prayed ever so many times with the Psalmist: "How long, O Lord! How long shall wicked prosper and the righteous suffer?"

The events of our country since September 1984 when the so-called New Dispensation was launched, have exercised the minds of all concerned. For Africans the affairs of State have taken a turn which seems to confirm the views of their fathers which they had almost come to regard as irrelevant in a plural community. But community is the community of all, and the forces of Divinity apply and are at work in it no matter how heterogeneous it may be. The principles that *Motho ke Modimo,* the human person is sacred and cannot be kicked around with impunity, or that *Molato wa khutsana o lowa ke ditshoswane* or that *Modidi ke Moloi* apply for all communities. That is why advocates of theology claim that it is not a theology for the blacks only. It is concerned about the totality of Being: Divinity, humans in/and nature. The new turn in the affairs of our State refers to the situation in which the rulers of the land and determiners of the fate of many lives find themselves, and have put all of us. Some negative element, ill-fate, seems to have overtaken us. "The funny thing", complain the whites through the commentator on the South African Broadcasting Corporation's English Service after the 7 o'clock news, "is that all this happens exactly when those in power admit the errors of the past and profess a desire and will to mend them." There is something in the working of Divinity with humans everywhere which makes the most convicting and convincing judge of any person his/her own conscience. All was sweet and rosy for the prodigal son until "he came to himself". In the meantime the arrogant idiot had caused many hearts to ache and many innocent people sleepless nights. For effective judgment and justice a common morality between the parties concerned must be accepted. Perhaps we are almost there: Today we hear more and more phrases like "the good of all" coming from high and official quarters. Is it not too late?

For many blacks *Badimo* — the Ancestors of the community, which are the peoples of this land, all the inhabitants, because they are *Beng ba Lefatshe* — the Owners of the Land, no matter who rules over it, seem to have risen up in vengeance against injustice, avarice, inhumanity, selfishness; and the pomp, power and glory of yesterday is being proven as empty and ephemeral. Moffat, the missionary, witnesses a similar happening among the BaTlhaping: Jacob Cloete, a KhoiKhoi, had terrorized the countryside; plundering and murdering the people with the guns he had acquired from the Cape Colony. At long last fate caught up with him and "his form haggard and countenance emaciated, looking wild, with halts and starts as if the very air he breathed was charged with spectres and arrows of death" he would walk among the villagers, his very victims of erstwhile, begging for a morsel. His illness was diagnosed, not by the knowledgable *ngaka*, but by the ordinary folk, for it was so obvious: *"O Tshwerwe ke Poitshe-go"* — The weird, numenous, *mysterium tremendum* has taken hold of him. Moffat in his superficial Western way, incapable of seeing deeper than the surface, mis-translates them as saying: "He is seized by the terrors" *(Missionary Labours and Scenes,* London, 1842).

As with Cloete, so our contemporary situation. Years of flouting justice and righteousness, disregarding human misery, have raised the ants of the earth *(ditshoswane)*, insignificant nothings, to threaten our very existence. Rich, powerful and mighty magnates start and halt at spectral shadows of disinvestment and trade sanctions; the recession is here. Gold, yes, gold, our hope, has fallen in price to an all-time low, and our security, the Gold Coin Exchange, crumbles like a pack of cards. Is it only African eyes which see these things? Then there are these black youths who go about burning everything, schools and the very administrative structures meant for use to cool and balm our communal conscience. Successes turn to tragic failures. For instance the Umkomati Accord. Our own people, in trusted positions, sabotage our intentions for their own private ideological reasons. Things just seem to be fatefully set against us. The attention of the world seems to be focused just on us. We cannot throw our weight and flaunt our power and authority as freely as we would like to in our own country. Now there is Crossroads, immediately followed by Langa, Uitenhage. What silly foolish negligence that normal riot control equipment was not made available. Then Cabinda! Putting us in such a bad light with our closest allies at a time when "constructive engagement" is so much under fire!

'Kgaba as Schapera observed among the Tswana has a tendency to leave the actual culprit seemingly unaffected, and rather exercise its effects on his/her offspring or property who are under the influence of his *"Seriti"* — *"Isithunzi"*. Did I hear you whisper "Westdene"? Well, on that tragic occasion Xhosa labourers on the ground of the University of Cape Town were heard remarking that: *Uqamata ukhauleza ukupendula:* Divinity is swift to reply. Which seems to echo Milton's hymn:

> The Lord will come, and not be slow
> His footsteps cannot err;
> Before Him righteousness shall go,
> His royal harbinger. *(MHB* 813)

It is a black theological perspective we have been assigned to ex-
pose here. The thing about African divination is that it quite often
appears so commonplace, and corroborated by other than African
knowledge and experience. And yet precisely there lies the claim that
while it is African it depicts the situation of all mankind, and affects
all. The bones declare *"Kgaba"*. According to Schapera, and the
Tswana "even unuttered but justified hurt by a member or section of
the community" is cause enough to call the wrath of Divinity upon
the perpetrators. The results is *"Ichabod!"*: The Glory is Departed,
and old men, seized by *"Poitshego"*, fall off their rocking chairs to
perish ignominiously.

Salvation in black perspective

This is not Salvation. Indeed not! But it does give us a direction as
to where to seek the meaning of "Salvation" in black theological
unerstanding: Salvation is a situation in which harmony and peace
prevail in community life. No one can have "Salvation" alone,
because it is always a matter of relationship:

> So if you are offering your gift at the altar, and there remem-
> ber that your brother has something against you, leave your
> gift at the altar, and go, first be reconciled to your brother,
> then come and offer your gift (Matt 5:23).

Otherwise, and I incurred the wrath and anger of "the fathers"
of my church when I said it twenty-six years ago, all the ensuing
worship is sham and empty, making our churches and cathedrals
"whited sepulchres".

If it is salvation we seek, the Old Testament prophets who
already prescribed the way to go about it in the "secular sphere"
so-called, viz:

> to lose the bonds of wickedness
> to undo the thongs of the yoke,
> to let the oppressed go free
> and to break every yoke.
> Is it not to share your bread with the hungry;
> (sorry if some of this sounds like The Freedom Charter!)
> And to bring the homeless poor into your house;
> When you see the naked to cover him
> And not to hide yourself from your flesh (Isa 58:6f)

But according to the African Tradition, there would need to be
a session of healing. The *Ngaka* (Diviner), or *Sangoma*. would pre-
scribe a Feast to the Ancestors — *Pha Badimo*, at which the victims of the sorcery will, in the company of the total community
(don't forget that this includes the unseen, *Badimo!*) under the
transcendence of *Modimo, Qamata, Umvelingqangi* — God, con-

fess the error of their ways, and then receive absolution, forgiveness and restoration and confirmation in their *Botho* (Human-ness) from the total community including the owners of the land. Only then will the Weird, the *Mysterium Tremendum, Poitshego,* release its hold on us and on the land, and *Lotsididi* be with us. Then only shall we be able to experience the longed-for *Fascinans* of Divinity, and able to understand what is meant by *Emmanuel* = God with us.

An after-thought:

Is not this *Pha Badimo* feast and come-together of all the elements of the community in the presence of Divinity (by whatever tradition, white, African, Asian, Coloured) which African divination reveals to us, the National Convention, which has been the cry of the aggrieved of this land for so many years?

MOKGETHI MOTLHABI

The Concept of Morality
in African Tradition

Few attempts have, so far, been made to look at the place of morality or ethics in traditional African life. This task has become primarily a concern of anthropologists, who, generally, merely glance at morality in the context of their other cultural explorations. Although in the last two decades African philosophers have been working hard to reclaim their traditional wisdom, depending on the work of anthropologists themselves, most of them also have dealt with questions of morality only in passing. Like the anthropologists, they have done this in the context of general, philosophical investigations or other concerns. They have thus not done justice to the study and illumination of the concept of morality in African tradition.

In recent years these "ethnophilosophers," as they have come to be called, have come under severe criticism from the younger generation of African philosophers. These later philosophers feel that there is more to African philosophy, in general, than memories of the past reflected in the anthropological approach. They have argued for a Western-style African Philosophy, distinguished from Western philosophy not by its "Otherness", its different view on life or on issues, but by the fact that it is a philosophical enquiry undertaken by Africans themselves, as opposed to its study by non-Africans. One of these recent philosophers is Paulin Hountondji, a Francophone African who has defined African Philosophy narrowly as "a set of texts, specifically the set of texts written by Africans and described as philosophical by their authors themselves."[1]

Hountondji admits that there was a time when the task fulfilled by "ethnophilosophy" was probably useful: "When what we badly needed, in the face of colonial power and its positive attempts to depersonalize us, was the restoration of self-confidence and the reaffirmation of our creativity. ... But today," in his opinion, "that discourse has lost its critical charge, its truth."[2]

Be that as it may, the fact remains that any current thought which does not take into consideration its past precedents and foundations may turn out to be repetitive. It may come up with "new" ideas which it considers to be original when these ideas have, in fact, already been scrutinized. To avoid this kind of oversight, the least that current African thought can do is to study whatever can be retrieved from its traditional past and acknowledge it, whenever necessary, in its new quests and discoveries. Because of the apparent lack of any systematic attempt to study the concept of morality, in particular, in African tradition, this paper aims to focus on this subject on these grounds. Because past "ethnophilosophers" do not appear to have given this concentration sufficient attention and current African philosophers do not see the need for such activity on the whole, the present attempt cannot but continue along the lines adopted by the "ethnophilosophers" themselves. There currently do not appear to be any other sources for this kind of study but the work of anthropologists. *

At the time when African intellectuals turned mainly West in their general quest for knowledge, it was the Western anthropologist who came to their continent and undertook the task of studying and disclosing their general, cultural background. Such an undertaking was initially negative and captive to Western ethnocentrism. However, anthropology later came to concede the value of other cultures chiefly as the result of the recognition of cultural pluralism and cultural relativity. "The idea of Western culture as a universal norm began to be abandoned by those anthropologists whose direct experience of other cultures had impressed them with the range of possibilities of human adaptation to the natural environment and of human potential for cultural creation."[3] This new openness of anthropology to other cultures and value systems made it possible for some African intellectuals to revalue and reclaim their past tradition. Early anthropology had done its best to make them loathe and wish to annihilate it from their minds.

It was this stage in the development of anthropology, ironically, which provided "both inspiration and ideas for a challenge to the

* The writings of African novelists may also serve as a useful, primary source in this kind of study.

colonial ideology with which it was bound up during an earlier phase."⁴ Thus came "ethnophilosophy" into being. In view of the current dispute among African philosophers regarding the status of African philosophy, the present essay amounts to questioning whether the task of "ethnophilosophy" has, indeed, been accomplished. If so, what texts, as suggested by Hountondji, can we learn from in the specific field of ethics? As there does not appear to be any immediate answer, particularly to the second question, there is nothing for us to do — in the meantime — but "regress" a little into "ethnophilosophy."

Western Definition of Morality

To discuss our present subject meaningfully, we must first have a clear understanding of some of the accepted definitions of morality or ethics as such. We must, particularly, be aware of the distinction often made between these two terms themselves: "ethics" and "morality" or "morals." These terms are a source of much confusion, particularly among "laymen" in ethics.

In philosophical discussions the term "ethics" is often reserved for the theory of morals, while "morals" refers to the practice of or to practised morality. It is thus common to speak of ethical theory and moral practice.⁵ The distinction is perhaps rendered more comprehensible by the common philosophical terminology. Philosophers generally speak of "moral philosophy," as opposed to "moral behaviour," to refer to ethics and morality, respectively. So distinguished, ethics (as moral philosophy) is then defined as the *"normative science of the principles (or laws) of the best types of human conduct."*⁶ Alternatively, it may be defined as that branch of philosophy which investigates "the fundamental concepts and principles underlying (or governing) our judgements of good and evil, right and wrong, the obligatory and the optional."⁷ Morality or morals, accordingly, becomes the actual practice or actions resultant from these principles and, in turn, leading to them.

According to this definition, it may be possible to act or behave morally without any systematic theory of morals. It is entirely inconceivable, however, so to act without at least a simple knowledge of good and evil, right and wrong, and other simple moral values. In other words, there must be some form of basic, no matter how simple, ethic to any kind of moral behaviour if such behaviour is to be regarded as moral at all. With this understanding of ethics in relation to morality, then, is it possible to speak of either a concept of ethics or of morality — or both — in traditional African life?

The Traditional African Concept

That we can speak of the concept of morality in African tradition has been little disputed among writers on African culture. This is because, as already hinted, moral behaviour can be engaged in without a rigorous, systematic theory of morals. There are those, however, who have argued that the traditional African does not have a clear concept of morality. They claim that his behaviour is governed and determined completely by so-called tribal custom and the mores of his community with its taboos and sanctions.[8] The impression given is that these customs and mores are followed blindly, without any deliberation or decision. Such an argument fails to realize that while customs and mores may form the basis for morality — as they do for law — they cannot take its place or make it irrelevant. To conform to given social obligations without any personal commitment or decision can have no moral significance whatsoever. For an act to be significant morally, it must involve some individual responsibility: the freedom to say yea or nay.

It must be borne in mind, however, that social obligations deriving from customs and mores are not directly imposed by society on individuals. This renders response to them distinct from response to legal obligations or certain legalistic moral codes which are directly and explicitly imposed under pain or threat of specifically defined sanctions. Customary and moral obligations are, rather, implicit and response to them is more self-regulated than determined by external factors which are characteristic of heteronomous obligations. The self-regulation implied in such obligations is what accounts for their moral nature.

Where there has been more dispute is on the question whether the traditional African has any concept of ethics as a rational code of conduct governing his/her practice of morality. The dispute seems to arise from a narrow or restricted interpretation of the terms "science" and "philosophy" as associated with ethics. It stems from the question whether the traditional African can philosophize at all or grasp concepts. If the words "science" and "philosophy" are understood in their etymological sense, however, and if Malinowski's seemingly superfluous study of magic, science and religion[9] among the so-called savages is anything to go by, it would be ridiculous to hold on to the view that traditional Africans had no basic life-philosophy or even a technical approach of their own to life.

This dispute also follows the belief by some, mainly anthropologists, that traditional African morality was concerned more with overt behaviour than with character.[10] Thus Hammond-Tooke, writing on the Bhaca, claims that their morality "involves the more or less meticulous observance of certain ritual acts, failure to perform which lays one open to the displeasure of the shades." Hence there is seemingly no need for a form of theory, however basic, that moulds character into harmony with accepted social norms. These experts seem to overlook the fact that behaviour not based on character and personal decision grounded on principles cannot be moral. If the people described, knowing the full consequences, are able to decide for or against those rituals, then it is not clear why the actual behaviour should be abstracted from the whole of the moral act and considered as by itself constituting the main focus of morality. Does not, for instance, Christian morality also lay emphasis on the performance of certain actions? Can we, because of this, say that it has less consideration for the moulding of character? Morality is a matter of both character and behaviour. The first is generally attained through up-bringing and moral education or "conditioning." The second is its application.

The Basis of Morality in Traditional African Thinking
Philosophical
Questions whether the traditional African has any concept of morality have a bearing on whether he/she has any philosophy which is distinctly African and traditional. If this question is answered in the affirmative, there can be no doubt that he/she has a concept of ethics, for ethics is generally a part of philosophy. In considering the question of the distinctness of African traditional philosophy in this section, we will overlook the objections raised in the foregoing sections, coming mainly from recent African philosophers.

John Mbiti, in his study, *African Religions and Philosophies,* is among those scholars who have argued for a distinctly African traditional philosophy or philosophies.[11] In discussing morality, however, Mbiti lays more emphasis on its religious rather than its philosophical basis. Placide Tempels, among other foreign anthropologists, was perhaps the first to speak explicitly of the existence of a (traditional) African ethical theory based on African philosophy. His work on Bantu Philosophy has, however, been one of the chief sources of the dispute between current African philosophers and those they have come to call "ethnophilosophers". Nevertheless, Irele notes that "quite apart from [its exaggerated claims and] ideological significance which it assumed in the colonial context, *Bantu Philosophy* provided a conceptual framework and reference for all future attempts to formulate the constitutive elements of a distinctive African mode of thought, to construct an original African philosophical system."[12] According to Tempels, the Bantu "turn to their philosophical concepts and no less towards their knowledge of God to draw out the principles and the norms of good and evil."[13] Indeed, to suggest that there can be some kind of *moral* practice which is not necessarily based on a theory of some sort is beyond comprehension.

Tempels emphasizes his point by suggesting that in African eyes, "to renounce one's philosophy is to renounce ethics and law." Contrary to those who have emphasized the relative nature of African morality, he affirms the universality of the moral order in African philosophy. This "idea of an universal moral order, of the ordering of forces, of a vital hierarchy, is very clear," according to him, to all Bantu.[14] One need not, of course, agree with Tempel's interpretation of African philosophy as a philosophy of forces, but his basic thesis in support of a traditional African philosophy seems to make sense.

Similarly, Jahn also sees the African concept of justice as related to the philosophical notion called "life influence". According to this concept, liability is not, as in the European sense of justice, measured by material damage. Rather, it is the "loss in force, in joy of life, that is evaluated, independently of material considerations."[15] These allusions to the philosophical basis of morality in African tradition — notwithstanding their shortcomings — show that it cannot be true to say that Africans traditionally are "thoughtless," externally controlled actors. It is paradoxical that though moral claims are made in the name of African morality, such claims are at the same time contradicted by another claim that Africans, before their exposure to Western values, had no idea at all of morality.

Religions
This question — whether the traditional African has any concept of ethics — also has a bearing on the obviously rhetorical question whether the traditional African has any religion. If so, and if it is generally agreed that religion has moral implications, then no one can doubt that these implications, which are necessarily drawn rationally, are by that very fact ethical (i.e., in the sense of pertaining to the theory of morality). Jahn affirms that there is no contradiction between traditional African religion and philosophy and goes on to declare: "Their ethics are also derived from the philosophical system." Further, the *"bazimo,"* the departed, are the guardians of morals."[16] This basic argument is substantiated by Mbiti. He writes of the Ashanti that they believe God has "created the knowledge of good and evil in every person and allowed him to choose his way. An evil man [however,] . . . cannot sucessfully escape his punishment."[17] It seems obvious from these statements, therefore, that to speak of

moral practice without some form of ethical theory is absurd, however "primitive" the society examined may be thought to be.

In his discussion of concepts of God in Africa, Mbiti continues his examination of the ethical implications on African belief in God. He observes that the Abaluyia believed that the world was created perfect by God. In it God established "a good order in which man could live". The Abaluyia thus found it repulsive that God could have created evil.[18] They might have agreed with the Vusugu that evil is produced by some evil spirit almost the equivalent of Satan in the Christian teaching or the Greek Demiurge. Equivalents of the Ten Commandments are also encountered in the traditional African concept of morality.[19] Thus the Bachwa held that God "has laid down a code of morals and a rule of life" to be obeyed by all.[20] Moral deviations were believed to be somehow punishable by God.

This last line of thinking touches upon the problem of moral autonomy, as opposed to theonomy and heteronomy; but this problem is not unique to traditional African thought. Even the Jewish Christian tradition of the Ten Commandments is open to the same challenge. Walter Muelder has attempted to solve it by suggesting that for those who accept a given set of religious (in his case, Christian) principles as meaningful and who make them normative for their lives, there is no contradiction between autonomy and theonomy.[21] Muelder was trying to check Kant's categorical imperative, lest an extreme interpretation of its emphasis on autonomy inhibit the acceptance of Christian norms. The categorical imperative commands one to act "only on that maxim which you can at the same time will that it should become a universal law".[22] Muelder finds no room for heteronomy, however, in ethics.

Equivalents to the Ten Commandments in traditional African morality often form the basis for "natural law ethics,"[23] that is, where they are not explicitly ascribed to God or some divine authority. Generally, however, it is in the world order that the divine will is seen to express or reveal itself. We have thus a basis for some "natural revelation". This "revelation," however, depends on its accessibility to human intelligence.[24] What is important in all this is that the human being is not seen as the ultimate judge of its deeds. It does not find the justification of its acts and omissions in itself. Transcending the free will of human beings is a higher force that knows, assesses and judges human acts.[25] There is also the concept of appeal from the supreme human authority to the transcendent authority. It is from this authority, according to Tempels, that human beings are understood to have received their power of judgment. Consequently, they have the obligation to give account (to this authority) of their use of the power bestowed.[26]

The idea of the religious basis of African traditional morality is supported by many anthropologists, who seem to be the main contributors to the subject. The African (Ghananian) philosopher, Kwasi Wiredu, however, has warned that traditional African thinking about moral foundations is "refreshingly non-supernaturalist". While immoral conduct was held to be hateful to God, the thinking was not that "something is good because God approves of it but rather than God approves of it because it is good in the first place."[27] Monica Wilson sees a direct relation between African traditional religion and morality. She is supported by Adegbola in his reference to the morality of West Africa.[28] For Wilson this connection can be denied "only if the symbolism is not understood or morality is narrowly interpreted". In certain cases a condition similar to the one in the New Testament — of making peace with one's injured fellowman before the offering of sacrifice or worship — was adhered to. Failure to do this was believed to render the sacrifice inefficacious.[29] Wilson asserts that because the religion of most African societies centred not on God but on shades and heroes, "it was the shades and heroes who were [considered to be] the bulwark of morality".[30] For our purpose it is not important who the centre of religion was but only that it served as a basis for morality.

Socio-Cultural

The philosophical and religious bases of morality have, of course, socio-cultural considerations as their infra-structure. Hence we may see society and its cultural outlook as the primary bases of morality. Geoffrey Parrinder states that morality, as the behaviour of many in society, is in fact governed by social custom in African tradition. This custom is usually ascribed to the positive command of an ancestor or a god.[31] Writing on the Batswana — and this is not only true of the Batswana or Africans in general but of all societies — Schapera also observes that throughout a man's life, "his behaviour is being either deliberately or unconsciously moulded into conformity with social norms making for law and order."[32] He goes on to point out that the development of Tswana law, which is true also of morality, is associated with social taboos. Taboos are, in fact, seen as the negative aspect of morality,[33] its "Thou shalt nots" or its "don'ts". We may say here also, as implied earlier, that the punishment associated with the contravention of taboos can be either morally or legally motivated. Emphasizing the point that most of African morality is reflected in social taboos, Wilson concludes that the argument "that observance of taboos has nothing to do with morality is only tenable if taboos are taken literally and the symbolic association ignored."[34]

The social basis of morality, not only in African tradition but in all cultures, has been demonstrated by social scientists such as Emil Durkheim, and recently by Peter Berger, Andrew M. Greely (the latter being also a theologian), and others, as well as by theologians such as Gordon Kaufman. Kaufman's view of the three moments in theology is very similar to that of Berger regarding the process of socialization.[35] This process, as described by Berger, includes three dialectic aspects: externalization, objectivization, and internalization. It is the basis of a cultural process where ideas originate internally, after the individual's encounter with the external world, before they become *sui generic* entities — through the process of externalization — which can then be internalized by successive generations for the moulding and directing of individual and social life. The dialectic nature of socialization inheres in this process. As far as morality is concerned, we may imagine a "primordio-perennial" stage in which moral ideas are born internally from the mind's contact with the social reality. These ideas are then externalized as moral knowledge and objectified, assuming a nature of their own, now independent of the mind. They then constitute the moral principles, norms and values which are internalized by individuals in the "final" stage of socialization as preparation (character formation) for moral practice. It is in this stage that moral education takes place, both formally and informally.

(a)*Moral Education*
In African tradition, informal education normally took place predominantly in the home, through parents and by example. Formal education — including moral education — was associated with the initiation school. Later in life, the individual informally improved his/her moral understanding through application as he/she participated fully in social life.[36] At the initiation school the "links between observance of taboo and morality" were explained and "certain definite rules of behaviour . . .firmly impressed upon the minds of the young people concerned."[37] We find, then, confirmation of the earlier argument that not only is there a conception of morality (as practice) in African tradition, but also of ethics (as theory).

(b) *Universality*
Looking at the social basis of African morality, in particular, a number of anthropologists have wanted to emphasize that it is rel-

ative or "ingroup morality". Monica Wilson also shares this claim.
"The shades," she alleges, "were concerned with obligation to
kinsmen; they were not concerned with behaviour towards other
people." Yet, ironically, she goes on to admit that "300 years ago
the Mpondo already recognized a traveller [naturally a foreigner]
as under the protection of the chief."[38] A similar view is held by
Hammond-Tooke on the Bhaca. He asserts that the dictates of
Bhaca morality are "relative to the social group involved." He goes
on to state: "There is not the application of a universalized code of
moral rules to mankind in general, [such as that] "found in Christian teaching".[39] Such a narrow interpretation of the African traditional concept of morality is tantamount to claiming that the
Christian command to love one's neighbour as oneself restricts
Christian morality to one's immediate community, if not to the actual neighbour. Perhaps we need to ask of the traditional African
view, "Who is my kinsman?" in order to come to a clearer understanding of the African position.

In his book, *Intlalo Ka-Xhosa,* T.B. Soga expresses amazement
that the Christian view to love one's neighbour as oneself should
be regarded as alien to African morality. *"Thina ma Afrika,"* he
writes — and note that he does not say, "Thina amaXhosa," but
"amaAfrika" — *"singumzi wobuhlobo nobuzalwana obunzulu ngo-
kudalwa."*[40] It is already obvious from Wilson's quotation, despite her
interpretation, that the friendliness and neighbourliness were not
confined to kinsmen or other Africans but also extended to foreigners. Tempels is the one who seems to grasp this aspect of African
morality, therefore, when he says that universality is not an alien concept to it. Statements such as, *"Motho ke motho ka batho"* —literally,
"a person is a person through other people" — are universal and are
key to the traditional African's attitude towards his neighbours — irrespective of who they are — and determine his behaviour in relation
to them.

Values, Norms and Moral Codes
Neighbourliness was at the very centre of traditional African morality. Good interrelations among persons implied also a good
standing with God.[41] Neighbourliness led to solidarity and mutual
helpfulness, which were central to the value of humanity, i.e.,
ubuntu or *botho*.[42] The concept of *ubuntu* placed emphasis on the person as the highest and intrinsic value. Some of its implications were
mutual respect, harmonious social and interpersonal relations, stability, kindness, gentleness, co-operation, and conformity to accepted
customs.[43] A person with these qualities was said to be in possession

of *ubuntu* or *botho*. Nothing captures the significance of this value better than Soga's expression that black people had "learnt it deeply in their blood to be mutually helpful day by day."[44] This point finds further emphasis in Wiredu.

He states that anyone who reflects on the traditional way of speaking about morality is bound to be struck by the preoccupation with human welfare: "What is good morally is what befits a human being; it is what is good for man — what brings dignity, respect, contentment, prosperity, joy, to man and his community. And what is morally bad is what brings misery, misfortune, and disgrace."[45] Hammond-Tooke, in fact, goes so far as to say that morality for the Africans "has been defined as the 'right and generous' way of acting towards one's fellows."[46] Two ways of judging actions were, according to him, whether an action was harmful to the smooth functioning of interpersonal relations, and whether it conformed to custom. Consequently, the central moral norms were the maintenance of harmonious relations within the community as well as conformity to custom.

It needs to be restated that conformity to custom as a moral source need not imply a relative ethic. Custom may have universal implications, as already suggested in the earlier argument against the relativity view regarding traditional African morality. Relativity as such, in morality, generally pertains to moral content (what should actually be done in certain circumstances) or to moral codes. It does not pertain to the form or goal of morality. For instance, that self-contradiction in willing and selection of values should be avoided is a universal moral principle. One cannot both will and not will at the same time; nor can one will and not will the same ends simultaneously.[47] On the other hand, there may, in considering moral content, be various conceptions of who, for instance, one's neighbour is in a particular situation.

Within the traditional African moral content are included codes similar to the Ten Commandments, as already noted: prohibitions to steal, murder, commit adultery, neglect one's ageing parents, tell lies or deceive; of uncontrolled anger, greed, witchcraft or sorcery, incest, covetousness, hatred, jealousy, and speaking ill of others.[48] Not only, therefore, did the traditional African have a concept of morality and ethics, but he also had — whether implicit or explicit — moral codes learnt both formally and informally, as also already indicated.

Moral Sanctions
Moral codes are normally accompanied by certain sanctions, which serve as conditional punishment or threat to ensure their fulfilment. In the first of the ten Jewish-Christian commandments, for

instance, idolatry is forbidden under the sanction: "for I the lord your God am a jealous God, visiting the iniquity of the fathers upon the children to the third and fourth generations of those who hate me" (Exod 20:5): It may be argued, of course, that the Ten Commandments are not genuinely moral but legal in tone. Their form is categorical, stipulative, and final, leaving no room for moral deliberation and decision which is ultimately regulated by reason and conscience rather than by external threats. Further, the fear of external punishment which accompanies their contravention would seem to retract from their moral significance for people, as they appear to interfere with their autonomy. In this sense one might find those moral codes more acceptable, the sanctions of which are implicit in them rather than explicit. This was the point being made in distinguishing between moral sanctions and legal sanctions earlier.

In the traditional African approach to morality both morally oriented and legally oriented sanctions were applied, as done in most forms of morality and moral codes. One must admit that failure to distinguish these orientations is a source of confusion in the study of morality in general. The time for its correction is long overdue.

Adeolu Adegbola speaks of the morally oriented religious sanction when he writes: "Everywhere in Africa, morality is hinged on many sanctions. But the most fundamental sanction is the fact that God's all-seeing eyes scan the total areas of human behaviour and personal relationship . . . Those who do evil in the dark are constantly warned to remember that God's eye can pierce through the dark of human action and motive."[49] The moral nature of this sanction is in that it contains no explicit threat of external punishment in case of non-conformity. One may dare God and commit an immoral act intentionally to find out the consequences, since these are not explicitly stated. The ancestors also provided some form of moral sanction. The "rights and duties sanctioned by [them] both define[d] and regulate[d] basic social and political relations."[50] The main moral sanctions, however, were social controls which worked upon the conscience, such as social disapproval or ostracism. Such sanctions are implicit in moral codes *qua* moral rather than, so to say, legalized or concretely threatened from without. To these might be added Wilson's statement that witchcraft also acted as some form of control. It was believed that a good man had little to fear from witches or sorcerers because he did not arouse enmity.[51] Moral uprightness might thus be cause for boasting against their evil spells.

Other types of sanctions were similar to those described in the Old Testament. God was believed to bless the good and punish the wicked. The wicked were often believed to be punished with sickness, hunger, or plagues.[52] Generally, misfortune was "linked with sin," and many of the "afflictions that befell men were attributed to their own wrong-doing."[53] It is noteworthy, however, that the Old Testament idea of corporate punishment for the sins of a minority does not appear to have been accommodated, in spite of the many other similarities.[54] Though one's moral integrity and social concern might benefit others, as in cases described by Soga, one was solely responsible and liable for one's own moral depravity or irresponsibility.

Sanctions must necessarily be viewed as the last aspect, if brought into play at all, of the moral process before the choice of the moral act to adopt. They should not be seen as part of "meta-ethics" or as constituting the grounds for moral behaviour. To do so would be tantamount to introducing heteronomy into ethics, thus encouraging legalism or a legalistic approach to morality. The religious, philosophical and socio-cultural bases of morality together provide sufficient substance for the inference of meta-ethics. All show that morality is, ultimately, oriented to interpersonal relations or to persons in community. Its goal is to ensure harmonious relations among persons both as individuals and as part of a community, as well as respect of their God-given personality. This can be done by letting them be who and what God intended them to be and by allowing them to achieve maximum fulfilment of this personality in accordance with their ability and through whatever possible assistance they can obtain as members of a human community. These grounds for morality are reflected in one way or the other in all the three bases of morality considered. They are as true for the traditional African concept of morality as they are for Western morality or any other kind of ethics, for that matter. Bernhard Haring summed up this fact of morality very well in the title of one of his books when he wrote, *Morality Is for Persons*. This, indeed, is what morality is about.

Conclusion
This essay may have sounded rather apologetic so far. However, my intention was not to act as an advocate or defender of the traditional African view of morality. Rather, it was to discover (in the light of the need to find the roots if one is to determine how firmly a tree is based in the ground) how Africans traditionally solved their moral problems and where they derived their standards for

doing so. The conclusion is that their approach was not significantly different from that of any known human morality and their meta-ethics generally coincide with those of other moralities.

The study is not meant to imply that current African views on morality have not changed — for the better or for the worse — from the traditional one. This would imply that African culture is static, which I believe is not true. The emphasis of the current paper's title is, therefore, on the word "traditional" rather than "African". This is stated advisedly, in agreement with the warning given by Wiredu in the article entitled: "How Not to Compare African Philosophy with Western Philosophy."[55] Wiredu, in this article, refers to the fallacies which have been committed by enthusiasts of African philosophy in trying to prove its worth by comparing it with Western philosophy.

It has been seen that the same case has been made by those who have labelled some of these enthusiasts "Ethnophilosophers." It has also been seen that while I generally agree with them on this and other positions, this essay itself is a protest against the *total* condemnation of so-called "ethonophilosophy". "Ethnophilosophy" is, indeed, still a valuable and principal source of the concept of morality in African Tradition.

REFERENCE NOTES

1. Paulin J. Hountondji, *African Philosophy: Myth and Reality,* translated by Henri Evans (London: Hutchinson & Co. (Publishers) Ltd, 1983), p. 35.
2. Ibid., p. 171
3. Abiola Irele, "Introduction," in Hountondji, *African Philosophy*, p. 14.
4. Ibid.
5. See Edgar Sheffield Brightman, *Moral Laws* (New York: Abingdon Press, 1933), p. 11.
6. Ibid., p. 13.
7. Kwasi Wiredu, *Philosophy and an African Culture* (Cambridge: Cambridge University Press, 1980), p. 171.
8. See below.
9. See his *Magic, Science and Religion and other Essays* (Garden City, N.Y.: Doubleday Anchor Books, 1954).
10. See W.D. Hammond-Tooke, *Bhaca Society: A People of the Transkeian Uplands South Africa* (Cape Town: Oxford University Press, 1962).
11. London: Heineman Educational Books, 1969.
12. Irele, "Introduction," p. 17.
13. Placide Tempels, *Bantu Philosophy* (Paris: Presence Africaine, 1959) p. 116.
14. Ibid., p. 135.
15. Janheinz Jahn, *Muntu: An Outline of Neo-African Culture,* Translated by Marjorie Green (London: Farber & Farber, Ltd, 1958), p. 116.

16. Ibid., p. 115.
17. John S. Mbiti, *Concepts of God in Africa* (London: SPCK, 1970), p. 248.
18. Ibid., p. 247.
19. Geoffrey Parrinder, *West African Religion* (London: Epworth Press, 1961), p. 176.
20. Mbiti, *Concepts of God*, p. 247.
21. Walter G. Muelder, *Moral Law in Christian Social Ethics* (New York and Toronto: The Edwin Mellen Pess, 1966), p. 73.
22. Emmanuel Kant, *Fundamental Principles of the Metaphysic of Ethics* (New York: Appleton-Century-Crofts, Inc, 1938), p. 38.
23. Tempels, *Bantu Philosophy*, p. 118.
24. Ibid., p. 115.
25. Ibid.
26. Ibid.
27. Wiredu, *Philosophy*, p. 6.
28. Monica Wilson, *Religion and the Transformation of Society* (Cambridge: Cambridge University Press, 1971); E.A. Adeolu Adegbola, "The Theological Basis of Ethics," in *Biblical Revelation and African Beliefs*, edited by K.A. Dickson & Paul Ellingworth (London: Lutterworth Press, 1969).
29. Wilson, Religion, p. 87
30. Ibid., p. 88.
31. Parrinder, *West African Religion*, p. 176.
32. I. Schapera, *A Handbook of Tswana Law and Custom* (London: University Press, 1955), p. 36.
33. Parrinder, *West African Religion*, p. 176.
34. Wilson, Religion, p. 82.
35. See Gordon Kaufman, *Essay on Theological Method* (Montana: Scholars Press, 1975), and Peter L. Berger, *The Social Construction of Reality* (London: Faber and Faber, 1967). Berger lately seems to have abandoned his earlier views for a more conservative approach.
36. Schapera, *Tswana Custom*, p. 36.
37. Ibid.; Wilson, Religion, p. 82.
38. Wilson, *Religion*, p. 90.
39. Hammond-Tooke, *Bhaca Society*, p. 241.
40. "We Africans are a deeply friendly and neighbourly family by origin." T.B. Soga, *Intlalo KaXhosa* (N.P.: The Lovedale Press, 1974), p. 102.
41. Mbiti, *Concepts of God*, p. 250.
42. B.A. Pauw, *Christianity and Xhosa Tradition: Belief and Ritual among Xhosa Speaking Christians* (Cape Town: Oxford University Press, 195), pp. 316, 320.
43. See also Hammond-Tooke, *Bhaca Society*, p. 241.
44. Soga, *Intlalo KaXhosa*, p. 104, translation mine.
45. Wiredu, *Philosophy*, p. 6.
46. Hammond - Tooke, *Bhaca Society*, p. 241.
47. Muelder, *Moral Law*, p. 62.
48. See Mbiti, *Concepts of God*, p. 247.
49. Adegbola, *The Theological Basis*, p. 116.

50   Benjamin C. Ray, *African Religions: Symbol Ritual, and Community* (Engel-
     wood Cliffs, N.J.: Prentice Hall, Inc., 1976), p. 147.
51. Wilson, *Religion*, p. 86.
52. Mbiti, *Concepts of God*, p. 247.
53. Wilson, *Religion*, p. 89.
54. This statement is, however, contradicted by Bonganjalo Goba. He tries to
     prove the opposite by quoting a Zulu saying: *"Zifa ngamvunye,"* literally, all
     (sheep) die because of one. See his "Corporate Personality in Israel and in
     Africa." This article is in a book which may not be quoted in South Africa.
55. Wiredu, *Philosophy*.

BENJAMIN WITBOOI

Liminality, Christianity and the Khoikhoi Tribes

In this paper we will focus on the rites of passage, as defined by van Gennep, with special reference to the Khoikhoi people of South Africa. (This group is now extinct and the descendants are referred to as the Coloured people). We will also reflect on the role that Christianity played in the process of de-culturalization. In my present research I have not come across an anthropological work that deals with the tremendous dislocation and confusion that must have followed the transition from a pastoral life free from foreign white interference to a life in subjugation to a foreign power. Anthropologists writing on the Khoikhoi normally adopt a functionalist analysis. But a functionalist anthropological approach (sociology sometimes adopts a functionalist approach because there is no need to "rock the boat") with its bias in favour of well-integrated societies would certainly not be an adequate tool for the analysis of the Khoikhoi disintegration.

We agree with Geertz that both culture and social systems must be taken seriously. "On the one level there is the framework of beliefs, expressive symbols, and values in terms of which individuals define their world, express their feelings, and make their judgements: on the other level there is the ongoing process of interactive behaviour, whose persistent form we call social structure. Culture is the fabric of meaning in terms of which human beings interpret their experience and guide their action; social structure is the form that action takes, the actually existing network of social relations."[1]

A.W. Hoernle, who did extensive research among the Khoikhoi
and especially among the Naman tribe in Namibia, follows a functionalist approach and therefore does not attempt an analysis of
the interrelationship between culture and social structure, but simply records her empirical findings. She does not examine why the
"Hottentots [another name for the Khoikhoi, yet unacceptable
because of the derogatory connotations attached to the name] are
now passing people, who have practically given up the struggle to
keep alive their own traditions. What vitality is left is spent in the
absorption of the ways of the incoming Europeans."[2] It is therefore
difficult to assess what immediate effects a change in the social
structure had in the disappearance of the entire Khoikhoi culture.

It seems that Christianity has played a vital role in the "liminality" that existed between the separation from the past and aggrega-
tion into white society. In shedding light on the meaning of the
word liminality and its root "limen", Victor Turner explains as follows: "a limen is a threshold, but at least in the case of protracted
initiation rites or major seasonal festivals, it is a very long threshold, a corridor almost, or a tunnel which may, indeed, become a
pilgrim's road or passing from dynamics to statics, may cease to be
a mere transition and become a set way of life, a state that of the
anchorite, or monk."[3]

The Europeans had a negative view of the Khoikhoi. Richard
Elphick makes the following observation: "Most Europeans, regardless of their personal level of piety, were interested in religion
and tried perfunctorily to inform themselves of Khoikhoi beliefs.
Since the Khoikhoi had no obvious temples or elaborate ceremonies, and since the language barrier made communication on philosophical topics almost impossible, many visitors reached the
ludicrous conclusion that Khoikhoi had no religion at all . . . It
seemed deplorable, as Wouter Schouten noted in 1665, that Khoikhoi, although descended from our father Adam, yet show little of
humanity that truly they more resemble the unreasonable beasts
than reasonable man . . . having no knowledge of God nor what
leads to their Salvation. Miserable folk, how lamentable is your
pitiful condition! And oh Christians, how blessed is ours!"[4]

It is our thesis that Christianity itself has become, in the case of
the Khoikhoi people, the second phase of Van Gennep's tripartite
processional structure, the limen, or in Turner's words, the "very
long threshold, a corridor almost," from one level to another. Culture and rituals cannot be judged to be higher or lower on a hierarchical scale. Each ritual has an important function to perform in
maintaining the equilibrium within that culture. The Christians

from the West rejected a whole culture using as a yardstick its own Western cultural prejudice.

I would like to illustrate this objection in a graphic fashion by refering to what the Khoikhoi were before Christianity and what they became subsequently: Prior to the influence of Christianity, according to H.A. van Reede ". . . they live under one another according to the laws, which they hold unbreakable . . . manslaughter, adultery, lying, incest are forbidden and punishable among them: reverence for the dead and their burial place . . . are strictly maintained."[6]

Christianized as they were, they became, what Johannes Wilhelm de Grevenbroek describe as follows: "From us they have learned blasphemy, purgery, strife, quarrelling, drunkenness, treachery, brigandage, theft, ingratitude, unbridled lust for what is not one's own, misdeeds unknown to them before, and among other crimes of deepest die, the accursed lust for gold."[7] These are observations made by human beings who sympathized with the Khoikhoi, but ironically, these are the accusations brought against the Khoikhoi for their non-acceptance into European society.

Contemporary society still reflects that, having undergone the process of transformation, they are still unacceptable to white or European society. We will not look at some of the common characteristics of all the transition rites among the Khoikhoi. We will make use of the empirical data collected by Hoernle from which we will draw certain conclusions. The analytical approach is not done in order to return to the "glorious past", but rather to make sense of beliefs that still persist up to the present. According to Hoernle, "All periods of crisis in the lives of the Hottentots (Khoikhoi), whether of individuals or of groups, afford admirable illustrations of those rites which A van Gennep has called 'rites de passage'."[8]

1. There is always the separation of the person from his/her normal surroundings.
2. There is preparation to enter a new group in society.
3. There is the reception into the new group.

A person in such a crisis acquires a characteristic unknown in the group to which he/she has belonged before. He/she is no longer protected by any group solidarity and is therefore exposed to danger on everyside. He/she must retire from contact with other people and "Karesin" (take care of himself in this special way. The word is used only in this connection, both of the individual himself and of others who, knowing they may be a source of danger to him, are considered on his behalf.) He/she is a danger to other people and as such is *!nau.*

The *!nau* person must be restored to the community and only people who have already undergone the process can do the initiation, e.g. an old man or a woman past the age of childbearing. It is also important that the person, the officiating officer, has the same characteristics as the person undergoing the transition; he/she must have experienced the process of *!nau.* The crisis attached to the transition may differ in terms of intensity. Let us group them as follows:

a) Childbirth, marriage, puberty, bereavement rites. These are the kind of crises that can be met with some preparation for the next stage, culminating in a sacrificial meal that will mark the transition from the *!nau* person to a fully aggregated person.

b) Remarriage, puberty ceremonies for boys, reception into the ranks of hunters, treatment of disease. Here a preliminary step is necessary in which incisions are made on the body of the *!nau* person, followed by the rubbing in of grease and the dirt scraped from the body of the officiating officer.

This transition period further involves the renunciation of all that represents the past life; in a very real sense the person is reborn. A further step involves the cleansing ceremony by which the person is touched by water and a new set of clothes is put on. The house of the *!nau* person must also be purified, after which an "expiatory" meal is eaten. Re-introduction to familiar daily tasks must take place and a new life in solidarity with a new group is established.

A brief reference to the state of *!nau* may be of help. It so happens that some people are immune to the dangers of *!nau,* e.g. older men who have undergone the stage of *!nau* and older women who are past the age of childbearing. The *!nau* person can make other people or things *!nau* or contaminated, e.g. the fire in the hut is *!nau* and must not be allowed to go out; the ashes of that fire must not be removed until the house is purified and a new fire is lit; also, nothing can be cooked on the *!nau* fire. The *!nau* person is not allowed to touch cold water or to touch raw meat, because doing that may involve great danger to himself. To illustrate the importance of not touching cold water, Hoernle states: "The Hottentot (Khoikhoi) witchdoctor or *!gai-aop,* never touches cold water and never washes from year's end to year's end. His power resides, as it were, in the dirt which clings to his body and this is always an ingredient in any medicine he gives. Should he touch water this power would be diminished, and complete immersion has proven to destroy that power."

The clothing and utensils of the *!nau* person also becomes *!nau* and is a great danger to others.

Details about various rites of passage could be found, but we will concentrate on only one in order to draw the conclusions. We will look at the rite that involves the purification of the survivors after the death of a relative.

It must be noted that not only were the immediate relatives affected, but also the larger family circle. When returning from the grave, everybody washed their hands in cold water in front of the dead person's house. Hoernle observed that *before* they had wailed their lamentation, but at the time of her research they sang hymns. The relatives were required to slaughter according to their means. Blood of the slaughtered animals were collected in a separate pot, the entrails in another, and yet another pot or pots for the meat. The pots were provided by all the families taking part in the ceremony. The blood was heated to boiling point and a herb called *//ganap* was mixed with it. A chopper which had been heated red-hot was then used to stir the blood to the point when the steam evaporated. The immediate family, men, women and children, (the woman, in the case of a male deceased, and her relatives were excluded) were then requested to cover their heads, stand over the pot and to perspire. An old man, not related to either husband or wife then proceded to take the black from the pot and drew a line on the stomach of each person, "in order to prevent them from getting pains from eating the food". All this was done in the dead man's house. The eating of the slaughtered animals was also important. The relatives ate only the meat or flesh and the other members the entrails, while the officiating person and others of the same age and experience used the blood. Those who were too poor simply had coffee.

The wife of the deceased was *!nau*. Purification had to be done. An officiating person had to be found — a woman who had experienced *!nau* i.e. lost a husband. First of all she was cleaned from head to toe with cow dung, after which the body was rubbed with *!naop* which is a face paint made by grinding a soft red stone to powder and mixing it with fat. The hair was cut from the top of her head. A piece of the hair was spat upon with the words "The next husband you get must be a lucky one, and get him quickly". She was also required to put on a new set of clothes. The officiating woman had in the meantime fetched a piece of meat from the cooking pots, which was cooking in the pot inside the hut. With the black from the pot the widow was marked: first under each eye, "so that everything the widow meets may be nice to her". Next she was marked in the same

way on the chest "so that her food may go down nicely". The meat in
the pot was eaten by the officiating person. The remaining hair was
mixed with the ashes of the old fire, removed from the hut, and a new
fire was lit.

The next morning the old woman took the /*arap* which was the contents of the animal stomach, and with the officiating person leading
the way, it was scattered over the cattle kraals with the saying: "Let
there be plenty of milk." A cow was milked, and the widow was re-
introduced to water. Clay was rubbed on her legs with the saying:
"Don't get thin, get fat like the *!aba,* onion." Finally, now fully restored, a pot of water was placed on the woman's head and with that
she returned to her home. In the case of a widower the same proce-
dure was followed, except for a few changes: Two cuts, incisions,
were made on his forehead and a certain juice was rubbed into it
(//ubus). Hair was cut off from the back of the head. Some herbs were
mixed and left overnight. The next morning, accompanied by the officiating officer (as in the case of the widow) he sprinkled the herbs
among the cattle and sheep.

When a child died, both parents were considered *!nau* and under-
went the rite of purification.

Some traces of these rites are still observed among the Christians,
though they are no longer a pastoral people. In contemporary society
the corpse is greeted before the burial by placing a hand on the forehead of the deceased and the placing of flowers around and on the
face. After the funeral, which is now a Christian burial, everybody re-
turns to the house of the deceased. (Note: the grave is not left open
for the gravediggers to close. First the close relatives step forward to
put sand in the grave, and all the others at the graveside are then allowed to cover the grave). They return to the house of the deceased
and the washing of hands takes place. Tea, coffee and cake are then
served to everybody, and a meal is served to those who travelled from
far off to attend the funeral. If the family can afford it, everybody is
served a meal. The relatives are identified as the mourners by, in the
case of men and boys, the wearing of black suits or black armbands.
The women wear black dresses. If a close relative has died, the
mourning is observed for a full year, and in other cases the mourning
period is less. A relative who was not able to attend the funeral, will
afterwards go to the grave to bid farewell to the grave and place a
stone on the grave. On arriving at the house, purification is done by
the washing of the hands.

How is one to explain the almost total loss of cultural observance
among the Khoikhoi; and why is the past to be erased from memory?
When Hoernle interviewed an old lady, she made the following ob-

servation: "One of my best informers, a woman, reproached me bitterly for encouraging her to think of things she had spent half her life in trying to forget: 'You have made me live the old life once more; soon you will be going, and what shall I do then?'"[11]

It appears that the ingredients for a successful transition are present in the Khoikhoi culture. Separated as they were from cattle, land and uprooted from their places of abode when they entered the service of the white settlers or were forced to move to mission stations, the whole fabric of their lives had to undergo change. A change in the entire social structure must be followed by a change in the culture. The missionaries and mission stations did not perform a neutral role, but they acted in support of the *status quo*, whether consciously or unconsciously. To apply the terms used in the period of liminality, we could say that in the separation they had become *!nau*. An officiating person was needed to help in the process of transition. None of the former people were able to help in the process because nobody remained who could resist the danger of *!nau*. The choice of the officiating person was always a careful process, and the missionary could fill that position. They also needed a place of separation from others who were not *!nau* and the mission stations filled that place.

The liminarians had to be instructed, and this was done by giving them the Western culture; they had to learn a new language, Dutch or English; they had to wear Western dress; they had to discard their religious beliefs. They were purified by the water of baptism, and so immersed, the *!nau* person exprienced rebirth. The fact that the persons who were *!nau* had to be exposed to humiliation offered a good opportunity for missionaries with a strong hell-fire slant in their preaching. The missionaries were accepted as people who could perform the role of officiating officer because, just as the former officiating persons, they had to undergo the period of *!nau*; they had to receive baptism in order to be reborn as Christians. Further instruction followed through confirmation instruction and I suspect that the process of confirmation replaced the puberty rites. Andries Stoffles, no doubt with some price, a Khoikhoi convert, remarked: "The word of God has brought my nation so far, that if a Hottentot young lady and an English lady were walking with their faces from me, I would take them both to be English ladies."[12]

The acceptance of culture also becomes easy. The former officiating person scraped dirt from the body and rubbed some of it on the *!nau* person, thereby giving something of himself/herself to the person. The missionaries had no dirt, but they could offer their culture as a part of themselves. In other words, Christianity equals civilization, equals nineteenth century Britain. In the words of Kate Crehan:

"Bethelsdorp and the other mission stations were, right from their very foundation, because of the ideology of their founders, dedicated to transforming radically the entire way of life of their converts. Ultimately what institutions like Bethelsdorp were doing was transforming social institutions and practices alien to a capitalist system into social institutions and practices compatible with capitalism."[13]

The last part, in which I pointed to the role of missionaries and mission stations is based purely on assumption. It seems clear to me, however, that the successful transfer of culture could have contained elements of those beliefs.

There are important conclusions to be drawn from the consideration of liminality. Those involved in Black Theology or Contextual Theology may well consider liminality, and how Christianity may or may not have addressed the culture of particular Africans. (I apply the term in its wider sense.) Does Christianity take seriously the liminality which occurs during child-birth, puberty, death, mourning etc? There are many transitional rites still being performed and the church often turns a blind-eye to it. Black Christians are often forced to engage in secret or midnight escapades in order to avoid discovery by church leaders. The result — half-baked Christians and half-baked Africans. Cultural observance should not be ignored, but should be integrated in the life of the church in order for people to be fully integrated.

If the State denies human beings their dignity, the church must restore it. One way of restoring dignity must be a recognition of transitional rites and the socio-economic and political context of human beings. No culture could be superimposed on another without considering the ritual processes within the culture. Such an imposition creates an alienated people. The Coloured people is a classical example. They are not white, yet many aspire to be white and are rejected. They are not certain of a past they have rejected. The Coloured people, to use the sick South African term, remain in the *liminal* stage. We must not allow ideology, religion or cultural imposition to place others in this liminal state.

REFERENCE NOTES

1. Geertz, Clifford; 'Ritual and Social Change: A Javanese Example.' from Schneider Louis;*Religion, Culture and Society*. John Wiley and Son, Inc. 1964. P. 123.
2. Hoernle, A.W. 'Certain Rites of Transition and the Concept of *!nau* among the Hottentots.' from Bates Oric, *Harvard African Studies II* Varia Africa II; The African Department of the Peabody Museum of Harvard University, Cambridge, Massachusetts. 1918, p.66
3. Turner Victor, *Secular Ritual:* 'Variations on the Theme of Liminality'. p. 37

4.   Elphick Richard, Kraal and Castle: *Khoikhoi and the Founding of White South Africa*. New Haven and London, Yale University Press 1977 P. 195
5.   Turner Terence S. *Transformation, Hierarchy and Transcendence:* Reformulation of van Gennep's Model of the Structure of Rites de Passage. P.57
6.   Elphick Richard, op. cit. P. 197
7.   Ibid. p. 198
8.   Hoernle A.W. Op. cit. P.67
9.   Ibid. P. 67
10. Ibid. P. 71
11. Ibid. P. 66
12. Elphick Richard, op cit. P. 176
13. Crehan Kate: 'Ideology and Practice, A Missionary Case: The London Missionary Society and the Cape Frontier 1799 — 1850,' from Centre for Southern African Studies. University of York: Collected Papers: 4.

K.E.M. MGOJO

Church and Africanization

Ecclesiastical Background

Most missionaries were partners with both the imperialists and commercialists in the exploration and exploitation of Africa. Nearly the same problems that were present in the political field were also evident here. We refer, first of all to the reluctance to encourage indigenous leadership, which is why many countries in Africa called for a *Moratorium*. They asked the missionaries to go home from whence they came, at least, for the time being, to allow Africans to develop their own leadership instead of being eternal juniors. Hence as far back as the 1920's there was already tension growing between white control and African initiative, a tension which was one of the leading factors in the creation of independent churches and a tension which the church is facing today. I refer you to the Hammanskraal *ultimatum*. We, as the church in South Africa are a carbon copy of the system. There are a White Church, a Coloured Church and an Indian Church and the so-called African Church. I say, "so-called" because for many years even those whites who have never travelled even 300 kilometers outside South Africa, and those who have been here for three generations, have accepted and clung to a tag "European", just because it gives them political, social and economic benefits. And this becomes a real cancer when such a practice is found in the church. How can a person born and bred in Africa be European and not an African? I have to reiterate the statement made some time ago by my friend, brother and colleague, Stan Mogoba at a Methodist post Sacla Consultation in Zululand: "Blacks per-

ceive whites as still regarding themselves as Europeans."
No wonder churches in Africa never became true African
churches but merely became extensions of the churches in the
mother countries. In fact, some churches became more Methodist
than Methodists in England or America.
The last number of years have witnessed an increasing call for a
shift of perspective in the theological enterprise. Expressions like
localization, contexualization, indigenization, inculturation, Africanization have proliferated. The attempt to establish a theological
expression for a local church of course stems from Apostolic times.
Paul was a champion of this approach. Hence his theology is not
consistent because it is solely concerned with the local situation of
the churches. This theme, Africanization, assumes that all people
of Africa, i.e. those who have come to stay in Africa, are Africans.
Theologically speaking, Africanization tries to adapt through translation models, what is perceived as the Christian message to local
contexts and situations. Characteristically, these models would
speak of a core Christian kerygma or kernel of Christian truth or a
basic Christian revelation which is wrapped in cultural expressions.
The task of Africanization, as these models see it, is to free the
"data revelation" from those cultural accretions of the West in
order to allow the Christian message to acculturate itself in new
situations. Such a translation or adaptation of the Christian message can take on a variety of forms.
One kind might be called the indigenization approach. Much
liturgical adaptation is on this level — things like prayers and mu-
sic are allowed to take local forms. A second sort of translation
model might be called a biblicist approach. This approach manifests itself among those who pursue what is known as a "biblical
theology". This approach realizes that much of the Western tradition has been generated by Western categories (European or
Americanization) rather than a fidelity to the Scriptures. This approach tries to return to the Scriptures to find a framework for a
local theology. This approach is aided by the recognition of the
similarity between cultural situations in the Bible and local cultural
situations in many cases. The obvious strength of this approach is
its fidelity to the Scriptural witness. A genuine Christian Identity,
often surpassing that found in the older churches in the West,
seems assured — it also seems to provide a way out of Western
cultural hegemony. Let us be reminded that the Bible is a cultural
document representing the response in faith by a variety of communities. An ideal type of a New Testament church is a cultural
creation of a given era.

The Gospel does not fall from the sky. Our faith is a *fide ex audito*. The presence of the Gospel is tied up with the mystery of the incarnation. The Gospel is only a living reality when it is incarnated in a concrete context and partakes of the ambiguities and limitations of history. Only then is the Lord truly present in his community.

Thus a local theology becomes very important in Africanization. It has always to ask a number of questions: Does the faith expression of a community really grow from the experience of that community, grow in such a way as to be truly its own? Does the community allow its expression of faith to be concrete enough to the situation, to radically challenge the quality of life within that situation? But does this expression of faith also rise above a cultural romanticism and accommodation to allow it to be understood by others who are willing to listen? Does the expression of faith urge the community into concerns wider than its own context?

These are the questions of the powers of Africanization that a local theology needs to ask itself, to maintain both its catholicity and its incarnational character.

Education
One point with which Africanization should concern itself is the question of the Christian leaders who have the ability to express themselves in genuinely local terms. Unless theological colleges or seminaries can train people to approach the question of leadership in the expression of faith in such a way as to make it available for a genuine local theology, then theology remains an academic exercise.

It is crucial that students not only learn about truth and culture, but be taught to think theologically within a shifting cultural context. The call for a method in local theology cannot be addressed solely to professional theologians; it must become a method practicable for the pastor, to enable a theological conscientization to come about in the community.

The Gospel incarnates itself and takes on flesh. The church is a complex of these cultural patterns in which the Gospel takes on flesh, at once enmeshed in the *local situation* and at the same time taking on eschatological significance. Culture is the context in which this happens. It, too, represents a paradesis, values, symbols and meanings, and a concrete way of life for the people within a given time and place. To abstract from the realities in order to establish a "universal" church or a *theologia perennis* can only lead to one or other form of paternalism and oppression. Without a sensitivity to the cultural context, a church and its theology become docetistic.

The Community as Theologian

Africanization bases its theology on the community. The community acts as a formulator of theology. The amazing and profound things that have emerged when professionals have taken time to listen to the experience of the people within the community certainly underscores this assertion. Faith is not meant to be dependent on professional theologians, since theology is rooted in the community's experience of faith, rather than in theological *monograms* and *lexica*. The problem with professional theologians seems to be that such persons are often removed from the day-to-day struggles of the people. What the professional theologian gains in expertise in the *traditions* and *experience* of other communities ends up in a *loss of contact* with the local community. The theologian not only needs the experience of the community, but must also share, in a significant way, in the experience of comnity and join *with the community* in giving voice to that exrience of faith.

Liberation Theology

Perhaps, for us caught up in the South African situation, Africanization should promote liberation theology which is a method for analyzing the oppression and struggle of a people and for giving it voice within the biblical witness. Oppression, racism, poverty, unemployment, class struggle, etc are key terms in the liberation approach. We have already observed that theology rises out of a community, not out of an academy. A sign of living theology is the enhancement of praxis from which it has arisen.

Liberation theology locates the genuine need; it respects and builds upon it; it provides an alternative to the consciousness of the oppressor. It brings forward aspects of Scriptures long submerged.

Liberation theology reminds us once again that what Christians do is central to understanding who Christians are. While the concept of praxis reaches beyond simple action, and includes reflection upon action, the action part does maintain a certain priority: "by their fruits shall you know them" has been one of the oldest ways for discerning Christian identity in the Christian churches.

The preaching of the Gospel is always a big risk. The contact of culture and Gospel never has a clear outcome if it is to be successful. The form of the Gospel emerging from a community may call into question previous forms of the Gospel in a most serious fashion. If one takes the radicality of the incarnation seriously, one is left with this risk. God's risk with Jesus remains paradigmatic for us in our churches. If this risk does not take place the Gospel may have been betrayed. Christianity has more often than not taken the risk, beginning with the admission of the gentiles into the Christian communion. This was the programme of Gentilization to free itself from the Judaization. This was a radical Christian response to apartheid. One of the tasks of Africanization is to continue the risk and to continue the deep-structure encounter between Gospel and culture.

"Africanization has now become a vogue, and frantic attempts are being made to dress Christianity in an African garb, without, however, totally stripping off the dress in which it cloaked itself on its way to Africa from Europe."[1]

We are warned by some African writers that if the churches in Africa are to grow and develop, they must be allowed to take root in the soil of Africa where they have been planted. Our attention is drawn to the breakthrough that has been made in the independent African churches.

In the established Western-oriented churches, we are told that medical practice has become so specialized and secularized that the ordinary pastor has been radically excluded from service for the sick. Thus healing and worship have become separate. Africanization seeks to integrate the two, and to make prayer, healing and a very simple evangelical preaching the centre of its religious life. Let us not forget that the spiritual hunger, which in our days characterizes most of the European churches overseas and possibly here has been one of the main causes of the emergence of Indigenous African Christian churches.

Support and Sharing
Africanization attempts to teach individuals to respect one another in a certain sence as siblings; hence the use of the terms "brother" and "sister" by members who are in no way related. The members are encouraged to behave as a family, to support and sympathize with one another. After all, theologically speaking *Koinonia* has to do with common sharing and equity among the members of a Christian family. I wish to remind all the Christians that the corollary term *adelphotes* (brotherhood) or *adelphoi* (brothers) in Christian holy greetings actually means nothing, unless respect, equity, and common sharing become a reality in *toto*.

"The idea and the ideal of partnership (brotherhood, Christian family, co-responsibility, fellowship, community, sharing, give-and-receive relationship) were actively present from the very beginning of the church."[2] This is what has lately been taken up by the Black Methodist Consultation (BMC), a movement often misunderstood in some circles of our church, and a movement whose emphasis is on the need for equal partnership — bearing the responsibility as equals. It asks nothing less than the costly rupture with a past in which life seemed secure and comfortable for some within the Christian family, while others in the same Christian family ate the crumbs of the bread under the table. You are aware just as I am, that this desired aim cannot be bought at a cheap price.

Africanization, through its spokesmen like the BMC, is geared to the full participation of the majority in the life of the church. The needs of the majority, their aspirations and problems will determine what their pastoral priorities will be. Africanization encourages the majority to become active, and through their activity determine from below, from inside, the real shape of the church. Finally, Africanization seeks to catch the spirit of that African Christian spiritual tradition which was slowly sung by Tengo Jabavu as he lay dying on his death bed — Tiyo Soga's Great Hymn: —

> *Lizalis' idinga Lakho*
> *Tixo, Nkosi yenyaniso*
> *Zonk ' intlanga Zalelizwe*
> *Mazizuze usindiso.*

Translated:
> Fulfil thy promises
> O God, Lord of Truth
> Let every tribe of this land
> Obtain salvation.

It is this kind of background in pursuit of Africanization which has nourished one of the greatest sons of Africa of our time, Archbishop Desmond Tutu. It is true that if great things are to happen two elements are necessary. It is necessary that there should exist a *man* who has three qualities: (a) mind; (b) heart; (c) spirit. These three elements make him a real instrument in the hands of God.

It is also true that it is necessary that there should exist a set of circumstances which makes it possible for that man to act. Sometimes there has existed in history a situation which was crying out to be used, but there was no man to use it. And sometimes there existed in history a man who might have done great things but who was frustrated and hindered and held back because the time was not yet ripe. If great things are to happen, it is necessary that the hour and the man should come together. We say the hour is now and such a man is our

Archbishop Desmond Tutu. We salute him with thousands of *shaloms*.

REFERENCES NOTES

1. Kofi: Appiah-Kubi, and Sergio Torres (eds.) *African Theology en Route*, Orbis Books, New York, 1979, p. 16.
2. Ibid, p. 48

ITUMELENG MOSALA

Ethics of the Economic Principles: Church and Secular Investments

I want to point out at the outset that the present political and especially ideological climate in South Africa does not permit a single black perspective on anything, least of all on "Economic Issues". It is an atmosphere in which ideological lines are fairly well drawn. If there had been any doubt, say in 1984, as to the serious-ness of the merging ideological demarcations, the experience of the "necklace" in 1985, at least within the black community, erased it with a brush of fire. Thus in the aftermath of 1985 any black re-sponse to any issue must identify itself more specifically in terms of *which* black response it is. There are black responses and black responses.

Being professionally a black biblical hermeneutician, working within the wider framework of Black Theology, committed to liber-ation defined as the struggle by black people to recover control of the development of black history, black culture and black destiny, I can only make a *black theological* response to "Economic Issues" in my church and country.

To the extent that it is appropriate to speak of sources of theology in Black Theology, two such sources may be identified. They are the biblical and the African roots of Black Theology. By the biblical roots of Black Theology it is not implied that the entire Jewish-Christian

Bible is on the side of the struggle of the black oppressed people of South Africa. On the contrary as I have argued elsewhere, there are significant parts of the Bible that militate against the struggle for liberation and are usable as ideological support for maintaining the interests of the ruling class.[1]

Black Theology has roots in the Bible insofar as it is capable of linking the struggles of oppressed people in South Africa today with the struggles of oppressed people in the communities of the Bible. The oppressed people in the Bible did not write the Bible. Their struggles come to us *via* the struggles of their oppressors. Thus Black Theology needs to be firmly and critically rooted in black history and black culture in order for it to possess apposite weapons of struggle that can enable black people to get underneath the biblical text to the struggles of oppressed classes.

Dialectically, Black Theology needs to be firmly and critically rooted in the Bible in order to elicit from it cultural-hermeneutical tools of combat with which black people can penetrate to the underside of black history and culture on the one hand, and beneath contemporary capitalist settler colonial domination on the other, to the experiences of oppressed and exploited working class black people. Only a strategy that issues out of this black theological method seems to me capable of providing an adequate black response to the issues of church and secular economic investments. I am of course painfully aware that neither the individual churches in South Africa, nor the South African Council of Churches, have officially adopted Black Theology as the legitimate theology of liberation of the black Christians of South Africa. With the increasing politicization and mobilization of the black communities since 1976, however, Black Theology has increasingly also been becoming a material force capable of gripping the black Christian masses of South Africa.

The "Ethics of Economic Principles" in black history and culture.
By history I mean far more than the exploits of prominent individuals and families. That way of looking at history is characteristic of bourgeois science. I refer, rather, to the relations that humans enter into the environment and with one another in the necessary business of eking out an existence. In this I concur with those scholars who hold that:

> the first premise of human existence and, therefore of all history is that 'men' (sic) must be in a position to live in order to be able to 'make history'. . . life involves before everything else eating and drinking, a habitation, clothing and many other things. The first historical act is thus the production of

the means to satisfy these needs, the production of material life itself.[2]

A reconstruction, therefore, of the "ethics of the economic principles" of black history is an iniquity into "the social-historical organizational structure of the production and reproduction" processes of black life.

There are at least two stages which can be delineated with reasonable precision in the development of black history prior to its distortion and exploitation by white history.

The first is the communal stage. This mode of social and economic production was characterized by a low level of development of the economic forces of production. Land and cattle were the fundamental means of production and, therefore, of livelihood. Ownership of the means of production was communal. This means that families had equal access to the basic means of livelihood. Members of families contributed their labour on family fields and shared equally in the pastoral activities of the community. Egalitarian control over the means of economic production ensured equal, egalitarian distribution of the products of social labour.

Production in this society was strictly of use-values, i.e. production was based fundamentally on human needs. Because of the low level of development of the forces of production which was itself a function of an undeveloped division of labour the human needs that controlled production were structured around the *household* as a unit of economic production. There was therefore no permanent collective or communal labour organization on a national level. Co-operative productive activity was confined to the basic unit of production, the family. Consequently, not enough surplus production was generated at this stage of African society to enable a further development of the technological capability of the nation, which would itself necessitate new methods of labour organization. There is a dialectic relationship between the forms which this labour sets in motion. On the one hand what forms of labour organization there are, are dependent upon the nature of the technology available to this labour. On the other hand, the technological capabilities of a society have a structuring effect on the labour organizational possibilities. The point I am making, therefore, is simple: Peasant production as represented by the communal stage of black history did not enable a further development of the *same* society because it confined its best form of labour organization, co-operative activity in production, to too small a unit of economic production, the peasant household. Nevertheless the egalitarianism of the communal mode of production has not been paralleled in subse-

quent history. Instead, now and again contemporary black people
take a nostalgic launch into this distant past history to seek weapons of struggle from it. For as one scholar has so rightly observed:

> Men make their own history, but they do not make it just as
> they please; they do not make it under circumstances chosen
> by themselves, but under circumstances directly encountered,
> given and transmitted from the past. The tradition of all the
> dead generations weighs like a nightmare on the brain of the
> living. And just as they seemed engaged in revolutionizing
> themselves and things, in creating something that has never
> yet existed, precisely in such periods of revolutionary crisis
> they conjure up the spirits of the past to their service and bor-
> row from them names, battle cries and costumes in order to
> present the new scene of world history in this time-honoured
> disguise and this borrowed language.[3]

Often this borrowing from the past is done by us, as has been
done by other people in other histories and cultures at other times,
as a way of finding "the ideals and art forms (and) the self decep-
tions that (we) need in order to conceal from (ourselves) the . . .
limitations of the content of our struggles."[4]

This danger we must avoid in our attempts to root ourselves in
black history and black culture. In our reappropriation of the economic systems of our own history we must show the intellectual
integrity that Frederick Engels exhibited in his assessment of primitive communism. Ross Gandy has this to say about this:

> "Engels speaks well of early communism, but he is not guilty
> of primitivism. He argues that this stage was inferior to civili-
> zation. He notes the war between tribes, the cruelty of the
> warfare, the stunted productive forces, the religious supersti-
> tion, and the power of nature over people. Primitive com-
> munism, he thinks, was better than civilization in only one
> way: its morality".[5]

That then is the fundamental strength of this mode of production, this economic system: *its morality*. The morality of this system is not abstract, it is not tagged on from outside. The ethics of
the communal mode of economic production is the condition of
existence of this mode. It consists in the fact that production is for
meeting perceived human needs. *Human beings* and their well-
being, are the starting point and the goal of production in this
mode. *People* are the basis and the content of the morality of this
economic system.

Thus when Black Theology speaks of being critically and firmly

based within the black history of struggle it has in mind the conflicts and harmonies between people and nature and between
people and people that revolve around the morality of production
for human needs, production of *use-values*. Economic investment
in the communal mode of production took the well-being of people
as a point of departure and the goals of economic production and
development were structured around the issue of the *wellbeing* of
people. It is this economic *morality* which Black Theology wants to
base itself upon in its struggle for a new South Africa.

Black history and black culture are, like all other histories and
cultures, not static. The cummunal mode of economic production
was altered and replaced by another mode around the 14th and
15th centuries A.D. The new mode was based on the tributary social relations of productions. By this I mean an economic system
where tribute paying was a basic means of surplus extraction. It is
under this mode of production that the chieftainship developed as
the dominant political structure. In this system of production ownership of the means of livelihood (land, cattle, implements) is still
largely communal, but the generation of a surplus in economic production has already allowed the beginnings of class and state formation. The relative development of technology and labour
organization in this mode

> necessitates the end of the dominance of kinship (which can
> continue to exist but only as a vestige dominated by another
> rationality). The forms of property corresponding to this sec-
> ond step are those which enable the dominant class to control
> access to the land and by means of this to extract tribute from
> the peasant producers. The extraction of this tribute is con-
> trolled by the dominance of ideology, which always takes the
> same forms: state religion or *quasi* religion.[6]

Hence under the influence of this mode the chief rather than the
fathers of the households becomes the priest; medical and psychiat-
ric activities are also alienated from the household to a specialist
group of *Nyangas/Dingaka*/traditional doctors who are now responsible first of all to the chief; military service is no longer a cooper-
ative activity of the above bodied persons of each household but
the drafting and mobilization of age regiments. *Mephato* under the
control of the chief or the chief's deputies; the ancestors of the
chief become the chief-ancestors in an hierarchical structure of ancestors. While under the communal system "the central contradictions were between elders and juniors and between elders and
women (Cooper, 1982, p. 65)", under the tributory system the contradictions are between the chief, nobility, retainers, on the one

side, and the elders, commoners, foreigners and slaves, on the other side.

At this early stage of the development of tributory relations in Africa, production, however, was still production of use-values, and not exchange values. As Samir Amin puts it:

"The product kept by the producer is itself directly a use value meant for consumption, in general, for the producer's own consumption. But the product extracted by the exploiting class is also directly a use-value for this class. The essence of this tributary mode then is a natural economy, without exchange but not without transfers (tribute is one) and redistributions".[7]

The immorality of this social-economic system consists in its practice of the social relations of dominance which were sealed by social and religious ideology. Samir Amin is right in asserting that:

"It is worth recalling that this domination aids in the extraction of the surplus, while the ideology of kinship in the communal mode, where ideology is also dominant, aids in the reproduction of relations of cooperation and domination but not of exploitation".[8]

The morality of the tributary economic system remains in its retention of the purpose of economic production, namely, production for *use,* for meeting human needs. Incipient economic exploitation in the form of transfers is offset by the redistributive economic justice. The irony and inherent contradiction of this set-up is captured by Jean Comaroff when she writes:

"The encompassment of the household within the political economy was actually conceived of in terms of the 'natural' progression of kin groups into the nation (*morafe*); and chiefly extraction was couched in the terms of agnatic seniority, a relationship idealized as one of paternal responsibility as well as authoritative licence. The chief, after all, was the 'father of the people'."[9]

In this social-economic system we already find the seeds of later morally suspect modes of production.

Having identified the morality and immorality of economic principles in the history and culture of its own people, Black Theology must enter the terrain of the biblical traditions to test morality against morality. To this we now turn.

The "Ethics of Economic Principles" in Yahwistic biblical history and culture.

I have chosen to address the Yahwistic biblical history out of considerations of space and time as well as for reasons of ideological congruence. A black theological projection of the ethics of economic principles must necessarily seek marriage with the just revolutionary traditions of the Bible. New studies of the biblical texts in the light of human struggles for liberation are showing increasingly that the revolutionary traditions in the Bible are themselves in struggle with the reactionary traditions in the Bible. This conflict explains why some people can find justification for oppression in the Bible while others find liberation in the same Bible. Harvey Cox, in a foreword to George Pixley's book, *God's Kingdom*, states the problem well when he writes:

"Throughout Christian history the argument over just how earthly the Kingdom of God is supposed to be has been fought along quite predictable lines. Those who are rich or content or powerful or comfortable here and now prefer a kingdom to come that will not alter our earthly reality very soon or very much. They like it the way it is now. They have devised theologies of inward, figurative, or post-historical kingdoms, or kingdoms that begin only after death. No wonder . . .

The disinherited, on the other hand, have frequently insisted on a much more commonsensical and straight-forward reading of what Jesus was saying and doing when he speaks of emptying the prisons, they refuse to reduce this to 'spiritual prisons', since the cell blocks they and their friends and loved ones languish in are made of stone and steel. When he talks of cancelling debts, they think first of all not of infractions of social decorum but of their unpaid bills and the hot breath of their creditors. When he speaks of filling the hungry, they think not of communion wafers, but of rice and beans and bread: 'Thy kingdom come'.

Who has been right and who wrong in this age-old hermeneutical class struggle? Not surprisingly . . . the weight of scribal evidence seems on the side of the wealthy and well-situated."[10]

Yahwistic Israelite society from which Black Theology takes its biblical cue originated from the revolutionary withdrawal of the Moses group from Egypt on the one hand, and from the resistance struggles of the lower or marginal Canaanite social classes on the other hand. The first Israelites were people of mixed origins ethnically and culturally. "Socio-economically, they were mostly peasants —whether as serfs or as impoverished freeholders — but they also included shepherds, artisans, professional soldiers, and priests."[11]

N.K. Gottwald has characterized the social relations of production in Ancient Israel succinctly when he writes:

"The people of Israel were of *approximate equality,* living in large extended families and protective associations (often called clans), a people with basically the same rights to life resources, which for them meant land and its produce and raw materials. They paid no taxes in kind, nor did they render military service or draft labour to kings or ruling classes . . .

The sharpest form of cultural self-expression among the Israelites was a *people's religion.* This religion, often called Yahwism (after the name of the deity, Yahweh), affirmed the unity of the people and their determination to prevail in history as a society of mutually supportive equals".[12]

Gottwald has rightly identified Deuteronomy 33:2-5, 26-29 as containing a vivid summary of the egalitarianism of early Israel:

"Yahweh came from Sinai,
and dawned from Seir upon us;
he shone forth from Mount Paran,
he came from the ten thousands of holy ones,
with flaming fire at his right hand.
Yea, he loved his people;
all those consecrated to him were in his hand;
so they followed in your steps,
receiving direction from you,
when Moses commanded us a law,
as a possession for the assembly of Jacob.
Thus Yahweh became king in Jeshurun,
when the heads of the people were gathered.
There is none like God, O Jeshurun,
who rides through the heavens to your help
and in his majesty through the skies.
The eternal God is your dwelling place,
and underneath are the everlasting arms,
And he thrust out the enemy before you,
and said, Destroy!
So Israel dwelt in safety,
the fountain of Jacob alone,
in a land of grain and wine;
yea, his heavens drop down dew.
Happy are you, O Israel! who is like you,
a people saved by Yahweh,
the shield of your help,
and the sword of your triumph!

Your enemies shall come fawning to you;
and you shall tread upon their high places."
(Deuteronomy 33: 2-5, 26-29)

Again the issue of the morality (ethics of the economic system of early Israel) must be posed. In my opinion and in those of an increasing number of biblical scholars the fundamental difference between early Israel and the surrounding Canaanite States, and early Israel and later monarchic Israel lies in the morality that underpinned the purpose of economic production in these social entities. Economic production and the organization of social labour in premonarchic Israel was based on the production of use-values in order to meet fundamental human needs.

Later on in the history of Israel when things had gone really bad; when the poor had been sold for a pair of sandals; the temple had been used as an ideological power base for buttressing the interests of rich landowners against depressed peasants; production of necessary products had been replaced by the production and importation of luxury goods for exclusive use by the ruling classes; human relations had been distorted and turned into commodity relations; when things had gone this bad we hear a terse but probably most important voice out of the prophetic text:

"He will settle disputes among the nations,
among great powers near and far.
They will hammer their swords into ploughs
And their spears into pruning-knives.
Nations will never again go to war
never prepare for battle
Everyone will live in peace
In his vineyard and under his fig trees
And no one will make him afraid". (Micah 4:3-4)

This, it seems to me, should be the basic morality of economic production: that the natural and human resources of a nation must be invested in productive rather than destructive technology; that people should learn how to live and work together rather than go to war with one another; that each family unit should have equal access and control over the fundamental means of livelihood; that living without fear of anything is integral to the existence of a just economy. Frankly, I do not think that the capitalist economic system under which we and the Western world live can contain this fundamental biblical and black theological morality of economic production. Neither the churches nor the theologians have faced squarely the problem of the morality or more exactly the immorality of the capitalist economic order. I submit that the capitalist economic system, often euphemistically called "free enterprise", is, when looked at from the moral perspectives of African history and biblical Yahwistic ideology, simply immoral. It is a system based on *wage-slavery*. Describing one aspect of this slavery Marx states:

> *In the first place,* the raising of wages gives rise to *overwork* among the workers. The more they wish to earn, the more must they sacrifice their time and carry out slave-labour, completely losing all their freedom, in the service of greed. Thereby they shorten their lives. This shortening of their life-span is a favourable circumstance for the working class as a whole, for as a result of it an ever-fresh supply of labour becomes necessary. This class has always to sacrifice a part of itself in order not to be wholly destroyed.[13]

There is an urgent need to describe, explain and change the morality of the economic systems on which our societies are based. The churches have been eloquent by their collusive silence as far as a theological assessment of capitalism is concerned. Black Theology, for itself, was born in war against capitalism. As a criticism of the weapon of struggle for a true humanity, that is, as a criticism of Christianity as an instrument of liberation, it has faired very well. It is rather as itself the weapon of criticism against capitalism and in the hands of struggling black working class people that it has performed poorly. The little contribution which the churches could make in an effort to establish a moral economic system, is to create conditions for the black working class people to participate without fear and meaningfully, within the churches, in the process of fashioning black theological weapons of struggle against the immorality of capitalist production, exchange and distribution.

REFERENCE NOTES

1. For an elaborate statement of this position see Itumeleng J. Mosala and Buti Tlhagale, *The Unquestionable Right to be Free,* Skotaville, Johannesburg, (1986) pp. 175-199; For a similar position in relation to liberation theology see N.K. Gottwald, "Socio-historical precision in the biblical grounding of liberation theologies", *An Address to the Catholic Biblical Association of America,* San Francisco (August 1985).
2. K. Marx and F. Engles, *The German Ideology,* edited by C.J. Arthus, Lawrence and Wishart, London, (1970), p. 48.
3. K. Marx, "The Eighteenth Brumaire of Louis Bonaparte" in Marx and Engels *Selected works,* Lawrence and Wishart, London, (1968), p. 96.
4. Ibid, p. 97.
5. R. Gandy, *Marx and History,* University of Texas Press, Austin and London, (1979), p. 17.
6. Samir Amin, *Class and Nation, Historically and in the Current Crisis,* Heinemann, London, (1980), p. 49.

7. Ibid, p.51.
8. Ibid, p. 52.
9. Jean Camaroff, *Body of Power Spirit of Resistance, The Culture and History of a South African People*, Univ. of Chicago Press, Chicago and London, 1985, p. 60f.
10. G.V. Pixley, *God's Kingdom*, Orbis Books, N.Y., (1981), pp. VIIIf.
11. N.K. Gottwald, "'Church and State' in Ancient Israel: Example or Caution in our Age?", *The Department of Religion Lecture Series*, University of Florida, Gainesville, (1981), p.2.
12. Ibid, p.3.
13. K. Marx, *Economic and Philosophic Manuscripts of 1844*, Lawrence and Wishart, London, (1977), p. 19.

Part 4

Prophetic Theology

ALBERT NOLAN

Theology in a Prophetic Mode

It is not without reason that Archbishop Tutu has been hailed throughout the world as a modern day prophet. His sermons, talks and many public statements can be aptly described as theology in a prophetic mode. What does this mean? What are the characteristics of a prophetic theology and what does it imply for South Africa at this moment of its history?

It would not be possible to attempt a comprehensive outline of prophetic theology in this brief essay. However, there is a fundamental characteristic of this mode in theology that underlies everything else and that distinguishes it from every other theology or mode of theology. And this is the characteristic of being *timebound*. All prophecy and prophetic theology speaks of, and speaks to, a particular time in a particular place about a particular situation. This is the aspect of theology in a prophetic mode that I would like to examine in this essay.

The Kairos Document has drawn our attention quite recently to the theological significance of a particular moment in history, a crisis, a *kairos*. And it has hailed it down to the particular crisis in which South Africa finds itself today. This alone would make the theology of the Kairos Document prophetic in character or mode. But unfortunately the document devotes no more that a page and a half to this all important notion of a *kairos* or moment of truth. Much more needs to be said if theology in a prophetic mode is to be taken up and developed fully, effectively and powerfully in South Africa. Moreover, it is no mere coincidence that this path of investigation would also be one of the ways of liberating ourselves from the dominant Western world that still imprisons and entombs our theology in South Africa. Western theology is singularly unprophetic because it understands all truth to be timeless and universal. This understanding, among other things, became a very convenient tool for colonizing the minds of much of the human race and for excluding all possibility of prophetic thinking. The biblical prophets were far removed from our Western intellectuals in many ways including the fact that their message was *not* timeless and universal.

Gerhard von Rad, after many years of research on "the message" of the prophets, draws this conclusion:

"It is all important not to read this message as if it consisted of timeless ideas, but to understand it as the particular word relevant to a particular hour in history, which therefore cannot be replaced by any other word. The prophetic word never tries to climb into the realm of general religious truth, but instead uses even the most suspect means to tie the listening partner down to his (sic) particular time and place in order to make him understand his own situation before God."[1]

There is a typically non-Western way of conceiving time that is not only Hebrew and Biblical but also, in at least some ways, African. The Western concept of time, however, has been part and parcel of our education in South Africa as elsewhere. And it has its uses. But it would not be possible to speak theologically and prophetically about a particular moment of time without going beyond the Western concept of chronological time.

The simplest and briefest way of making this clear and of developing a basis for a prophetic theology in South Africa today would be to make a clear distinction between three kinds of time. The three kinds of time might best be designated by the three Greek words *chronos, kairos,* and *eschaton.*

Chronos:
This is the typically Western concept of time. *Chronos* means time as a measurement. It is the time of measured hours and dates, the time that is recorded on clocks and calendars. An historical epoch in this way of thinking is something that is identified by the date when it began and the date when it ended. Time is conceived of as a measured and numbered empty space that can be filled with events of greater or lesser importance. It is what one might call *qualified time.*

This is what comes to mind immediately and almost exclusively in Western thinking when the word time is mentioned. A quantified measurement. However, this is *not* the way the Bible thinks of time. In the words of Von Rad, "Today one of the few things of which we can be quite sure is that this concept of absolute time, independent of events, and, like blanks on a questionnaire, only headings to be filled up with data which will give it (time) content, was unknown to Israel."[2]

Kairos:
This word on the other hand, refers to time as a *quality*. A particular *kairos* is the particular quality or mood of an event. This is clearly and succintly expressed in the famous passage from Ecclesiastes (3:1-8):

> There is a time for everything;
> a time for giving birth,
> a time for dying,
> a time for planting,
> a time for uprooting,
> a time for killing,
> a time for healing,
> a time for knocking down,
> a time for building,
> a time for tears,
> a time for laughter,
> a time for mourning,
> a time for dancing...
> a time for loving,
> a time for hating;
> a time for war,
> a time for peace.

For the Hebrew, to know the time was not a matter of knowing the hour or the date, it was a matter of knowing what kind of time it was. Was it a time for tears or a time for laughter, a time for war or a time for peace? To misjudge the time in which one was living might be disastrous. To continue to mourn and fast during a time of blessing would be like sowing during harvest time (see Zech 7:1-3). Time here is the quality of mood of events.

This concept of time is not entirely foreign to us. It is particularly meaningful to those who inherit an African culture and even more meaningful when we are involved in an intensified struggle to change the times. We know about times of mourning that make it inappropriate to celebrate a joyful Christmas. We have discussed about whether it is a time for boycotting or a time for returning to school. There is a time for conflict and confrontation and a time for reconciliation and peace but, unfortunately, we do not relate each different *kairos* to God as easily and as naturally as the people of the Bible did. This indeed is where prophetic theology comes in and where we have much to learn from the Bible.

In the Bible the prophet was someone who could tell the time. He (or she) could see what kind of time it was and what kind of action would be appropriate now. The prophets could read the signs of the times, which means they could interpret the *kairos,* interpret the signs that would indicate what kind of time it was (compare Mt 16:3 with Lk 12:56).

Prophecy, however, was not just a matter of knowing one's *kairos;* it was also a matter of finding God in it. For the prophets, God determined the different times and therefore it is He who speaks to us and challenges us through our particular *kairos.* Revelation has a tremendous immediacy here. God is directly involved in the changing times. God speaks loudly and clearly through this crisis or that conflict or some victory over the forces of evil. Theology in a prophetic mode is a theology that can find and experience God as alive and active in the excitement or the sadness or the suffering of our present *kairos.* This is not to say that every moment of chronological time is equally important or significant and that God can be found equally in every and any event. Every event in history is not a *kairos.* A divine *kairos* is a very special and significant time. There are lulls in history when nothing of significance happens. For the Bible such chronological times are simply not history. History is the succession of God-inspiring events. The gift of the prophet is the ability to recognize such events, such critical times and to spell them out as moments of truth, as challenges, as opportunities, as times for decision and action. A *kairos* is privileged time that not everyone is called to witness or participate in. Such was, of course, the time of Jesus and that is why he could say to his disciples: "Happy the eyes that see what you see, for I tell you that many prophets and kings wanted to see what you see and never saw it" (Lk 10:23-24). The time of Jesus was of course a unique and unrepeatable *kairos.* But that does not mean that there can be no other specially privileged times. Today in South Africa, according to the prophetic theology of the Kairos Document, is indeed for us an unprecendented *kairos.*

It is at times like this that God visits his people, that God walks down our streets and enters right into our homes. Everyday life is turned upside down and inside out and nothing will ever be the same again. These are the favourable times, the times of grace when God offers us the kind of opportunity that our predecessors might have longed to see but never saw. And woe betide us if we do not rise to the challenge.

But even this is not all. The real specialness and seriousness of a prophetic *kairos* is determined by its relationship to another kind of time: the *eschaton*.

Eschaton:

Eschatological time or the *eschaton* is a notoriously difficult concept. Biblical scholars crack their heads over it and come up with a whole range of different theories from realized eschatology to consistent eschatology and existential eschatology. I have no intention of delving into these theories because I think that the present crisis in South Africa can provide us with a simple and practical appreciation of what the prophets had in mind.

Put quite simply, an *eschaton* is an event of the near future, an act of God, that determines the quality, the mood and the seriousness of our present time, that is to say, it turns the present moment into a particular kind of *kairos*. This way of thinking about God and time requires some unpacking.

A very important characteristic of all prophetic thinking is that it turns the attention of the people from the past to the future. Prophets are called prophets precisely because they speak about the future. Instead of trying to understand the present in terms of the events of the past (for example, Exodus, Mount Sinai or King David), the prophets ask the people to think of the present time in terms of a future act of God. They challenge the people to break with the past and to look forward to something new: "Remember not the former things," says God in Isaiah, "I am going to do a new thing" (43: 19-19).

An *eschaton* is a qualitatively and radically *new* event. It is interesting to notice how often the prophets use the word "new": the new covenant, the new age, a new heart, a new spirit, the new heaven and new earth, the new Jerusalem or simply the fact that God is going to do a new thing. They looked forward to a future in which new and unprecedented things would happen and even when they looked back to the past and the traditions of the past they would interpret them anew in view of the new future. Thus the covenant makes them think of the new covenant to come, the exodus turns their attention to the new exodus and Jerusalem to the new Jerusalem and so forth.

The prophets did not use the Greek word *eschaton*. When they spoke of the new future they called it "the day of Yahweh", "the day of vengeance" or "the latter days" or "the days that are coming" or simply "the day". At a later stage the *eschaton* was referred to as "the coming of the new age" and Jesus is making use of the same idea when he speaks of "the coming of the kingdom of God."

The first and most important thing that all the prophets, and Jesus, have to say about this new future or *eschaton* is that it is "near", "at hand", "coming soon". The prophets stand up to make the momentous announcement that "the day of Yahweh is near" (See for example Is 13: 6,9; Jer 46: 10; Ezek 7: 7,12; 30: 3; Joel 1: 15; 4: 14; Zeph 1: 7, 14; Zech 14: 1) and Jesus comes to proclaim that "the kingdom of God is near" (Mt 4: 17 and par). Of course they are not all referring to the same day nor are they all speaking about the last day. The *eschaton* is a new saving act of God that was imminent or near for them at that time.

The new saving act of God that will happen on the day of Yahweh is an act of judgment and salvation. Not that they have in mind what we call the last judgment or eternal salvation. They have in mind a particular day or time when God will punish those who are presently doing evil and save or vindicate or liberate those who are now enslaved or in exile or suffering oppression. The Hebrew verb "to judge" means literally "to put right what is wrong". We can say then that the *eschaton* is an event of the near future in which God is going to put right all that is presently wrong. That will mean punishment for those who are doing wrong and salvation for those who are being wronged.

In the minds of the Old Testament prophets this future event will take the form of a mighty war [3] in which the forces of evil will be destroyed so that peace and justice may reign on earth. Many of the prophets give vivid and terrifying descriptions of this mighty war of liberation. For but a few examples, one can read about the imminent destruction of Babylon and Edom in Isaiah 13 and 34 and the terrifying massacre of the Egyptians by the Babylonians in Jer 46: 1-24 and Ezek 30, not to mention the many descriptions of the slaughter of the Jewish ruling class in Jerusalem on the day of Yahweh because of all their sins (See for example Joel 2: 1-11 and Ezek 37).

The prophets found no pleasure in describing all this horrific bloodshed. They trembled and shuddered at the very thought of it and they describe the fear and suffering of so many of the people with great compassion. Theirs is not a dispassionate and objective description of a war, but a prophetic warning about a world-shaking event that will be experienced as a cosmic upheaval:

> "The earth quakes, the skies tremble,
> sun and moon grow dark,
> the stars lose their brilliance"

(Joel 2:10).

We know this apocalyptic-type description of a cosmic upheaval and we come across it again in the Gospels (for example Mk 13: 24 25). It is fundamentally the experience of a terrible war that changes the face of the earth and is a turning point in human history. It is an *eschaton*.

But the day of Yahweh is not only a day of vengeance, a time of gloom and doom. The prophets were in no doubt about the terrifying seriousness of what was going to happen, the awful seriousness of God's anger. But they never lost hope. On the contrary the peace, the salvation, the justice and the equality that they were always hoping for would be the outcome of these very wars and upheavals. They have equally vivid descriptions of the peace and happiness that God will bring: when the lion lies down with the lamb (Is 11: 6-9; 65:25) and swords are melted into ploughshares (Is 2: 2-5); (Mi 4: 1-5) when there will be nothing more to fear (Zeph 3:13) and peace and justice will reign supreme (Is 32: 16-17) because the law will be written in the hearts of the people (Jer 31: 33) and the spirit of God will be in them (Ez. 36: 26). On that day God will put right all that is now wrong. The oppressors will be destroyed or converted and the poor and oppressed will live in peace (Zeph 3).[4]

This same idea of an *eschaton* appears in the New Testament when Jesus speaks about the coming of wars and rumours of wars (Mk 13) and the destruction of Jerusalem (Lk 19: 43-44; 21: 20-23; 23: 28). This he speaks of as the birth pangs of God's kingdom (Mk 13:).

However, for Jesus and the prophets the destructive side of the *eschaton*, the bloodshed, is not inevitable and absolutely unavoidable. As far as the Jewish prophets were concerned there was probably very little, if anything, that they could do about the massacre of the Egyptians by the Babylonians or later of the Babylonians by the Medes except to see that it would be to the advantage of Israel. (But when the Israelites themselves, or at least their ruling class, are the oppressors, then at least the prophets can appeal to them in the name of Yahweh to change their ways before they are destroyed.) This is where Jesus' and the prophets' oft repeated call to repentance and conversion comes in, the element of *metanoia*. And this is what constitutes their present moment as a special divine *kairos*, a moment of truth.

A *kairos* is a moment of grace, a unique opportunity precisely because the *eschaton* or day of reckoning is near. It is a time for decision and action, a time for oppressors and wrong-doers to be converted. And at the same time, the *kairos* is a time for rejoicing and for hope because the *eschaton* as the day of liberation is near at hand — whether the oppressor is converted or not, whether there will be bloodshed or not. The element of hopefulness and expectancy in any genuine *kairos* should not be overlooked. It is indeed one of the constitutive elements of a divine *kairos*.

The fundamental insight of prophetic theology, then, is the recognition that an *eschaton* or day of reckoning and liberation is near. It is this that turns the present moment into a *kairos* and everything else in prophetic theology follows from here. But one may well ask how anyone can be sure that an eschatalogical event is close at hand or how the prophets themselves could have known when their *eschaton* would occur.

Here again we would first need to be reminded that the nearness of an *eschaton* is not a matter of *chronos* or measured time. In other words, a prophet would not be able to tell you the day or the hour when all these things will happen. Jesus makes this quite clear when he says that nobody, nor even he himself, knows the day or the hour (Mk 13: 32 and par). But the impossibility of pinning the *eschaton* down to a chronological date did not make Jesus or the prophets any less certain about the central truth that their *eschaton* was near. What they are speaking about then, is another kind of time relationship, the extremely *close* relationship between the present *kairos* and a future *eschaton*. In fact, qualitatively speaking, the two events are so bound up together that they are almost contemporaneous. The *eschaton* is the event that determines and qualifies, or should determine and qualify, the whole mood and atmosphere of the present time.[5] If we believe that war, revolution, liberation or any other total upheaval is imminent, this will colour our whole understanding of our present reality. Once we realize that something totally new is about to happen, we are already living in a new time. Or if we come to believe that the day of reckoning is upon us, we are forced to decide to make our choices and take sides immediately. It is the approaching *eschaton* that turns our present crisis into a make-or-break *kairos*.

But that still leaves us with the question of how one is to know that there is an *eschaton* on the horizon. There answer is quite simply that we discover this, as the prophets did, by reading the signs of the time. If one interprets one's own time correctly and especially if one can see the events of one's time with the eyes of God, then one sees clearly what all the signs are pointing to. One can foresee what is going to happen sometime in the near future, even if one cannot calculate the exact day or the hour. Prophetic theology begins with some such insight or foresight.

South Africa Today

The Kairos theologians have drawn the conclusion that the present moment in South Africa is a *kairos,* but they have not spelt out very clearly and in a truly prophetic manner why this particular moment should be regarded as a divine *kairos*. Reference is made to the conflict between oppressor and oppressed and to the division in the church which claims the loyalty of both the oppressor and the oppressed. That indeed is a crisis and does indeed raise some serious questions about the meaning of Christianity but in and by itself it does not make our present time a *kairos*.

What is not explicit in the Kairos Document, although it is implied throughout the document, is that what we are now facing is an *eschaton*. What all the signs are now pointing to is that one way or another the day of liberation is near. Apartheid's days are numbered. In the near future this whole oppressive system is going to be utterly destroyed and a totally new, liberated and peaceful society will be built up in its place. The people are determined to do this and to do it soon and all the signs indicate that this drive towards liberation and peace through justice is now unstoppable. Of course it will be resisted, violently resisted, but it can no longer be stopped. This means that we must expect, unfortunately, more violence, more conflict and possibly more bloodshed before our society can be turned completely upside down to become a land of justice and peace.

In religious or theological terms, this is our *eschaton*. The day of Yahweh is at hand. The day of reckoning when God himself will put right what is wrong in our country is now very near. The terrifying seriousness of God's anger and his love, of God's justice and his mercy are about to descend upon us in a manner that might well make what the Old Testament prophets were talking about look like child's play. God is no less involved in our present crisis and in the upheaval that is about to take place here, than he was in the crisis and in the upheavals of the history of Israel.

That is what makes our present time in South Africa a truly prophetic *kairos*. A time of judgment and salvation. A time for real fear and trembling. A time when everything is at stake. A time for taking a clear stand. A time of tears and sadness that is nevertheless fraught with hope and joyful anticipation.

But it is also a time for us to act in the name of God, as the prophets did, to minimize the bloodshed. It is the sort of time when we should drop everything to proclaim from the rooftops that the day of reckoning is upon us and that the day of liberation has dawned. It is a time to appeal for immediate repentance and radical change; a time to call upon all in the world who can still hear the voice of God to do everything in their power; and at whatever cost to themselves, to hasten the downfall of the apartheid regime and so bring the violence of oppression to a speedy end. Now is the time. God is near.

FOOTNOTES
1. *The message of the Prophets,* SCM 1968, p 100.
2. op. cit., p 77.
3. op. cit., pp. 95 ff.
4. Norbert Lahfink, "Zefamja and das Israel der Armen." in *Bibel arid Kirch* 3: 3 (1984), 100-108, summarized in *Theology Digest* 32: 2 (1985), 113:124.
5. Albert Nolan, *Jerusalem before Christianity, The Gospel of Liberation,* David Philip (Cape Town), 1976, pp 77-78.

JAMES H. CONE

What is the Church?

Much has been written about the churches during the course of their historical development. Ernst Troeltsch, H. Richard Niebuhr, and Peter Paris[1] have written about the social origin and teaching of the Christian churches, and others, like Williston Walker, Carter G. Woodson, E. Franklin Frazier, and Sydney Ahlstrom[2] have concentrated on their institutional history. Systematic and historical theologians, like Karl Barth, Cyril Richardson, Jurgen Miltmann and Hans Kung[3] have focused their attention on the doctrine of the church, with special interest in its transcendent origin. None of these foci should be isolated from the others, because each is important for the formulation of a meaningful, contemporary definition of the church.

Every generation of Christians should ask: What is it that constitutes our identity and thus empowers us to live it out in the world? To answer this question, we must focus on the institutional and ethical activity that validates our ecclesiastical confessions. If we separate the doctrine of the church from its historical embodiment in our congregational life, we will also ignore the social and political significance of our credal formulations. Therefore, whatever else we may advance as our definition of the church, we should never separate the doctrine of the church from empirical, local congregations. While a theological doctrine of the church attempts to point to "more" than what can be empirically observed in local congregations, yet this theological "more" is itself obscured and distorted when it is separated from particular congregations and their behaviour in the world. This means that the "more" which may be disclosed in a theology of the church can only be found through a critical social analysis of the churches.

What then is the relationship between the church and local congregations, between a theology of the church and a sociology of the churches? Unfortunately theologians have tended to give an inordinate amount of attention to the doctrine of the church, an ecclesiastical perspective that seems to exist nowhere in society except in their minds and textbooks. This clever ecclesiastical sophistry enables pastors and other church officials to justify existing church institutions without seriously inquiring about their historical faithfulness to the gospel message that they claim as the foundation of the church's identity. By focusing their attention on a doctrinal understanding of the church that has little sociological relevance, theologians can ignore obvious historical contradictions and shortcomings of empirical churches. This abstract theological manoeuvre makes it possible for theologians to speak of the church as the "body of Christ" without saying a word about its relation to broken human bodies in society.

Focusing on the sociology of the churches, including their privileged political status in this society, makes it possible for church people to see themselves as others see them and thus partly guard against fatuous theological speech. Too often churches have been guilty of covering up their own sins behind sophisticated theological jargon. While saying that we are concerned about the poor, we do not analyze and fight against the socio-economic structures responsible for their poverty. To be sure, many congregations have food programmes, jail and hospital ministries, and other special projects designed to "help" the needy and the unfortunate. But such projects are not designed to challenge the capitalist system that creates human misery. Churches are often incapable of attacking the root cause of oppression, because they are beneficiaries of the socio-political system responsible for it. It is because churches are so much a reflection of the values of the society in which they exist that they also have a serious credibility problem among people who regard their poverty and imprisonment as a by-product of an unjust social order. A poem circulated at a poor people's rally in Albuquerque, New Mexico, entitled "Listen Christians," describes a perspective of the church that church people do not like to hear.

> I was hungry
> and you formed a humanities club
> and you discussed my hunger.
> Thank you.

I was imprisoned
and you crept off quietly
to your chapel in the cellar
        and prayed for my release.

I was naked
and in your mind
you debated the morality of
        my appearance.

I was sick
and you knelt and thanked God
        for your health.

I was homeless
and you preached to me
of the spiritual shelter of
        the love of God.

I was lonely
and you left me alone
to pray for me.
You seem so holy;
so close to God.
But I'm still very hungry
and lonely
and cold.

So where have your prayers
        gone?
What have they done?
What does it profit a man
to page through his book of prayers
when the rest of the world
is crying for his help?

This poem exposes the hypocrisy of the churches and forces one to ask whether any ecclesiastic confession is ever valid apart from a concrete, practical activity that validates it. How can one speak about the church as the body of the crucified Jesus of Nazareth when church people are so healthy and well-fed and have no broken bones? Can we really claim that established churches are the people of God when their actions in society blatantly contradict the one who makes that identity possible?

In this essay, it is not my intention to ridicule the churches. I am a member of the church, and I have been one of its ministers since I was sixteen years old, with pastorates in Little Rock at San Hill,

Spring Hill, and Allen Chapel A.M.E. Churches. It is because of
my love and concern for the church that I, as one of its theologians, must subject it to severe criticism when it fails to be in
society what it confesses in worship. Because our so-called theological jargon about the church has become so insensitive to human
pain and suffering, it distorts the theologian's authentic Christian
calling. In this situation it would be helpful to return to the concrete social reality of our existence, so that we may be permitted
to move to a deeper theological level. I do not believe that we can
experience the deeper level of our theological identity until we
have immersed ourselves in the social matrix in which our identity
must be actualized. For this reason, a social analysis of the
churches must precede a doctrine of the church. We should never
allow a theological interpretation of the church's transcendent
origin to obscure the empirical behaviour of churches that deny
what church people affirm in their ecclesiastical confessions.

While a sociology of the churches should serve as the starting
point for an analysis of the theology of the church, it none the less
is important to point out that theology and sociology in the context
of the church and the churches are not identical. Despite what
some persons may think, I still believe in the transcendent foundation of the church. I only wish to emphasize that I think that we
church people, especially theologians and pastors, have been too
carried away by that theological option, and as a result have distorted its true meaning. The transcendent origin of the church has
been used as a camouflage to cover up the gross shortcomings of
so-called Christian churches. As church people, is it not claiming
much too much to say that what we represent is of God when our
actions clearly originate from the values of a racist, classist, and
sexist society?

Furthermore, even if it is agreed that the church has its origin
beyond the context of this world, it is still necessary to face honestly the question: What is the relation between the theology of
the church and a sociology of the churches? The way out of this
dilemma is not a bold theological affirmation that "the Christian
church is the Church of Jesus Christ." Rather, the acid test of any
ecclesiastical statement is whether it has taken sufficient account of
the actual world in which liturgical confessions are made. For the
transcendent can be encountered only in the particularity of a
human situation. Whatever else the transcendent may mean, it is
always relevant to and for human beings. This is the significance of
the Incarnation, God becoming human in Jesus. It is the Incarnation that necessitates our sociological starting point. To be sure,

the sociological without the theological reduces the church to a social club of like-minded people. But the theological without a critical sociological component makes the church a non-historical, spiritual community whose existence has no effect on our social and political environment. In this essay, my concern is to examine the theological understanding of the church in the context of its socio-political existence in the world.

The Inter-relationship of the Church, Jesus Christ, and the Poor
The Christian church is that community of people called into being by the life, death, and resurrection of Jesus. The beginning and the end of the church's identity is found in Jesus Christ and nowhere else. He is the one who is the subject of the church's preaching, and also the one who embodies in his person the meaning of its mission in the world. To ask, "what is the church?" is also to ask, "who is Jesus?" for without Jesus the church has no identity. That was why Paul referred to the church as the body of Christ, and also why many theologians, past and present, would adhere to the claim that every ecclesiastical statement is at the same time a christological statement.

The differences among the churches, therefore, have not focused at the point of whether Christ is to be regarded as the head of the church. All churches who bear the name "Christian" would adhere to the confession that "Jesus Christ is Lord". Rather the differences among the churches that prevent their unity arise from the theological and sociological implications of that christological confession. When the churches begin to spell out the structural meanings of Jesus's Lordship for congregational life and for participation in society, they often find themselves in sharp disagreement. What does it mean to declare that Jesus is the head of the church whose sovereignity extends to the whole world? Not all churches answer that question in the same way.

Another factor worth noting has been the churches' inordinate pre-occupation with the *theological* side of their identity as if their transcendent origin legitimated their privilege in society and also bestowed upon their ministry a similar privilege in judgment regarding how the society should be politically, socially, and economically arranged. From the early church to the present, there have been intense debates regarding the precise meaning of the *ekklesia*. But the discussions have focused primarily on the church's specifically *divine* origin in order to defend its privilege against "heretics" rather than in defence of the poor which the divine origin entails. This distorted emphasis on the theological, almost to the exclusion of the need to make political solidarity with the poor and against their oppressors, has often blinded churches to their responsibility to implement in society what they sometimes confess in worship.

In his debate with the Donatists, Augustine, for example, defined the church in terms of the four marks of unity, holiness, catholicity, and apostolicity, with an emphasis also on its visible and invisible nature. John Calvin and his supporters of the Magisterial Reformation added the two additional marks of "the Word of God purely preached and heard and the sacraments administered according to Christ's institution".[4] The Radical Reformation added several additional marks, one of which was obedience to the "Cross of Christ which is born for the sake of his testimony and Word."[5] Menno Simons, a representative of this Radical tradition, rejected the inordinate emphasis on the invisibility of the church. According to him, "as long as the transgressors and wilful despisers of the Holy Word are unknown to the church, she is innocent, but when they are known and then not excluded after proper admonition, but allowed to remain in the fellowship . . . then . . . she ceases to be the church of Christ."[6] Simon's concern, along with other Anabaptists, was the *restitution* of the church along the lines of its apostolic pattern. That was why *discipline* became one of the essential marks of the church. Unlike Augustine and Calvin who contended that the true church was invisible and thus known only to God by virtue of divine election, the Anabaptists insisted that the church of Christ is an "assembly of the pious". While Calvin could say that "the pure ministry of the Word and pure mode of celebrating the sacraments" are sufficient for the church's identity "even if it otherwise swarms with many faults."[7] Menno Simons contended that "we know for sure where . . . there is no pious Christian life, no brotherly love, and no orthodox confession, there no Christian church is . . . ."[8]

While there are sharp differences between Augustine and Calvin, on the one hand, and Menno Simon and his Anabaptists supporters on the other, yet there is a striking similarity among them from the perspective of their concentrated pre-occupation with the theological or the transcendental origin of the church. This transcendent focus has often prevented church people from seeing the correct relationship between theology and politics, the preaching of the gospel to the poor and its implementation in society. During the sixteenth century, the Anabaptists appeared to come the closest to recognizing the cross of Jesus as essential for the church's life of suffering. For they insisted that "the True Church was a suffering church whose changing patterns were ever cast in the shadow of the Man Upon the Cross."[9] But unfortunately they tended to become too sectarian by withdrawing from social and political responsibility and thereby reinforcing the idea that the church is a specifically spiritual institution.

It was Karl Marx and later the sociologists of knowledge who pointed out that the churches' emphasis on the specifically theological was in fact a camouflage for their support of the existing social order. The churches are not really non-political, even though they often have said that "the church should stay out of politics". As the active participation of the Moral Majority in electoral politics has demonstrated, this dictum holds true for many white conservative church people only as long as the existing social order is not disturbed. If a threat to the "law and order" of the system exists, the churches will take the lead in providing a sacred justification for all so-called good people to take up arms against the forces of evil.

It was because the churches and their leaders provided a theological justification for an unjust social order that Marx defined religion as the opiate of the people. Whether Marx was correct in his judgment is still a much debated issue, with church people insisting that they represent more than a "sacred canopy"[10] of their social environment. Regardless of what church people claim about themselves in their worship and intellectual life, it seems that the burden of proof is upon them to validate their claims of transcendence. And this validation must involve more than intellectual or pious appeals to God. Church people must be able to point to something in their congregational life that is not simply a religious legitimation of the values of the social order in which they live.

The need for the church to act against itself in order to be its true self has been pointed out by both theologians and social ethicists. For example, Langdon Gilkey has said: "Since the church is in secular culture, . . . the life of the congregation cannot in any sense express transcendence of the culture around it unless it is willing to challenge the injustice . . . of the wider community in which it lives."[11] With a firmer grasp of the tools of social analysis, James Gustafson manifests even more insight in his comments about the churches. Gustafson is concerned about the sharp distinction made between the public and private life and the limitation of the church to the latter. But even in the private sphere, the church's "role has become supportive, therapeutic, pastoral and even idolatrous, for its functions to give religious sanctions to a culturally defined pattern of life that is itself not sufficiently subjected to theological and moral criticism."[12] One test of the au-

thenticity of the church's claim to transcendence is its capacity to
represent in its congregation a "socially heterogeneous" people. If
it is not possible for blacks and whites to worship and practice the
Christian faith in the world as one community because of radically
different cultural mores, can we not conclude that their respective
racial groupings are due to each people's values and not due to the
work of God's Spirit? Jesus Christ breaks down the barriers that
separate people (Gal. 3:21).

> The physical presence of heterogeneity makes it more difficult
> for a congregation to confuse a particular social mode of life
> with the religiously acceptable and divinely ordained one . . .
> Moral concerns brought under the conditions of social and cul-
> tural diversity could not be simply the projection of the ideol-
> ogy of a particular interest group on the screen of divine
> approval.[13]

It is unfortunate that Gilkey's and Gustafson's points about transcendence have not been forcefully advanced so as to shake up the
social and political complacency of white churches. Established
white churches have almost always focused on the specifically theological understanding of their identity which also has usually led to
a conservative approach to politics, especially in race relations.
One can examine the attitude of white churches toward African
slavery, and with few exceptions, their views functioned as a religious legitimation of their social and political interests. Many
whites openly justified slavery as ordained of God, quoting Paul's
"slaves be obedient to your master" as the evidence. Others, being
a little more sophisticated, ignored the issue altogether, as if one's
attitude toward human servitude had nothing to do with the gospel
of Jesus. Another group, while admitting that slavery was immoral
and should be abolished, advocated a gradual, peaceful approach
to its abolition. It is revealing that similar attitudes were found
among white church people regarding lynching, school integration,
civil rights, black power, and poverty. In regards to justice and
peace for persons who are not of European descent, the great
majority of white church people (conservative and liberal, right
and left, theologians, pastors and lay people) seem to reflect in
their religion the values of the existing racist and capitalist socio-
economic order.

Gustafson explains the support of white clergy and theologians
of the existing social order in this way:

> "Like all beings, the clergy and the theologians are more com-
> fortable if they can blame what is wrong on forces outside
> themselves. . . . Clergy and theologians can find as good ex-

cuses as any man to deny any responsibility for what is happening to the community and mission with whose leadership
they are charged. If there is any sense of repentance, it is all
too often, like a general confession of sin, vague and undif-
ferentiated. It leads to a certainty of guilt for the ills of the
Church but does not move in the direction of overcoming
those ills."[14]

I believe that whatever the Christian faith may be, it is never a
reflection of the values of the dominant culture. That was why
God elected Hebrew slaves and not Egyptian slavemasters as the
covenant people. That was also why the prophets defined God's
justice as punishment of the oppressor and the liberation of the
poor. In a similar vein, but at a much deeper level, the birth, life,
teachings, death, and resurrection of Jesus means that God turns
the world's value system up-side down. No one expressed this
point any clearer than Apostle Paul:

"It was to shame the wise that God chose what is foolish by
human reckoning, and to shame what is strong that he chose
what is weak by human reckoning; those whom the world
thinks common and contemptible are the ones that God has
chosen — those who are nothing at all to show up those who
are everything" (I Cor. 1;27-28 JB).

If the white churches expect to be taken seriously about their
claim to be of God, then they must begin to act against the social
order and ecclesiastical structures that do not affirm the humanity
of people of colour.

It is important to note the contrast between black and white
churches in the United States during slavery and the civil rights
movement of the 1950's and 60's. For example, when white
preachers and missionaries introduced their version of Christianity
to African slaves, many slaves rejected it by contending that God
willed their freedom and not their servitude. Separate and independent black congregations began to develop among slaves and
free Africans in the North and South because black people did not
believe that a segregated congregational life in which they were
treated as second-class Christians was reconcilable with their view
of the Lordship of Jesus over the church. If Jesus Christ is the
Lord of the church and the world, as white confessions claimed,
then church institutions that claim the Christian identity must reflect their commitment to him in the congregational life of the
church as well as in its political and social involvement in society.
When northern black Methodists and Baptists formed independent
church institutions in Philadelphia, New York and Baltimore, and

when southern blacks created a secret, "invisible institution" in
Alabama, Georgia, Arkansas and Mississippi, their actions in both
contexts suggested that some black people recognized the connection between theology and politics, between the confession of faith
in church worship and the political commitment that validated it in
society. Expressing her reaction to the sermons of white preachers,
Hanna Austin, an ex-slave from Georgia, said: "We seldom heard
a true religious sermon: but we were constantly preached the doctrine of obedience to masters and mistresses."[15] One white preacher interpreted Christian obedience as follows to black slaves: "The
Lord says . . . if you are good to your masters and mistresses, He
has got a kitchen in heaven and you will all go there by and by."[16]

But African slaves knew that God had more than a kitchen waiting for them, and their experience of this "eschatological more" in
Jesus Christ necessitated the formation of a congregational life so
that their christological encounter could be liturgically celebrated.
Minnie Ann Smith, an ex-slave, reflected on her presence in the
church as an "invisible", secret but historical institution: "We slips
off and have prayers but daren't 'low the white folks to know it
and sometimes we hums' ligious songs low like when we's working.
It was our way of prayin' to be free, but the white folks didn't
know it."[17] In this quotation, a different perspective on the invisible church is suggested. It is an invisibility grounded not (as with
Augustine and Calvin) in divine election, but in a religious conviction about the Lordship of Christ that had to be lived out in history and in the the midst of an extreme situation of political
oppression.

It is unfortunate that many black churches of today have strayed
from their liberating heritage. Instead of deepening their commitment to the poor in their community and in the Third World,
many have adopted the same attitude toward the poor as the white
churches from which they separated. Too many black churches are
more concerned about buying and building new church structures
than they are about feeding, clothing, and housing the poor. Too
many pastors are more concerned about how to manipulate people
for an increase in salary than they are about liberating the
oppressed from socio-political bondage. If black churches do not
repent by reclaiming their liberating heritage for the empowerment
of the poor today, their Christian identity will be no more authentic than the white churches that segregated them.

It is revealing that the modern search for unity among the
churches focused on *confessional* unity and neither white nor black
churches of the United States objected to that limited focus. When

the World Council of Churches (WCC) was organized in Amsterdam in 1948, its unity was based on the confession of "Jesus Christ as God and Saviour." There was no reference to the political and social significance of this confession. But the subsequent increase of Asians, Africans, and Latin Americans as member churches has called this narrow theological understanding of the church into question. It is not that Third World Christians reject the christological focus of the WCC. On the contrary, they insist that the christological confessions of the WCC must be validated by a political commitment that is necessitated by it. In the christologies of Asian, African, and Latin American liberation theologies,[18] Jesus Christ is defined not so much with the substance language of Greek philosophy as found in the Niecean and Chalcedonian definitions of 325 and 451. For many Third World theologians, Jesus is the Liberator who came, as the gospel of Luke says,

"... to bring good news to the poor,
to proclaim liberty to the captives
and to the blind new sight,
to set the downtrodden free,
to proclaim the Lord's year of favour."   (4:18 JB)

The church is that people who have been called into being by the life, death, and resurrection of Jesus, so that they can bear witness to Jesus' lordship by participating with him in the struggle of freedom. This means that the primary definition of the church is not its confessional affirmations but rather its political commitment on behalf of the poor.

To liberate the poor requires social analysis that explains the origin and nature of human poverty. Why are people poor, and who benefits from their poverty? This question places the church in the context of society and forces it to be self-critical as it seeks to realize its mission of bearing witness to God's kingdom that is coming in and through the human struggles to liberate the poor. The church bears witness to Christ's Lordship not only in preaching about justice but also in being the agent for its implementation in society.

The Church as the Servant of God's Coming Future.
If Jesus Christ is Lord of the church, then the church is His servant. It is that congregation of people whose identity as the people of God arises from a definition of servanthood that is derived from Jesus' life, death, and resurrection. By definition, the church exists for others, because its being is determined by the One who died on the cross for others.

The others for whom the church exists are the poor and not the rich, the downtrodden and oppressed and not the proud and the mighty. Because the church is a community called into being by the "Crucified God,"[20] it must be a crucified church, living under the cross.

The servanthood of the church is defined by the cross of Jesus, and nowhere else. To be a servant of the Crucified One is to be his representative in society, bearing witness to (in words, actions, and suffering body) the kingdom that Jesus revealed in His life, death, and resurrection. We must be careful not to spiritualize servanthood so as to camouflage its concrete, political embodiment. To be a servant of Jesus means more than meeting together every Sunday for worship and other liturgical gatherings. It means more than serving as an officer or even a pastor of a church. Servanthood includes a political component that thrusts a local congregation in society where it must take sides with the poor. Servanthood is a call to action that commits one in struggle for the poor.

Servanthood is the opposite of the world's definition of Lordship. That was why Jesus said to his disciples:

> "You know that among the pagans their so-called rulers lord it over them, and their great men make their authority felt. This is not to happen among you. No; anyone who wants to become great among you must be your servant, and anyone who wants to be first among you must be slave to all" (Mark 10:42-44 JB).

The task of the church is more than preaching sermons about justice and praying for the liberation of all. The church must be the agent of justice and liberation about which it proclaims. A confessional affirmation of peace is not enough. The church must represent in its congregational life and seek to structure in society the peace about which it speaks. When a congregation does not even attempt to structure in its life and in the society the gospel it preaches, why should anyone believe what it says? "To affirm that [people] are persons and as persons should be free, and yet do nothing tangible to make this affirmation a reality, is a farce."[21]

It is the cross of Jesus that connects the church with the victim. "We cannot speak of the death of Jesus until we speak of the real death of people," writes Gustavo Gutierrez. Unnecessary starvation in Ethiopia, staggering poverty throughout the world, and rich American churches continue to sing and pray to Jesus as if the gospel has nothing to do with feeding the hungry and clothing the naked. In 1980 the World Bank reported that, "excluding China, approximately 750 million persons live in 'absolute poverty'" of which "40,000 small children die" each day "from malnutrition and infection."[22] All of this is unnecessary. But we live in a nation that is more concerned about using food as "a tool in the kit of American diplomacy," to quote the former Secretary of Agriculture, Earl Butz, than using it to save the lives of starving human beings. The United States feeds people missiles. According to Arthur Simon, the writer of *Bread for the World:*

> "In 1984 the United States devoured approximately $663 million each day in direct military spending — more than the entire annual budgets of the World Health Organization and the UN Development Programme combined. The United States allocates about 40 times more for military defence than it does for development assistance."[23]

With so many people dying in the world, how can the churches continue their organizational routine and still expect sensitive people to believe that they are concerned about the cross of Jesus? That is why Hugo Assman has said that "the church cannot be the reason for its own existence."[24] To preserve itself is to destroy itself. Nothing is more applicable to the church's identity than Jesus' claim that the one who would save his/her life shall lose it, and the one who loses his/her life for My sake shall find it. The church's distinctive identity is found not in itself but in the crucified Jesus whose Spirit calls the church into being for service on behalf of victimized people.

When the church makes its political commitment on behalf of the poor, the historical actions of the church bear witness to an ultimate hope grounded in the resurrection of Jesus. The church is a hoping community. It believes that the things that are, can and ought to be otherwise. How is it possible to hope in hopeless situations? That is the question that all oppressed people must face when their projects of freedom end in failure? How can they believe that they are what they shall be when their history seems to be closed to the future?

It is in the historical context of the apparent closed future that Jesus Christ "makes a way out of no way" by creating a people who believe that because of his resurrection "that which is, cannot be true." This is God's distinctive gift for the oppressed who otherwise would not have the courage to "keep on keeping on" even though the odds are against them. Max Weber has expressed this experience of the poor in sociological terms.

> The sense of honour of disprivileged classes rests on some concealed promise for the future which implies the assignment of some function, mission or vocation to them. What they cannot claim to *be*, they replace by the worth of that which they

one day will *become*. . . . Their hunger for a worthiness that has not fallen their lot . . . produces this conception from which is derived the rationalistic idea of a providence, a significance in the eyes of some divine authority possessing a scale of values different from the one operating in the world of man.[25]

According to Weber, "since every need for salvation is an expression of some distress, social or economic oppression is an effective source of salvation beliefs. . . ."[26] Because the hope for salvation is always related or derived from situations of distress, Weber has a different sociological evaluation of the religion of privileged classes.

> Other things being equal, classes with high social and economic privilege will scarcely be prone to evolve the idea of salvation. Rather, they assign to religion the primary function of legitimizing their own life pattern or situation in the world. This universal phenomenon is rooted in a certain basic psychological pattern. When a man who is happy compares his position with that of one who is unhappy, he is not content with the fact of his happiness, but desires something more, namely the right to this happiness, the consciousness that he has earned his good fortune, in contrast to the unfortunate one who must equally have earned his misfortune. Our everyday experience proves that there exists just such a psychological need for reassurance as to the legitimacy or deservedness of one's happiness, whether this involves political success, superior economic status, . . . or anything else. What the privileged classes require of religion, if anything at all, is this psychological reassurance of legitimacy."[27]

"Correspondingly different", according to Weber, "is the situation of the disprivileged. Their particular need is release from suffering."[28] They look forward to the time when the things that are no longer will be. Because there is so little in their history that reflects their humanity, they are forced by the unrealized vision in their historical struggle to look beyond history in the hope that the truth which is not present in their situation will soon take place in God's eschatological future.

This eschatological hope of the oppressed is not an opium or a sedative, because it is a hope derived from historical struggle and never separated from it. God is the power who transforms the suffering of the present into hope for the future. The reality of God's presence in the lives of the poor empowers them to affirm their humanity, by looking to another world where they will be treated as human beings.

No people have expressed the Christian hope in the midst of suffering and struggle, in our contemporary situation, with greater depth than the black poor in South Africa. Living under the wretched condition of apartheid, with its forced removal ("homelands") and destruction of black family life (migratory labour), the black poor of South Africa "keep on keeping on", because they believe that the "God of Moses and of Jesus has not brought them this far to leave them" in the hands of their enemies. No one has been a greater symbol of the Christian hope than the life and thought of Archbishop Desmond Tutu. Despite the continuous threat of banning, imprisonment, and even death, Archbishop Tutu, Nobel Laureate and a leading interpreter of Black Theology, has taken a radical stand against apartheid, describing it as an evil similar to Nazism and therefore a heresy of the Christian gospel. His courageous stand for justice, along with other South Africans, many blacks (like Steve Biko, Robert Sobukwe, Nelson Mandela, and Alan Boesak) and a few whites (like Beyers Naude), has been an inspiration for liberation struggles throughout the world. Authentic Christian hope is not an opium or an otherworldly pie-in-the-sky religion. It is rather, as Alan Boesak has said:

"Our dreams for the liberation of humankind, our dreams of justice, of human dignity, of peace . . . meant for this earth and for this history . . . . So, let us dream. Let us prophesy! Let us affirm with humility, with joy, with faith, with courage: *Jesus Christ is the life of the world.*"[29]

Boesak's hopeful proclamation is similar to Archbishop Tutu's "crying in the wilderness".[30] In the face of the enormous power and increasing violence of the South African government, Tutu said to the South African Minister of Law and Order: "Mr Minister . . . you are not God." And to his people, he has said:

"We must not be surprised that suffering will come our way . . . (because) it is the other side of the coin to witnessing . . . . To uphold faith and hope in these dark days of crises is what it means to be servants of God. Our servanthood and our witness are urgently necessary and must be translated into action hallowed by prayer, the sacraments, worship and meditation shot through and through with the Holy Spirit of God. . . . (For) the Resurrection of Our Lord and Saviour declares for all to know that life will triumph over darkness, that goodness will triumph over injustice, and that freedom will triumph over tyranny. I stand before you as one who believes fervently what Paul wrote when he said, 'If God be for us, who can be against us?'"[31]

REFERENCE NOTES

1. See Ernst Troeltsch, *The Social Teaching of the Christian Churches,* 2 volumes, trans. by Olive Wyon (New York: Harper Torch Books, 1960); H. Richard Niebuhr, *The Social Sources of Denominationalism* (Cleveland: Meridian Books, 1957); and Peter Paris, *The Social Teaching of the Black Churches* (Philadelphia: Fortress, 1985).

2. Williston Walker, *A History of the Christian Church* (New York: Charles Scribner's Sons, rev. ed., 1959); Carter G. Woodson, *History of the Negro Church* (Washington, D.C.: Associated Publishers, 1921); E. Franklin Frazier, *The Negro Church in America* (New York: Schocken Books, 1964); and Sydney E. Alstrom, *A Religious History of American People* (New Haven: Yale University Press, 1972).

3. Karl Barth, *Church Dogmatics,* Vol. IV, Pt., 1, trans. by G.W. Bromiley & T.F. Torrance (Edinburgh: T & T Clark, 1956); *Ibid.,* Vol. I.V. Pt. 2; Cyril Richardson, *The Church Through the Centuries* (New York; Charles Scribners, 1950); Jurgen Moltmann, *The Church in the Power of the Spirit* (New York: Harper, 1977); and Hans Kung, *The Church* (New York: Sheed & Ward, 1967).

4. John Calvin, *Institutes of the Christian Religion,* Vol. 2, trans. F.L. Battles, Library of Christian Classics, (Philadelphia: Westminister Press, 1960), p. 1023.

5. *The Complete Writings of Menno Simons,* trans. by Leonard Verduin (Scottdale, Pennsylvania: Herald Press, 1956), p. 741.

6. *Ibid.,* p. 746.

7. Calvin, *Institutes,* Vol. 2, p. 1025.

8. *The Complete Writings of Menno Simons,* p. 752.

9. Franklin H. Littell, *The Origins of Sectarian Protestanism* (New York: Macmillan Co., 1964), p. 53.

10. See Peter Berger, *The Sacred Canopy,* (New York: Anchor Books, 1969).

11. Langdon Gilkey, *How the Church Can Minister to the World Without Losing Itself* (New York: Harper, 1964), p. 71.

12. James Gustafson, *The Church as Moral Decision-Maker* (Philadelphia: Pilgrim Press, 1970), p. 63.

13. *Ibid.,* p. 122, 123.

14. *Ibid.,* p. 151.

15. Cited in Olli Alho, *The Religion of the Slaves: A Study of the Religious Tradition and Behaviour of Plantation Slaves in the United States, 1830-1865* (Helsinki: Soumalainen Tiedeakatemia, 1976), p. 140.

16. *Ibid.,* p. 170.

17. *Ibid.,* p. 125.

18. Although liberation theology is largely associated with the continent of Latin America, it is important to emphasize that similar developments are found in the churches and theologies of Africa, Asia, and among minorities and women in the United States. The best sources for an examination of these theologies and their relationship to each other are the books that have been produced by the Ecumenical Association of Third World Theologians (EATWOT). EATWOT was organized in 1976 in Tanzania and has held subsequent meetings in other countries of the Third World, focusing on African, Asian, and Latin American liberation theologies. See Sergio Torres and Viginia Fabella (eds.), *The Emergent Gospel* (Maryknoll, NY: Orbis Books, 1978); Kofi Appiah-Kubi and Sergio Torres (eds.), *African Theology En Route* (Maryknoll, NY: Orbis Books, 1979); Virginia Fabella (ed.), *Asia's Struggle For Full Humanity*

(Maryknoll, NY, 1980); Sergio Torres and John Eagleson (eds.), *The Challenge of Basic Christian Communities* (Maryknoll, NY, 1981); and Virginia Fabella and Sergio Torres (eds.), *Irruption of the Third World* (Maryknoll, NY: Orbis Books, 1983). Orbis Books is well-known for it publication of books on liberation theologies in the Third World and also among minorities in the U.S.

19. See Leonardo Boff, *Jesus Christ Liberator*, trans. by Patrick Hughes (Maryknoll, NY: Orbis Books, 1987); Hugo Echegaray, *The Practice of Jesus*, trans. by M.J. O'Connell (Maryknoll, NY: Orbis Books, 1980); James H. Cone, *God of the Oppressed* (New York: Seabury Press, 1975); Bishop Joseph A. Johnson, Jr. "Jesus Christ: Liberator," in his *The Soul of the Black Preacher* (1970).

20. See Jurgen Moltman, *The Crucified God* (New York: Harper, 1974).

21. Paulo Freire, *Pedagogy of the Oppressed* (New York: Herder and Herder, 1970), p. 35.

22. Arthur Simon, *Bread for the World* (New York & Grand Rapids: Paulist & Eerdmans, rev. & updated, 1984), p. 7.

23. *Ibid.*, p. 144.

24. *Theology for a Nomad Church*, trans. by Paul Burns (Maryknoll, NY: Orbis Books, 1975), p. 81.

25. Max Weber, *The Sociology of Religion*, trans. by Ephraim Fischoff (Boston: Beacon Press, 1964), p. 106.

26. *Ibid.*, p. 107

27. *Ibid.*

28. *Ibid.*, p. 108.

29. Alan Boesak, *Black and Reformed* (Maryknoll, N.Y.: Orbis, 1984), p. 154.

30. See his *Crying in the Wilderness: The Struggle for Justice in South Africa* (Grand Rapids, Michigan: William Eerdmans, 1982).

31. Desmond Tutu, *Hope And Suffering* (Grand Rapids, Michigan: William Eerdmans, 1984), pp. 66, 158; Skotaville Publishers, Johannesburg, 1983.

DAVID BOSCH

Processes of Reconciliation and Demands of Obedience — Twelve Theses

More than ever before the Afrikaner is in the dock, not only here in South Africa but around the globe. He is held responsible for the most brutal oppression and the most pernicious political system ever devised by the human mind. It is further argued that the Afrikaner church has been playing a crucial role in shaping and upholding this system. How then could I, who happen to be both an Afrikaner and a Christian, dare to write on this theme? Perhaps the answer to this question is that I should do it precisely because I am an Afrikaner!

There is probably little point in asking once again why our history has unfolded the way it has and why it has come to the situation we have at the moment. Nevertheless, let me plead with you to bear with me while I give you in an extremely condensed form my version of what has brought us to where we are today. I do this, asking for your understanding of what has happened, not your endorsement.

Who and what are the Afrikaners? What do they perceive themselves to be? They — or let me rather say, we — are a small white tribe, in the extreme southern tip of a vast black continent, cut off from the mother country almost three centuries ago, threatened with extinction from two sides, the British and the blacks, determined to maintain and defend our identity. The majority of Afrikaners are convinced that — for at least a century and a half — they have been engaged in a battle for survival and that this battle is today being fought more fiercely than ever before. They have

lost much of their self-confidence in recent years. They are far less
certain about the outcome of the battle than they used to be; in
fact, despondency is the dominant emotion in many Afrikaner circles. This does not mean, however, that they are close to surrender. What is developing, rather, is a kind of "Masada complex".
Masada, you will remember, is the mountain in the desert of Judea
where a group of Jewish fanatics held out against the Roman at-
tackers for an incredibly long time. When eventually the Romans
conquered the mountain at awesome cost they found that hardly a
single Jew had remained alive. This — if I am not mistaken — is
what some people are preparing the Afrikaners for today, particularly Afrikaner children. The challenge presented to our children
in essence seems to be: "Are you prepared to die for South Africa?", rather than "Are you prepared to live for South Africa?"

It should be understandable — even if not pardonable — why
Afrikaners could for such a long time — in the first stage of our
history — only think of themselves and their own survival but
hardly of the interests of others. During the second stage we convinced ourselves that it was our divine calling to uphold and safe-
guard the separate identities of other groups as well; in order to
implement this we appointed ourselves their guardians and set out
to restructure the entire fabric of South African society. To what
has all this led? Let me quote from Willem Nicol's monthly column
in Beeld:

> "It has now become clear that our designs of recent decades
> did not work out, but have, rather, merely aggravated South
> Africa's problems. We have torn apart families, uprooted
> communities, made discriminating laws and enforced them
> with harshness. We have made millions of people into ene-
> mies. We have estranged our coloured fellow-believers, with
> whom we should have experienced the most intimate unity.
> Why did our fine-sounding designs have such a negative re-
> sult? Because group selfishness has been one of the main mo-
> tives which urged us on and blinded us. Why did we persist so
> long with our impracticable and unjust designs? Because we
> believed that enforced racial segregation was consistent with
> the Christian gospel; we sometimes even went so far as to
> think that our faith demanded racial separation. We have hurt
> millions of people, hurt them deeply... . The gulf of misappre-
> hensions, fear and hatred between white and black has
> reached alarming dimensions ..."[1]

If Willem Nicol is correct in his analysis, if all that he says is
true, what then is the point in talking about reconciliation? Is this

debate not a classical case of an exercise in futility? I want to say immediately that this is a very real possibility, and one of which we constantly have to be aware. If, after what I have said in my pre-amble, I may nevertheless be as bold (or foolish?) as to talk about reconciliation, I want to do it by means of putting forward twelve theses and commenting briefly on each of them.

Twelve Theses

1. *Cheap reconciliation is the deadly enemy of the church.* Almost fifty years ago Dietrich Bonhoeffer taught us that cheap grace was the deadly enemy of the church. I want to suggest that the same is true of cheap reconciliation.

What then is "cheap reconciliation"? It is — as the phrase suggests — reconciliation that costs us very little, that can be obtained at a minimum of expense. It is a papering over of deep-seated differences. It is arguing that, after all, we are one in Christ — are we not? — and that, therefore, our existing differences do not really matter. Or it sees our being reconciled to one another only in spiritual categories, not in those of everyday life. Or does it suggest that, if only we are really reconciled to Christ we shall, almost automatically, also be reconciled to one another? I remember some years ago, sitting in a group where these things were being discussed; a white pastor said, "All we need is to be truly born again, then all our problems will get solved". To this a black pastor responded, "Brother, my greatest frustrations come from born-again Christians!"

Cheap reconciliation manifests itself in other forms as well. It is practised where one party wholeheartedly admits that they are wrong and the other party right, but nothing changes. It is also in evidence where one party attempts to ingratiate itself with the other party by constantly fawning on it. This happens at both ends of the spectrum: blacks buttering up whites, whites seeking favour with blacks. In both instances we have servility at the expense of honesty and real change.

Cheap reconciliation means tearing faith and justice asunder, driving a wedge between the vertical and the horizontal. It suggests that we can have peace with God without having justice in our mutual relationships.

In summary then, cheap reconciliation means applying a little bit of goodwill and decency to the South African society, but that is like trying to heal a festering sore with sticking plaster or treating cancer with aspirin.

2. *All of us are prisoners of history, and are, as such, challenged to become prisoners of hope.* We have in this country a terrible le-

gacy of faction fighting: black against white, Afrikaner against English, black against black, Afrikaner against Afrikaner, etc., etc. All this has driven us into so many different camps, or rather strongholds. We have built sky-high walls around us ... and, almost imperceptibly our strongholds have been transformed into prisons. Es'kia Mphahlele sums it up well when he says, "In South Africa we look at each other through a key-hole, blacks and whites." And you know, that is so very true if you are in a prison. Your only avenue of communication is the key-hole. So, squatting before our respective key-holes, we squint at each other.

Through the grace of God some of us then discover that we are in prisons, and we begin wishing those prisons away. "Oh, if only we had not been saddled with the legacy of our history! If only it were possible to start all over again!" But that is truly only wishful thinking. We all come out of the terrible South African tempest — black and white, Zulu and Sotho, English and Afrikaner. It is that hurricane which deposited us where we are today. It is that storm that gives our interhuman relations in this country such as peculiar poignancy. We cannot undo this; indeed, we should not. We cannot shake off our past and start anew at square one. We take our history with us into our future. A person without history has no identity; he suffers from amnesia. If you do not know who you are, you cannot help others; neither can you if you deny being who you are. I have heard of an American missionary who went to an African country and who used to go around saying: "I always try to forget that I am an American." The fact that he was constantly repeating this proved of course, that he never really succeeded in forgetting who he was. Besides, even if he would succeed in forgetting, would the Africans ever forget?

History is indeed a prison that locks us in. But it is, paradoxically, also the key that can open that prison for us. Then we move from being prisoners of history to being "prisoners of hope" — this is a phrase used by the prophet Zechariah to refer to the Judean captives in Babylon who are awaiting liberation (Zech. 9:12). Only by taking both the guilt and the grandeur of our history upon us, can we transform that history en route towards our common hope. Some people take only the guilt of their history with them; then they resemble that American missionary. Others take only grandeur of their history with them; then they absolutize it and make it normative also for the future. In neither case do they escape from their prisons.

Let me say it by means of a metaphor — that of a bird in a violent storm. If the wings of that bird are set wrongly, it will be smashed against the cliff. But if the wings are set correctly, the storm itself will lift that bird above the danger of the cliff and it will soar towards the sun. We do not need new wings, then. It is the setting of our wings that matters. That has to be made new. God takes us as we are, together with our histories and he "sets" our histories in a new way. Indeed, our histories could have smashed us against the cliffs. But they can also, under God, help us to soar into true freedom. The storm is necessary to carry the bird over the cliff. If there had been no wind, no storm, the bird would never have been carried into the blue.

3. *The biblical concept of reconciliation has as its corollaries the concepts repentance and forgiveness.* This means, simply, that we cannot talk about the one without at the same time talking about the other. It is therefore necessary to reflect on the meaning of repentance and forgiveness also since they can help us give a clearer profile to what reconciliation means.

4. *In ordinary inter-human communication people are usually more aware of the sin of others than of their own sins.* To use a biblical metaphor: I am more aware of the mote in my brother's or sister's eye than of the beam in my own. In a society such as ours, where groups are increasingly polarized and alienated, this phenomenon tends to take on ghastly proportions. In white circles the tendency is to blame everything that went wrong in our country on the blacks, or on Communist infiltrators and agitators, or on hooliganism. In black circles the opposite tendency prevails: whites are regarded as the authors of every conceivable evil in society.

"Reconciliation" in such a contest would mean, then, that the other party has to agree to my point of view, has to be won over to my position. Of course, he usually adopts the same position. And so we both remain unyielding. The fronts harden. We adopt the language of "winners" and "losers" and seem to suggest that the winner should take all.

Even Christians are not immune to this interpretation of reconciliation. In fact, we are often even better at this than non-Christians! Those of you who attended the Lausanne Congress (1974) will remember how the South African group met daily to discuss what we would do once we had returned to South Africa. We were not able to make any headway, however. We were too divided. Each group kept on calling the other group to repentance and change, for each group believed that they were right and the other wrong. Then, one day, Michael Cassidy pointed out that we had been confronting each other with two different but very muscular Christs. And if one group's Christ becomes too muscular, the

others either go back into their shells or they make their Christ
even more muscular. And if Christ becomes muscular, he ceases to
be the man of Calvary. The print of the nails disappears behind
the flexing of those powerful muscles.

5. *In the context of the Christian faith, by contrast, we judge ourselves before we judge others.* As Christians we can be critical
about others only after we have been critical about ourselves. If we
are truly prophetic, in the biblical sense of the word, we would
identify with the sin and guilt of those whom we, humanly speaking, would regard as our adversaries. We would hope and pray
that they would do the same with our sin and guilt but we cannot
make our solidarity with their guilt dependent on this kind of re-
ciprocity. We should be prepared to carry the burden of our own
guilt and of the other; and carrying the burden of their guilt means
forgiving it, wholeheartedly. This is the difference between the
critic and the prophet. The critic condemns from the outside, the
prophet confesses from within. The critic accuses, the prophet
weeps. The critic boasts, "Lord, I thank you that I am not like
other people"; the prophet beats his breast and cries, "Lord, have
mercy on me, a sinner!" The critic remains unscathed; the prophet,
however, is ridiculed, ostracised, even persecuted. Criticism is
easy, but therefore also cheap; being prophetic is terribly demanding, and therefore very costly.

6. *If we are followers of the One who was crucified we too will
have to be cross-bearers.* This is not a call to masochism but simply
to the normal Christian life. The Cross is the hall-mark of the
Christian church. And it is good to remember that it was the scars
of Jesus that were to his disciples the proof of his identity: because
of his scars they believed (John 20:20). Will an unbelieving world
identify us as followers of Jesus unless they recognize his scars in
us?

Reconciliation, so Hans-Ruedi Weber reminded us during the
Durban Congress in 1973, takes place when two opposing forces
clash and somebody gets crushed in between. This is what happened to Jesus, for in his body on the Cross he reconciled Jew and
Gentile; he demolished the middle wall of partition and thus transformed erstwhile enemies into a single new humanity (Eph. 2:14-
17).

Jesus did this not only in his death on the Cross but in his entire
ministry. Look at this man as he walks the dusty roads of Palestine
and ministers to the crowds! He could also — as we often do —
present argument upon argument to show that the people have
only themselves to blame, that the Jews only got what they de-

served or that the Romans were wicked and cruel. Jesus does not adopt this line, however. He disarms himself. He stands with a bleeding heart before Jew and Roman, black and white. He invites all of them in, even if it might mean that they would exploit him, trample upon him and deceive him. He accepts all of them unconditionally. He is the good Samaritan who risks his life for a Jew who is really supposed to be his arch-enemy. He is the good Shepherd who puts his own life in jeopardy for every obstinate sheep. He is the Servant who washes the feet even of his traitor. He is the Master who loves the rich young ruler while knowing that the young man would not be prepared to pay the price of discipleship. He is the one who reinstates Peter in his office, even if Peter has denied him in the hour of trial. He is the Master who trusts his disciples sufficiently to send them to the ends of the earth, even while knowing that they have all deserted him and fled in the hour of trial. Ultimately, he is the One who prays for those who crucify him: "Father, forgive them, for they do not know what they are doing."

It is of such a Man that we are called to be disciples. And it is totally out of the question that we shall be his disciples without getting hurt ourselves. Moreover, unless I get hurt, I can't help others who hurt. It is only through wounds that wounds can be healed. Isn't that what the prophet said? "... he was pierced for our transgressions, he was crushed for our iniquities; the punishment that brought us peace was upon him, and by his wounds we are healed" (Isa. 53:5). The early Christian church took up this ancient word from the prophetic tradition: it was Jesus, they said, who was pierced for our transgressions; it is by his wounds that we are healed. The soldiers mocked him, "He saved others; he cannot save himself." But this is just the point. This Christ who saved others but did not save himself reveals the fundamental character of the true God. False gods save themselves; they do not save others. By implication the same is true of false Christians; they save themselves, not others. True Christians, however, bear on their bodies "the scars of Jesus" (Gal. 6:17), inflicted by other people. They carry around in their mortal bodies the death of Jesus (2 Cor. 4:10). They are like people condemned to death in the arena, a spectacle to the whole universe, fools for Christ's sake (1 Cor. 4:9-10). Where the world demands violence, they bring peace. Where the world cries for vengeance, they offer forgiveness. They thus turn everything upside down, almost as if nothing makes sense any longer! According to 2 Cor. 6:8-10 (in the inimitable New English Bible translation) it is impostors who speak the truth, the unknown people whom all people know. It is the dying who still live on and the sorrowful who have always cause for joy. It is the poor who bring wealth to many and the penniless who own the world. This is the paradox of the Christian life: it is when we are weak that we are strong (2 Cor. 12:10).

We have to go a few steps further, however, and attempt to become more concrete. What does all this mean in practical terms? Put differently: what is it we have to repent of and ask forgiveness for? This brings me to my next thesis.

7. *Repentance and conversion always affect those elements in our lives that touch us most deeply, which we are most attached or devoted to, without which — so we believe — we simply cannot exist.*

These elements are not necessarily bad things. On the contrary: they may be very, very good things. Our faith, however, challenges us to put them in jeopardy, to risk living without them. In the New English Bible "self-denial" is often rendered "leaving self behind": "If anyone wishes to be a follower of mine, he must leave self behind" (Matt. 16:24).

For Abraham this meant being willing to give up Isaac, his only son, whom he loved. He had to transfer his allegiance from his own ideas about the future to God's ideas. For Paul it was something similar. He used to judge everybody according to only two criteria: Was he a Jew? Was he circumcized? Years later he reminisced about this: "If anyone thinks to base his claims on externals, I could make a stronger case for myself: circumcized on my eighth day, Israelite by race, of the tribe of Benjamin, a Hebrew born and bred; in my attitude to the law, a Pharisee; in pious zeal, a persecutor of the church, in legal rectitude, faultless" (Phil. 3:4-6). But something happened to Paul. The centre of gravity of his entire life shifted. And he now says some truly shocking things about those two earlier criteria. Circumcision he now calls mutilation! (Phil. 3:2) As regards all his other assets: his Jewishness, his being a member of the party of the Pharisees, he says: "I have written those things off"; "I count everything sheer loss"; "I count it so much rubbish" (Phil. 3:8,9).

Abraham and Paul had to deny themselves; they had to "leave self behind". Paul in particular had to discover that he had it all wrong, that his zeal for God's cause was misplaced, that he was, in fact, acting contrary to God's will and in his blindness persecuting and oppressing God's people. This is why — when he discovered what his practice really had entailed — he used such strong language in distancing himself from his past convictions and actions.

How does all this apply to us? Naturally, I cannot speak for my black fellow-Christians : they have to decide for themselves whether this has implications for them and if so, what. I dare not even take it upon myself to say what it means for whites in general and Afrikaners in particular. At most, I can ask a few questions and make some tentative suggestions as regards this latter group.

The gospel then, I submit, challenges us to be willing to give up our privileges. As a matter of fact, the gospel goes further than that. It challenges us to "leave self behind", that is, to deny ourselves. It reveals to us that, in taking it upon ourselves to regulate the lives of other people in the minutest details, we have overstepped all limits. It urges us to stop all this and put it right, now, regardless of the consequences. We know that, at least as we perceive it, this involves tremendous risks. But the gospel challenges us to do justice now, even if the world comes to an end ... our world. We know that only if we accept this and get up and do it, shall we really be free to obey. We remind ourselves of Bonhoeffer's words: Only the one who believes, obeys; only the one who is obedient believes. We know that God does not ask about the extent of our successes but about the depth of our obedience.

Only if this is the road we walk — only if we truly "leave self behind" — shall we be free to live in a country in which we no longer have any say, live in it and serve in it while we truly experience and enjoy the freedom of the children of God, even if a future South Africa turns out to be one ruled by a corrupt and oppressive Marxist regime and we have to give up all those things to which we have always clung for dear life.

I do not say this out of defeatism. Neither am I suggesting that I would welcome a Marxist regime; I believe the Communist system is something abhorrent. So I am not saying anything about the desirability of such a regime. The statement I am making is about us, about white Christians, Afrikaner Christians. I am suggesting that we should begin thinking about the possible emergence of a situation where we become the underdogs. I am submitting that we should be able to continue being Christians even in such circumstances. And I remind you of the fact that the church is surviving today even in Russia and China and Vietnam and Iran. I suggest that the church in the catacombs is church in a truer sense of the word than the church in palaces; it is, for one thing, liberated from the guilt of privilege and from its bad conscience. I am aware that this may involve martyrdom; but martyrdom has always been one of the lesser threats to the church's survival — after all, the blood of the martyrs is the seed of the church, as Tertullian phrased it in the third century A.D.

I am saying all this truly with fear and trembling, not only because I know that what I am saying may be misunderstood and
misreported, but also, and perhaps particularly, because I know
myself and my own weakness too well to make in confidence this
kind of statement about willingness to be a servant in a context
where I am the underdog and the oppressed. I can only say I will
do it ... may God have mercy on me! Like the father of the boy
with an evil spirit, I can only say: "Lord, I do believe ... help me
overcome my unbelief" (cf. Mark 9:24): "Lord, I am willing... help
me overcome my unwillingness ... ." We are, after all, not only
talking about "processes of reconciliation," but also about "d-
emands of obedience". This was the terrible lesson Abraham had
to learn, and Saul of Tarsus. They saw their entire world crumbling down, before a new world could be rebuilt, out of the ruins,
piece by piece. Can we expect to get by with less?

More positively, all this would mean that we would then be freer
than we have been before. We would be empty-handed, but free
under God's wide open heaven.

Naturally, we would have preferred all these changes to come
about because of the promptings of God's Spirit rather than because of the terrible events around us — biblically speaking, that
change should come about because of the repentance of Israel, not
because of the batterings of Assyria. But this is often the way,
God works: if our hearts are hardened to his Spirit, he uses other
means. And the executors of his judgement may surprise us.

Let me now move on to my next thesis, which is intimately related to the previous one, but on another level.

8.   *Confession of guilt and repentance cannot be imposed by others
but is a gift of the Holy Spirit.* This should, in fact, be completely
evident. If repentance and restitution approximate even remotely
the kind of steps I have intimated in my previous theses, there is
no chance that demands from others will persuade me to take such
steps. I'll only take them willingly if God has changed my heart.

I can, however, challenge those who share my privileges to open
their hearts too. I may then be used by God's Spirit as a catalyst.
Ideally, then, it should be white Christians who challenge their
other white Christians, Afrikaners who challenge fellow-Afrikaners
to come to the recognition that we all share in the guilt of the sins
we have committed, that we should recognize that guilt for what it
is, confess it, and take deliberate steps at making restitution.

If, however, the challenge to confess our guilt comes from white
English-speaking South African Christians. Afrikaners will simply

label them hypocrites, in the light of their own history of oppression and exploitation. Neither should the challenge come from Christians outside South Africa; from their comfortable positions they make demands on us which cost them nothing, and precisely for that reason we will dismiss those demands with contempt. I daresay the main reason why Afrikaner Christians have been so slow in confessing their guilt is precisely that others — for whom nothing was at stake — have tried so frequently to bludgeon us into it. Gradually, however, Afrikaner Christians are beginning to express and confess their guilt, even publicly. They have been doing this for some time already, mostly as individuals or unofficial groups. Now, for the first time, a regional Nederduitse Gereformeerde Kerk body in its official capacity has done the same. The Presbytery of Stellenbosch, in its recent annual meeting (29 August 1985), released a statement which says, *inter alia* (I translate from the Afrikaans):

1. We recognize that, in the South African society, racial discrimination plays a fundamental role in both structural and personal matters; we confess that this is contrary to the biblical principles of love of one's neighbour and justice.
2. We also acknowledge that the ideal of apartheid did not succeed in creating social justice but has, on the contrary, led to human misery, frustration and injustice.
3. We confess that the Nederduitse Gereformeerde Kerk has often insensitively and uncritically tolerated the negative realities and consequences of apartheid.
4. We therefore hereby declare ourselves prepared
    (a) to assess the apartheid system in all its consequences truly, honestly and critically;
    (b) with all other people in our country, to seek prayerfully for a meaningful alternative for our land, and to do whatever we can to alleviate the suffering caused by the system.

At long last, then, the process has begun. Pray God that it will gain momentum! No longer dare we argue that the others also have guilt and that they, too, must confess their guilt and repent. Perhaps they have guilt. But that is of no consequence to us. We dare not make our confession of guilt and repentance subject to or dependent upon theirs. We dare not even demand forgiveness; we may not withdraw our confession of guilt if the other party fails to forgive us. Confessing our guilt is in itself a supreme blessing and a sign of grace. It opens up the fountains of new life and cleanses us.

9. *Our most terrible guilt is that of which we are unaware.* Jesus'

principle parables dealing with forgiveness and mercy were directed not to tax collectors, prostitutes and others clearly identifi-
able as "sinners" but to those who assumed that they were spiritually healthy and therefore thought that they were not in need of a
"doctor" (see Mark 2:17) They were oblivious of any guilt they
might have; they thought themselves completely innocent. The gospels are crystal clear, however, that this is no excuse. Their imag-
ined innocence does not lessen their guilt but aggravates it. The
Pharisees who believe themselves to be blameless and righteous
before God are not, because of this, less guilty, but more. The rich
man who is unaware of what he has been doing to the poor Laz-
arus, is not less culpable because of this, but more culpable. The people in Jesus' last parable in Matthew (25:31-46) who
did not minister to the hungry and the naked for the simple reason
that they never consciously "saw" those unfortunate victims of
society, are not acquitted by Jesus for not being aware of the others' needs; on the contrary, they are pronounced guilty and sent
into eternal punishment. All these are cases not of innocence but
of pseudo-innocence. If a pastor today attacks a colleague for referring to injustices in our society and then claims that he is totally
unaware of any injustice in South Africa, he is not just ignorant,
he is misguided and blind. Not being aware of our guilt may be
our most terrible guilt.

10. *God forgives us our debts as we also forgive our debtors.*
These words are, of course, from the fifth petition of the Lord's
Prayer. I quote them here as they intimately link reconciliation
with God to reconciliation with our neighbour. There is no dichotomy here.

The one who honestly confesses his guilt knows, categorically
and totally, that God forgives him. God's forgiveness is uncondi-
tional. He does not forgive us if we forgive our debtors. Still, there
is a link between the two. We cannot receive God's forgiveness
and remain unyielding to our human debtors. Leonardo Boff puts
it in the following words: "The lesson is crystal clear: if we ask
(God) for unrestricted pardon and receive it without reservation,
subject to no conditions, we shall also have to give unrestricted
pardon ... We cannot maintain two attitudes, one toward God and
the other toward our neighbour ... If we have really had the radical experience of forgiveness of our sins and our debts, if we truly
have felt the mercy of God at work in our sinful life, then we are
also impelled to forgive without limits, without reservations ... We
have no right to God's forgiveness if we do not want to forgive our
neighbours."[2]

11. *If we reject the road of reconciliation we are crucifying Christ anew.* Confessing our sins, repenting, forgiving and reconciling are not optional extras for those who claim to be followers of Jesus Christ. Those outside can afford to go without these, we cannot. If we refuse to walk this road, we are denying our Lord. We are saying, in effect, that what Christ did, is of no consequence. The middle wall of partition is as solid as ever. It is as though Christ had never come. Not to believe in the possibility of reconciliation and not to act as people who have found and embraced one another, act justly toward one another, actually means reinforcing and buttressing that wall that divides us. The question: "Are you prepared to be reconciled to your brother and sister?" is in essence the same as the question: "Do you believe in the Lord Jesus Christ?"

12. *Reconciliation is not a human possibility but a divine gift.*

At one stage during the Second Vatican Council there was a lot of discussion about the college of bishops being modelled on the community of Jesus' disciples — a body of colleagues with common functions and ideals, people of one mind and purpose, acting with one accord. During one of the breaks a Protestant observer asked a delegate: "You say the college of bishops has to be modelled on the community of disciples. But tell me, when did the disciples constitute a true community? When were they of one mind and one accord?" After a moment's reflection the bishop replied: "In Gethsemane, when they all abandoned Jesus and fled."

That is the kind of unity of purpose and solidarity in action we human beings are capable of. We can do no better in our own power. Still, in spite of the Gethsemane episode the band of disciples constituted a community of hope in the midst of despair; and so do we, not because of ourselves but because of our Lord who bound us together and enlisted us in the ministry of reconciliation. This ministry — we often say — is one of building bridges. That is true, but only in a secondary sense. Primarily, however, we are not bridge-builders but bridge-crossers. The Bridge is already there — our Lord, who in His own Body of flesh and blood has broken down the enmity which stood like a dividing wall between us. He is the Bridge over which we cross to each other, again and again.

REFERENCE NOTES
1.   Willem Nicol, *Beeld*, 27 August 1985. Translated by the author from the original Afrikaans.
2.   Boff, L. *The Lord's Prayer: The prayer of integral Liberation*, Orbis, Maryknoll, 1983 pp. 94-5.

SHUN GOVENDER

The Sermon on the Mount (Matt 5 - 7) and the Question of Ethics

Introduction

It is necessary right at the beginning to state one's intentions and in this regard the interpreter's position *vis-a-vis* the text must be made clear.

With the argument that the theological message of the text was paramount, theological students are normally urged to seek the ultimate christological significance and messianic intention of all.

This exegetical attitude was valid on the assumption that Calvinists interpreted scripture with scripture and further, it was a necessary form of biblical interpretation, since exegesis (and all biblical and scientific study) ultimately had to have a practical and homiletic result. Biblical hermeneutics thus, from the theological student's perspective, had to be subsumed under the great injunction of his being preacher and pastor. It formed part of the specialized equipment with which he was sent forth to "sow the seed of God's Word". That may all be well and good and necessary when Bible interpretation has to be given a perspective and a position within the theological curriculum, and within the wider aims of training people for the ministry. However, such an approach to the interpretation of the scriptures has usually (at least from the student's point of view) been dominated by ecclesiastical, dogmatic, confessional/denominational and homiletical considerations. In this atmosphere, students were drilled, for example —

- that all scripture points to and thus had to be made to point to Christ;
- that we should begin with the text and not with the situation, hence "exegesis" was blessed by God while "eisegesis" was of the devil;
- that the essential biblical principles have first to be established before any "application to today" could be made; *"sola scriptura"* was the unquestioned authority which determined the integrity of our scholarship and also sometimes the quality of our spirituality;
- that therefore the true interpretation of the Bible could only be a Christian interpretation, and the true interpreter could only be a person of Christian faith which was usually taken to mean a form of personal piety and commitment to give scientific enquiry a Christian character; we were therefore constantly at pains to distinguish ourselves from the fundamentalists with their biblicistic hermeneutics and we distanced ourselves from the blatant biblical criticism of the text which had no respect for the Bible as the Word of God and its divine authorship;
- that the only defence against the ravages of literacy criticism, source criticism, form criticism, the history of tradition schools, redaction criticism — all of which eventually leave the Bible ultimately as one heap of useless paper to be trampled upon — that the only defence against this Western scientific arrogance, is a theological commitment to the uniqueness of the Biblical message and its overall unity. In the relationship between faith and intellect, (*fide* and *intellectus, pistis* and *logos*) faith is the essential and necessary point of departure. In effect therefore, we were taught to counter the arrogance of Western hermeneutical method which took scientific rationality to its logical consequence by defending ourselves with the arrogance of Western theological formulations.

Thus our exegesis is determined by certain unquestioned presuppositions. The Bible is interpreted within the Christian church, and thus presumed to be a book of the church. And because we set the ecclesiastical boundaries of its function, we proceed to reduce its message to a justification of our own confessional or denominational emphasis. And then of course we experience the week by week sermon wherein the Bible or one tiny aspect of it is subjected to the personal whims and fancies of the preacher: e.g. his "need" to preach (that need becomes a crisis on Saturday evenings, something which directly influences his choice of text) his own theological slant, his emotions and state of mind, etc. — all of these of course we are told is equivalent to the leading of God's Spirit. And of course, every sermon ends on one or other moral note on the good life. And usually this is reduced to the personal life of the believer. Within the confines of the church, the function of all exegesis is thus reduced to a matter of how to live the individual Christian life better. So the Bible and preaching are often the main instruments used to preserve the *status quo*: whether it be the dogma of the church or church tradition, or the privileged position of the intellectuals or the power of the clergy or the seizure of power by men within the structures of the church. Within the church the Bible and its interpretation are usually the ally of adult male chauvinism, bourgeois values and morals, a white Western and capitalistic ideology. And because of such a co-optation of Bible and message, children, blacks, women, the poor and uneducated have usually suffered as the victims of its interpretation and ethical application.

A proposed reading of Matt 5-7

In the light of the remarks made above I wish to propose that a reading of Matt 5-7 should take serious cognizance of the following hermeneutical considerations:

2.1 The Sermon on the Mount cannot be read as an isolated block of ethical teaching, containing ethical principles of eternal value.

2.2 Matt 5-7 can be faithfully exegeted only in the conscious effort we make to understand our own time. There is, therefore, an intimate and reflective (dialectical) relationship between exegesis and eisegesis. The nature of this relationship is both linguistic and contextual. Linguistically, the meaning of the text can be explicated only in the light of its ability to "speak again" in a different set of circumstances and time far removed from its own. Its original and semantic significance becomes expanded in a later time without being a distortion of the original meaning. Contextually, the meaning of the text is a means on the part of the interpreter of giving a commentary on contemporary events. This hermeneutical circulation between text, context, interpreter is unavoidable.

2.3 Thirdly, both a textual and a contextual reading of Matt 5-7 seem to require that the boundary between church and world, sacred and profane, divine and human be ignored as points of departure. This is born out textually by the position, structure and language of Matt 5-7 and by its distinctive message; secondly, it is borne out contextually by the nature of the ethical questions being raised in today's world, questions which certainly go beyond the narrow and restrictive confines of the Christian church.

2.4 Fourthly, I propose that we read Matt 5-7 in a non-capitalistic fashion, even in an anti-capitalistic way. Here again I suggest that the contents of the message of the Sermon on the Mount warrant and justify this. Secondly, the nature of the crisis of morals today derives, to a great extent, from the church's message and presence in capitalistic society.

2.5 Fifthly, we should consciously reject an individualized and privatized reading of Matt 5-7 for the following reasons:

Objections to a Privatized Exegesis of Matt 5-7

1. Such a hermeneutics is based on the unquestioned assumption that the context of the individual (thus the social order) is either alienating or that it is unquestionably to be accepted. Besides, the text is totally absorbed into the realm of the private and non-real, and subtly rendered ineffective.

2. Both an alienating and an accepted social order are forms of private accommodation to the given social structures. It is possible for South Africans to preach a totally other-worldly ethic and castigate the rest of society for its total corruption and sinfulness, and yet at the same time to be totally absorbed in the pursuit of the good life as we know it in South Africa. Those who accept the social order, in effect accept the capitalistic basis of society as the only legitimate one in which to try and exhibit Christian obedience. Both these are in effect a denial of the radicality of the ethical mandate being espoused in the Gospel. Matt 5-7 is not an ethic of accommodation.

3. The proper understanding of personhood, individuality, responsibility and freedom as actually presupposed in the whole Bible and expressed in Matt 5-7, is substituted by a shallow and selfish egotistic individualism, which has its basis more in the ideological and hedonistic philosophical presuppositions of the present social order than in the biblical understanding of human beingness and community. The Bible, therefore, surely takes utterly seriously the individuality of our creation, our being the image of God, etc, but this is not to be equated to what we today understand by individuality in South Africa.

4. Privatized interpretations are usually the options of people with a reasonable amount of social security. They usually emanate from that class of people who had a reasonably well-off life with or without middle class cares. Thus, such an interpretation is more a revelation of the class positions of interpreters, than the understanding of the text from the social position determined by an

option for the oppressed classes. When we see that poor people in the townships make easy resource to private assessment of the Gospel and its ethical implications, this is usually because those who preach to and teach poor people come not from among the poor and/or present their injunctions as the only normative way of interpreting Scripture.

5. Private interpretations usually rob the text of their radical social protest character, render its message apolitical and avoid its revolutionary significance. Further they leave the true addresses of the Gospel, viz. the marginalized of our world, without any comfort from God's Word and without a chance to turn the Gospel into an instrument for their liberation.

6. Further, if we accept that the social position of the interpreter has a direct bearing on the meaning or unmeaning of the text, I propose, on both textual and contextual grounds, that today only a marginalized reading of the Sermon on the Mount, and for that matter of the Gospel as a whole, is possible. I suggest that this passage be read firstly on the basis of a conscious option on the part of the interpreter in favour of the poor and marginalized of our society, secondly that the text be read for and with them, and thirdly that the text be read in the light of their personal and communal historical project.

7. An exegesis which is based on the above-mentioned hermeneutical considerations, is not necessarily an anti-intellectual vulgar interpretation of the text, which will be satisfied with face-value meaning. And that is not what is being proposed here. Rather an attempt is being made to argue that the Sermon on the Mount be interpreted in such a way that faithfulness to one's own historical context and faithfulness to the actual intentions of Matthew in 5-7 are not sacrificed to each other in the process of interpretation. Jesus does have something to say according to Matthew, to the Jews in his day and the written witness wants to convey that message and its ethical implication to us. But we do not have Matthew or Jesus at hand to tell us exactly what either of them intended. We have only the text and our own situation. And because of this we need a scientific analysis of the text from a linguistic, literary and historical point of view. The synoptics themselves make this necessary. On the other hand, we have to remain faithful children of our time, charged with the task of faithfully interpreting the biblical message for our situation and at the same time understanding our faith in the context of our time. Thus we have not only to look "behind" the text (its structure, its sources, its editorial and redactional qualities, etc. etc.), but we have also to look in "front"

of the text to its accumulated and potential significance. I am proposing that we read the text not "from above", but from the context determine "from below".

The Ethical Message of Matt 5-7

Right at the outset of this section, we have to put the question: What is the ethical question being asked today? But I have the conviction that a more urgent and fundamental question needs to be asked, namely: Whose ethical question are we asking? or Who is asking ethical questions today? For instance: Do poor people ask ethical questions in the first place? Do they ask themselves ethical questions? And if they do, what are the questions?

I have the growing conviction that the ethical perspectives of poor and marginalized people on life and its options differ fundamentally from those of rich and secure people. The rich young man asked Jesus: "What must I do to inherit eternal life?" In other words: provide me with a programmative scheme of ethical principles which I believe I am capable of fulfilling. For middle class capitalistic society today, ethical options are reduced to the embroidery which must serve to make life personally acceptable. It would be nice to know that I am not too far off the moral mark. So too at the communal and national level. For example, in South Africa, the ethical question of the white powerful well-to-do is also "what must we do?" This is the ethical question behind the policy of apartheid and its theological justification. Thus when pressed, Afrikaner theologians will ask: "Well then, what more do you want us to do, we are doing all that we possibly and permissably can." And it is, I "think", also the same ethical question behind these so-called constitutional changes which theologians are trying to catch up with: "We are doing what we must do to give a better deal to blacks, and the morality of our deeds lies in our intentions."

The poor, in my opinion, don't ask the "what" ethical question, but the "why" ethical question. Their question finds its echo in the words of Jesus: "My God, my God, why have you forsaken me." It is not possible for the poor to be dilletantic about ethical options. Their life situation, constantly threatened as it is by the terror of non-being in the concrete form of hunger, homelessness, joblessness, illness, child-death, eternal misery of circumstances and anguish of soul, etc. does not make it possible for them to ask: "What must I do to inherit eternal life?" Rather, the questions which rack body and mind, and beat against God's heaven, are more likely to be: "God, why was I born? Why did you create me black and abandon me to cruelty of this O so white world? God why don't you want to see and hear what is happening to us?"

The ethical posture of the rich appears to be their assumption that the world in which they live does make life humanly tolerable. Their private, individual, or family or communal expression of human behaviour, gains an ethical quality because their morality has been historically built into the structures of their socio-political and economic world. From birth to death they have the advantage of experiencing life as being morally tolerable because the structures such as family, marriage, education, amenities, health facilities, work, church, suburb, communication, state, politics, etc. are all infused with the ethical qualities of their own choice. The choices open to such people for private or social ethical behaviour are many. Thus, very often the "what-more-must-I-do" ethical question is put as an extra option, as an intellectual exercise which has first to be debated and principal conclusions distilled. It is a morality whose philosophical framework is shaped by Kantian rationality and Hegelian idealism and undergirded by the safety of an economically secure life-style.

The poor in our society and our church do not and cannot tackle the issue of morality as a matter of abstract possibilities which now and then find a willing adherent. The way of living life which confronts the poor is directly linked to conditions under which life is encountered. Morality is thus often a matter of survival and the strategy for survival. The ethical choices are directly situational and expedient, being dictated to more by what is incumbent and necessary at a given moment than by the abstract "ought".

The inherent weakness of the moral mandate which accompanied the Christian mission into the world (thus into the black communities, traditional societies, into our townships) is that it preached and demanded a form of ethical behaviour and obedience based on the abstraction of the biblical "ought". There is something vile and abhorrent about a missionary in a black township or a preacher on a black pulpit or a church in a black area, which piously sounds forth the moral requirements of the good Christian life, of obedience and discipleship, of love for God and man, without giving a second thought to the life conditions, the myriad emotional and psychological contradictions into which the believer is plunged as a result of having to cope with the alienating circumstances of his/her life and then, even worse, of having to come to grips with such an alienation with the aid of Christian virtues which are preached in just as alienating a fashion. And the believer has to contend with both forms of alienation, i.e. the alienation of his actual condition and the alienation of his faith at the same time: is this humanly possible? Why should the Christian church teach black people for instance, to behave in a Christian way and respond to the challenge of a humiliating life by reference to the Christian virtue of love or the attitude of love, obedience, forgiveness, patience, humility, hope and faith? These qualities may be Christian, but the more one practices them in a mindless way, the more do they plunge our people into deeper and desperate self-alienation and a fleshless Christian existence. Can one be a Christian at the direct cost of one's being human? Can one believe in such a way that faith itself becomes the agent of oppression? The church is so busy getting black people to be and behave in a Christian way that it has forgotten that there are black people around.

A Brief Look at Matt 5, 6, and 7.
The Sermon on the Mount is the first of five discourses into which the teaching of Jesus has been arranged in Matthew's gospel (5.1-7: 27; 9.36-10.42; 13.1-52; 18.1-35; 23.1-39,24.1-25:46). Immediately after the temptations, and following the arrest of John the Baptist, Jesus began to preach. Matthew locates the preaching and healing ministry of Jesus as having its beginning, not in Jerusalem, but at the periphery of Capernaum. At the margin of occupied territory, Jesus begins to tell marginalized people that the Kingdom of God had come and to call them to repentance, healing their diseases and displaying the glory of God in their midst. In the presence of these crowds (4:24; 7:20-29), Jesus ascends a mountain and like a New Moses presents a new law to his disciples within hearing distance of the crowds.

Iconoclastic
There are several reasons to indicate that the way in which Jesus presents his ethical teaching in the Sermon on the Mount has a clear iconoclastic intention. Matthew wants to express this intention of Jesus clearly. Some indications are, for example
  (i) the message is addressed to affluent Jewish Christians in an urban rather than a rural setting, people it seems who are pre-occupied with their economic, religious and class positions within society.
  (ii) the teaching reminds one distinctly of Moses and Sinai and yet the "but I say to you" is clearly intended on the one hand, to take distance from the Pharisee upper class interpretation of Moses which presupposed the hoi polloi's ignorance and inability to keep the Law; and on the other hand, at the same time to challenge, deepen and radicalize

the old law. Such a teaching would have religious respect-ability.

(iii) The economic references in these chapters to the poor be-ing blessed, to the ostentatious giving of alms, to the stor-ing up of treasures, to serving God or money, to the cares of eating, drinking and clothing, to giving your coat to one who took your cloak, would have outraged the wealthy and business minded, but would have delighted the poor who depended upon the rich, for a chance in life. Here was somebody who did not teach like their teachers.

(iv) Croatto said: "The gesture of Jesus was to be in solidarity with the poor, to be one of them. Only on the basis of this identification could he carry out the work of liberation. Je-sus had the experience of being marginalized, denounced, accused and plotted against by the centres of power. He had no structural or institutional defence. He always moved about at the grassroots level....."

(v) The words of Jesus in the Sermon on the Mount are rather intended to make it possible for people to be more human rather than more religious, something which must have been an affront to the religious aspirations of the wealthy but a balm to oppressed humanity.

Of course this raises the question of the religious character of this teaching of Jesus. I do not wish to deny that the whole dis-course is certainly couched in a religious tradition and language. But I feel that the angle from which we want to read the religious significance of these words of Jesus is of great consequence. Thus for example those who felt themselves being castigated and judged by the words of Jesus would certainly conclude that what was be-ing taught here was nothing short of blasphemy of Jesus' words, about not praying in public, for example. And secondly, even the reader today can misunderstand the religious significance of these words of Jesus. If for example we read the Sermon on the Mount from within the confines of Christian church piety, then there is the great danger of reducing the religious meaning to within the church and individual piety. Over and against these dangers I wish to propose that we try to understand the religious significance of Jesus' words hand in hand with the conferring of gracious human dignity to the poor. Spirituality then will inevitably be understood as a dynamic call to dehumanized people to assert their God-given right to be human beings. This is a spirituality for combat.

Jesus' Announcement of the Kingdom of God:
The centrality of Jesus' message was the announcement of the im-

minence of the Kingdom of God. In Matthew's Gospel, there are
two aspects basic to this announcement. The one is the announcement of God's rule upon earth as a fulfilment of the Old Testament prophetic message; and the other is the significance of the
life, death and resurrection of Jesus himself for the eschatological
arrival of God's Kingdom.

So too, we must see the ethics of Jesus in the light of the announcement of the arrival of the Kingdom of God. We have,
therefore, to do with the announcement to the poor and marginalized of the eschatological presence of the Kingdom. The following
characterization of Jesus' preaching is necessary if we are not to
misunderstand his teaching on the Kingdom and the kind of ethics
he enunciates.

(i)   The good news of the Kingdom is announced to the poor;
(ii)   This announcement is directly limited to Jesus' own personal
        pilgrimage as the Suffering Servant and to his personal quest
        in life, word and deed for liberation.
(iii)   In line with the Old Testament prophets (cf. Is. 9.5-7; 11.1-9;
        Jer. 23.3-8; Ezek. 34.23-27) the Jewish expectation of the
        Kingdom was not the realization of an other-worldly reality,
        but rather the coming of the Kingdom was expected as a very
        historical and real earthly establishment of structures of jus-
        tice and liberation on behalf of the oppressed. Far from being
        a spiritual reality, the Kingdom of God was the presence of
        righteousness upon earth and among human beings, begin-
        ning with and in Jesus.
(iv)   The eschatological character of this announcement is linked
        to the eschatological expectation of the poor for true respite
        from suffering and longing for peace. The foreigners, who are
        pronounced "blessed" and are the true inheritors of the King-
        dom are not being called to endure their eternal agony.
        Rather, in the breaking in of the eschatological epoch, they
        are called to set out into the future, God's future and with
        God the "power of the future" into the future of liberation.
        Such a summons is frought with ethical implications. The
        ethical mandate for the poor is therefore not historicized in
        past tense, but instead is dynamized and provided the op-
        pressed themselves with the opportunity to become the cre-
        ators of their own history.

Conclusion
If such an understanding of Matt 5-7 as presented above is not
totally wrong, then we should try to conclude with an attempt to

relate all of it more directly to the
- socio-political scene at present in South Africa;
- the aspirations for liberation of the oppressed in South Africa today;
- whether the church in South Africa today has a role to play with such an historical project or not and if so, under what conditions.

I shall limit myself to some general remarks on all of these issues raised above rather than refer to each item individually.

Today in South Africa, Christianity is preached unashamedly in State and church, especially the Nederduits Gereformeerde Kerk. The policy of racial separation and economic exploitation and po- litical domination in its changing faces even today is held up as based on Christian principles and in accordance with the dictates of Christian ethics. The managers of such a policy are all members of the church. The moral injuction with which they make and execute policy is the Christian virtue of obedience, i.e. obedience to some or other historical calling, and obedience in accordance with some version of the preaching and teaching of the church.

The type of Christian reasoning which is advanced by State and church, makes it amply clear that this form of obedience is under- stood in terms of a stewardship over power, and more important, it is the stewardship of the possessors of power. The NGK, for ex- ample, is busy trying to fashion, in a tortuous theological exercise, a theological rationale justifying the possession of power, a posses- sion which has to be maintained also within a challenging policy intended to share that power.

We must point out that the more the NGK persists in this ven- ture, the more ethically bankrupt it will become. The possession and maintenance of power, which has been gained by unjust means, cannot be morally justified with the aid of biblical and theological arguments.

Secondly, Christian obedience from a position of power and Christian obedience from a position of powerlessness are funda- mentally different in quality and effect. Within the South African context, I would want to hazard the thesis, that given the funda- mentally unjust socio-political and economic system, that both white Christian obedience and black Christian obedience are in the final analysis forms of disobedience. I shall try to explain myself as carefully as possible.

If white Christians really want to understand and practise obedi- ence, then I am convinced that discipleship on their part must be understood in socio-political and economic terms. If they are really willing to contextualize their faith, then apartheid will not be able to survive and the white church will at last become an agent for change in South Africa. But one despairs of such a possibility in South Africa coming from white Christians, if their action in the last referendum concerning the tricameral-constitution is an indication.

SHEENA DUNCAN

A Fearful Time
for Peacemakers

This is a fearful time for peacemakers.

The people of South Africa are at war with one another. As 1986 began we moved rapidly into a new phase in the conflict, with land mines killing people in the north as they have been killing people in Namibia and Angola for years, with repressive action against Lesotho, with new kinds of targets being singled out for limpet mine and bomb attacks, blatantly open and ruthless attacks by vigilantes who are not being prevented by the police from beating, torturing and killing people. There is ongoing repressive security force action against people who are trying to bring orderliness into resistance and protest, such as the Soweto Parents' Crisis Committee, whose meetings were banned just as they seemed to be moving towards the beginning of a resolution of the education crisis.

Hardly a day goes by without some report of deaths and injuries. There are violent attacks on people all the time, violent reprisals, and more deaths as we bury those who died before.

The fear of attack is a reality for those who live in our neighbouring countries. At home there are no forces of law and orderliness. The rule of law has been destroyed and the forces of disorderliness reign unchallenged. Those whose job it is to protect the people and to preserve the peace are seen as predators to be avoided, feared and hated.

The horror of war is upon us.

The government continues to devise new ways of entrenching apartheid, wrapping it up in glossy paper and presenting it as "reform" to the international community and to white South Africans.

Almost everyone demands an end to the pass laws and influx control. Government calls a pass a "book of life" and extends the exemptions from influx control allowed to marriage officers, teachers and lawyers to include those few who are wealthy enough to move from a homeland and to buy a freehold title in a segregated black township.

The law is changed to make it easier for those who are inside the city walls to stay there but forbids their families to join them.

The law is changed to make it easier for insiders to move around. This is called mobility but every easing of controls on the insiders strengthens the exclusion of the majority who are outside.

The rich can rub shoulders in expensive hotels and restaurants. The poor remain on the streets outside struggling to and from the black ghettos in the search for survival.

The Mixed Marriages Act is repealed; but couples must get a permit to live together other than in a designated "coloured" area.

A new Constitution is presented as reform; but gives enormous power to an executive State President, removes power from elected representatives and entrenches Race Classification and the separate residential provisions of the Group Areas Act. These cannot be repealed until there is yet another new Constitution.

The homelands policy is being pursued without interruption. Consolidation proposals for the Transvaal have been accepted by the government. Those for Natal, which will entail the removal of thousands of people, are on the way to acceptance.

Moutse has been incorporated into Kwa Ndebele against the wishes of the residents in the area whose public representatives asked only that a referendum be held to test the desires of the people. This was refused and violence in the area is now a daily occurrence.

Kwa Ndebele with its sjambok wielding government-supported vigilantes, is to be brought to independence this year. A new tide of refugees will be forced out just as the last lot fled from Bophuthatswana after independence and the many before that from the Herschel district of Transkei.

Detentions continue both in terms of the Internal Security Act and the Emergency Regulations. Several detainees who have been released from emergency detention have been served with new-style banning orders which differ only in minor detail from the old kind of banning orders. They severely restrict the movement of the recipients, curtail their activities and in many cases prevent them from carrying on with their normal work.

The majority of the people are not interested in reforms which merely redraw the apartheid barriers so that they are no longer there only to separate black from white, but increasingly to separate the rich from the poor, to the exclusion of the majority of black South Africans who are poor.

So South Africans are arming themselves to kill and injure each other and are facing the real possibility of a long drawn out violent civil war which could last for years.

Soon we will know what it is to live in the midst of war as the people who live in the Namibian and Angolan war zones have come to know it.

Ordinary people live in daily fear. Every journey, whether it be to the local store or to far away places, is an occasion of terror. Those who go out from their homes in the morning may never return. Children and young people disappear and may never be heard of again by their grieving parents. No-one is safe even in bed at night behind locked doors. Children are born and grow up and die without ever knowing what it is to live free from fear. Families are broken, communities disrupted.

Crops are destroyed and the land is laid waste to create a no man's land between opposing forces. The people who once lived there have been driven away.

Refugees flee from one place to another seeking safety where there is no safety to be found.

Christians on both sides of the conflict sing their different patriotic/freedom songs. Prayers in parish churches are for very different things depending on whether the congregation is black or white. We all pray for peace but our separate understandings of the things which make for our peace are diametrically opposed.

What are people who will not take up arms do in such a situation? What should the churches be doing?

The Jewish faith has two criteria for the conduct of war which are helpful to those of us who know we are going to be amongst the many who will be caught in the crossfire.

One is the obligation to create cities of refuge for the victims of war. The other is that fruit trees should not be destroyed.

Our fruit trees have already been destroyed through the removals programme, the migratory labour system, the homelands policy, by all the evil structures of apartheid, but we can start planting again now.

We can, if we have the will to do so, begin creating the future, begin preparing for the time after the destruction.

We need to begin now to plant the seeds of a new and better education for all South Africa's children with pilot schemes for alternative education for those who will never complete a formal education within the official structures. We can plan and practice education which enables children to grow into whole persons. We can rethink the values which presently distort education for South African children of all races. Is education only to produce cogs for the great industrial machine or should it be more than that?

We can begin now to feed and water strong and sturdy trees which will bear the fruits of democracy, justice, the rule of law. If we do not teach these things, uphold them, practice them, work for them, they will be lost to our future. They are the foundations of justice and there will be no peace without justice. We use that phrase so often that it begins to lose its meaning. We have to understand ourselves what justice means and pass on our understanding to others. This will not be possible unless we are prepared to work for it with total commitment.

We can begin to plan now for the proper stewardship of the land so that it can be worked for the benefit of all, rather than for the enrichment of the few. We have not given this nearly enough thought. It is one of the most critical issues which will face us in the future.

We can begin now to plant the mustard seeds which will become the trees of the kingdom in the years to come.

Sir Robert Birley once said that the rapid reconstruction of post-Nazi Germany was only made possible because of the seeds planted throughout the years of the Hitler regime by the few who had the courage to go on steadily holding fast to the truth and to their vision of a new and better future. This must surely be what we strive to do in the years ahead.

What of the cities of refuge? Where are we building them? Every single parish church should be a sanctuary, a place of refuge where people can come for help in trouble, for food when they are hungry, for healing when they are sick or wounded, for legal help when the law offers no protection and redress, for shelter when they are homeless, for safety when they are afraid, for consolation when they grieve.

The vast majority of our churches are not like that at all. We are afraid to open our doors and our hearts. Our gates are locked at night when danger stalks in the hours of darkness. We hide from reality in our pulpits, measure our performance by the amount of our revenues.

Where is Jesus? In a pew for two hours on a Sunday morning or in the troubled fire-torn streets outside?

If we are to build cities of refuge we must be out there with him, with his healing in our hands and his kingdom in our hearts.

The grace is sufficient for what we have to do. Is our faith sufficient to know it?

Part 5

The Struggle in South Africa

JOHN W. DE GRUCHY

The Church and the Struggle for South Africa

Ten years ago I began preparing the lectures which were eventually published as *The Church Struggle in South Africa*.[1] During the intervening decade a great deal has happened in South Africa, and, in the process my perception of the nature of the church struggle has changed. My clue for its redefinition has come from the title and content of another book published the same year, 1979, Ian Linden's *The Church and the Struggle for Zimbabwe*.[2] The emphasis in my title was on the church struggle against racism, a struggle taking place within and between churches, as well as between some churches and the state. Linden's emphasis was on the role of the church in the political and military struggle for the liberation of Zimbabwe. The different focus is are highly significant. I now see more clearly that the church struggle in South Africa, which remains a very real matter, can only be understood in the context of the larger political struggle, the struggle for the future of South Africa. The struggle within the churches, as well as the struggle between the church and the state, is about the role which the church should play in the unfolding drama of the struggle for justice and liberation.

The Struggle for South Africa
The struggle for South Africa has to be understood in relation to the socio-political crisis in which the country presently finds itself. This crisis is the product of apartheid, the ideological attempt to divide South Africa so that whites, and especially Afrikaner nationalism, should control the country. This racist ideological project has permeated virtually everything in our society, and it continues to do

so despite the Government's attempt at reform and some improvement away from racial discrimination. The new constitution and its tricameral parliament, for example, while hailed as evidence of reform, remains based upon ethnic difference. The reason for this structured control in the face of massive rejection by the world community and the majority in the country, is undoubtedly the Government's perceived need to retain power in order to protect the material interests of the white community and its continued existence. These interests include the unjust distribution of land, resources and wealth, interests which are also increasingly shared by middle-class members of the "coloured" and Indian communities, and those blacks with power in the homelands.

In pursuance of the possession and control of these interests apartheid has meant the uprooting of peoples, social dislocation, bad housing, migrant labour, third-rate education, poverty and malnutrition and, despite the emergence of a black middle class, a growing gap between the rich and poor coupled to rampant unemployment especially amongst blacks. South Africa has long been a country in which first and third worlds have co-existed. This co-existence has become increasingly problematic and conflictual as first world privilege collides with third world need, and as those who are oppressed have become more urgent and radical in their demands.

These demands have been expressed during the past few years most loudly and clearly by the emergent black trade unions and young black students, whose anger and frustration burst so dramatically on the world's television screens during 1985. The majority of blacks are no longer willing to accept apartheid passively, and have quite categorically rejected the Government's path of reform as totally inadequate. This is reflected in the emergence and growing strength of new organizations like the United Democratic Front and the National Forum, the revitalization of the African National Congress and the re-appearance of the South African Communist Party. Of course, the situation is more complicated than it might appear at first sight because some blacks have accepted, or at least begun to participate in the reformist programme of the Government, and some whites have identified themselves with the black struggle for liberation. Within both racial groups there are different factions with different ideologies, hopes and fears. None of the segregated ethnic communities are united in the struggle; a fact which is vividly reflected in the life of the churches and their response to the struggle for South Africa.

Politics is ultimately the question of who has power, how it is exercised, checked and balanced. The majority in South Africa have been denied access to this power, and thus have begun to explore and use the power which they have, the power of numbers and labour, the power of social morality, conscience and world-wide support, the power of protest, of strike action, of shop and school boycotts, of civil disobedience, and, for some, the power of the gun. This movement for liberation, while a movement of diversity, has a common commitment to ending white power and hegemony, and ushering in a new non-racial democracy. The actual shape of the future South Africa is a subject of intense debate.

The response of the government to the emergence and activities of black or non-racial resistance movements has for a long time been forceful and violent. Security legislation, which includes banning and detention without trial for extensive periods, censorship and propaganda, violently repressive police action, and the militarization of the country, have been a reality for many years though they reached new depths during the recent state of emergency. The pattern established at Sharpeville twenty-one years ago has been exceeded and become almost routine in recent months. As a result, the rejection of apartheid followed by violent government repression, in turn followed by the radicalization of increasing numbers of blacks and more violent resistance, has created the familiar spiral of violence, and in the process society has become more and more brutalized. This brutalization is exacerbated by the fact that right-wing vigilante groups have emerged, both black and white, which have begun to take the law into their own hands, and there has been a frightful amount of violence exercised by blacks upon other blacks.

Whether or not it is strictly accurate to say that South Africa is now in the midst of a civil war is a moot point; it is near enough to the truth as troops patrol the townships and guerillas engage in acts of revolutionary violence. It is therefore no longer meaningful to ask whether social change will come about without it. For those who live in the black townships especially, violence is endemic to apartheid, it has become an everyday, terrifying reality. Many would argue, moreover, and with some justification, that violent reaction is the only language which speaks to those in power. The authorities use the same argument in reverse. To argue the case for non-violent change, to which I remain committed, can only be done in the light of this reality. Can fundamental social change come about without a violent conflagration, what people refer to as the Lebanese option?

The spiral of violence extends, of course, beyond the borders of South Africa. Since 1966 South Africa has been involved in an ever escalating conflict in Namibia and Angola, and is apparently covertly involved in other areas of conflict in the southern African region. The truth is, South Africa cannot be separated from southern Africa as a whole, nor from the globalization of the conflicts in the sub-continent. What is happening in Angola, Namibia, Mozambique, and Zimbabwe, but also in Washington, London, Havanna and Moscow, is now of considerable consequence for the conflict within South Africa itself. There is a regional and international conflict of interests which is integrally related to that within the country.

Fundamental to the conflict of interests now violently starting to engulf us, is a conflict of perceptions. South Africans differ from each other, and respond in radically different ways to what is happening, because each of us is, to a significant degree, the product of our history, culture and environment, and, more immediately, the product of an apartheid society. Our perceptions, the way we discern our society and its future, as well as the way in which we respond to other people and events, are profoundly affected by the conditioning of our culture, our education, or, to put it in other terms, the fears, hopes and interests of our class, group and race. South Africa is, historically, a country made up of many different cultures and ethnic groups. Even if apartheid had never been devised it would have been difficult to weld such diversity into a nation with a shared sense of identity and common goals. But it has created a bitter legacy which has reinforced these historic divisions so successfully that our society has become one of separated islands between which there is not only little meaningful communication, few common interests or shared perspectives, but mistrust and enmity. The exceptions, and there are significant exceptions, signs of hope amidst despair, prove the rule. But how does one build a united nation with common values and commitments in such a divided community?

While I do not believe that the end to apartheid and white dominance in South Africa has arrived, I do believe that the beginning of the end has been signalled. Apartheid is breaking down not so much through white altruism as through its own inherent absurdity, and through the immense pressure that is being brought to bear upon it both internally and externally. Of course, predictions about human history are perilous undertakings, and it is forseeable that something could happen, for example, a white, right-wing military coup which will clamp down on the process of change. But even that, I suggest, could only be a short-term digression towards the end of white oligarchic rule controlled by Afrikaner nationalism. But the road ahead is strewn both figuratively and literally with landmines. It is within this critical context that the church of Jesus

Christ which, being comprised of the same social groupings as those in conflict with each other, experiences the conflict within her own life, and has to bear witness to the gospel of justice and liberation, peace and hope.

Redefining the Church Struggle

Those familiar with the church in South Africa will already know that it is made up of many different groups and denominations reflecting, on the one hand, the divisions of post-Reformation Christendom which were imported into the sub-continent, and, on the other, the cultural plurality and historic divisions of South Africa itself. It is only possible to speak of the church as an article of faith; sociologically or empirically-speaking we have to recognize not only different churches which relate in a variety of diverse ways to the crisis in which we find ourselves, but also different responses within the same churches. The various historic tensions and conflicts between denominations and church groups, such as the South African Council of Churches (SACC), which I documented and discussed in *The Church Struggle in South Africa* are still very much with us.

The conflict of perception and interest which lies at the heart of the present socio-political crisis also permeates the life of the church itself both ecumenically and within each separate denomination. This affects the way in which the gospel is understood, the way in which ecumenical and socio-political issues are debated, and the resolutions and actions which result.[3] Hence the ongoing struggle within the church and, concomitantly, the ambiguity of the church's response to the struggle for liberation in South Africa.

Within the past decade several movements have arisen within the churches which attempted to overcome this ambiguity and identify fully with the liberation movement. Prominent amongst these are black confessing movement (e.g. the Alliance of Black Reformed Christians in South Africa (ABRECSA), and *Die Belydende Kring* within the black Dutch Reformed churches) and those identified with the Institute for Contextual Theology, which have articulated a more decisively radical theology and programme of action. The roots of these developments can be found in the emergence of Black Theology at the end of the sixties, and the development of liberation theologies in various parts of the world.[4] As a result, Christians in every major church are radically challenging their denominational leadership and membership, including even the South African Council of Churches itself. In the process the church struggle in South Africa is being redefined as a struggle within the churches related to the political struggle for the future of South Africa. In fact, Christian participation in and reflection on the political struggle has re-written the agenda for the church struggle.

This redefinition of the church struggle must, however, not be understood as something unprecedented. The debate within the churches as to their appropriate response to black political movements like the ANC has a much longer history. Already within the 1950's there was tension precisely on this issue as black Christian leaders such as Albert Luthuli, Z.K. Matthews and Robert Sobukwe, threw themselves fully into the political struggle, and as some whites like Fr. Trevor Huddleston identified with them. For many politically conscious blacks this is what the church struggle has always been about; but it is only more recently, as the struggle for liberation has escalated, that it has become the central issue on the churches' agenda.

Several earlier developments laid the foundation for and began this process of redefinition. I refer especially to the publication of *The Message to the People of South Africa,* in 1968; the rise of Black Theology; and the World Council of Churches' Programme to Combat Racism, launched in 1969. Each of these has also contributed to the growing polarization within the churches. But more recently, in the past few years, several important steps have led directly to the redefinition of which I am speaking. Firstly, in 1982 apartheid was finally declared a heresy by significant groups of churches in South Africa, including the Dutch Reformed Mission Church and many of those involved in the SACC. This completed the process already begun with the publication of *The Message to the People of South Africa* in 1968 in which apartheid was declared a false gospel. With the declaration that it is a heresy, apartheid was, once and for all, rejected as theologically and morally bankrupt, indefensible and beyond reform.[5]

Secondly, on June 16 1985, the ninth anniversary of the Soweto uprising in 1976, services of prayer were held in South Africa for "the end to unjust rule". In the theological rationale which accompanied the call it was stated:

Now, on 16 June, and twenty five years after the dawning of this phase of resistance (i.e. Sharpeville) it is right to remember those whose blood has been shed in resistance and protest against an unjust system. It is also right that we as Christians reassess our response to a system that all-right-thinking people indentify as unjust. We have prayed for our rulers, as is demanded of us in the Scriptures. We have entered into consultation with them as is required by our faith. We have taken the reluctant and drastic step of declaring apartheid to be contrary to the declared will of God, and some churches have declared its theological justification to be a heresy. We now pray that God will replace the present structures of oppression with ones that are just, and remove from power those who persist in defying his laws, installing in their place leaders who will govern with justice and mercy.[6]

Following on from this call to pray for an end to unjust rule came, thirdly, the publication of *The Kairos Document* in September 1985. Since the advent of apartheid as the governing ideology in 1948 there have been several important statements or confessions of faith emanating from those churches and Christians in opposition to it. Each of these statements has clarified the issues at the given moment and pushed the debate further. For example, *The Message to the People of South Africa* clearly stated that apartheid was a false gospel which contradicted the gospel of reconciliation in Jesus Christ. More recently, the Belhar Draft Confession of Faith of the Dutch Reformed Mission Church (1982) rejected apartheid as a heresy. *The Kairos Document* has gone further and, in important respects, represents most forcefully the paradigm shift in the Christian response to apartheid which redefines the church struggle.

This paradigm shift led, fourthly, to the *The Harare Declaration*, emanating from a conference on South African and world-wide church leaders meeting in the capital of Zimbabwe in December, in which churches inside and outside South Africa were called upon "to support South African movements working for the liberation of their country". In this way, what was implicit in the WCC Programme to Combat Racism has become explicit at a critical moment in the struggle for liberation. It has yet to be seen how the churches in South Africa will respond to *The Harare Declaration*, but if they do respond positively it will be the most far-reaching and concrete opposition they have hitherto expressed to apartheid.

As a result of this redefinition or paradigm shift in thought and action, the conflict within the churches and between Christians has intensified. For some the response to the liberation movement is unambiguous commitment, for others it ranges from one which is more qualified or reluctant to rejection and opposition. In this context we should note the small but vocal coalition of right-wing church groups which seek to oppose such commitment and often do so through misrepresentation and distortion of the facts. Thus the church struggle is very much alive within the churches, but the debate is not so much about apartheid as it is about how to change it and what role the church should fulfil in that process.

The Kairos Document and the National Initiative for Reconciliation

In order to show more concretely the way in which the church struggle has been redefined, but also in order to examine alternative ways in which the church might respond to the struggle for liberation in South Africa, I propose to examine two different responses which were articulated at the height of the crisis towards the end of 1985. Both have subsequently become embodied in programmes of witness and action. The first was the launching of the National Initiative for Reconciliation (NIR) at a conference held in Pietermaritzburg in September. This led to the formulation of a *Statement* which set out the position of those who attended, the goals to which they were committed and the means they were to employ in working towards them.[7] The second was the publication of *The Kairos Document*[8] a few weeks later. Significantly both of these were attempts by Christians in South Africa who reject apartheid and seek to respond to the crisis in a way which will facilitate a more just society in the future of the country. Yet a comparison of the two documents will show that despite some common ground and shared concerns, the approaches are significantly different.

The National Initiative for Reconciliation was sponsored by Africa Enterprise, an evangelical organization, which has attempted increasingly over the years to relate evangelism to social witness, and to include in its programme Christians and churches from across the sociopolitical, racial and theological spectrum. Present at the launch of the NIR were people like Archbishop Desmond Tutu, who did not sign *The Kairos Document* and other black theologians such as Dr. Bonganjalo Goba and Professor Simon Maimela who did. Also present were a number of white ministers and theologians of the Dutch Reformed church, as well as representatives from various other churches, including both SACC member churches and others such as Pentecostal denominations. The vast majority endorsed the *Statement of Affirmation* which was issued at the end of the conference. As already intimated, the *Statement* no less than *The Kairos Document* categorically rejects apartheid, and endorses a programme of action which will "take the necessary steps towards the elimination of all forms of legislated discrimination." Amongst those listed are the demand to the State President to:

- Release all detainees and political prisoners, withdraw charges against the treason trialists and allow exiles to return home.
- Begin talks immediately with authentic leadership of the various population groups with a view toward equitable power sharing in South Africa.

Both of these would also be regarded as priorities by the Kairos theologians and those who endorsed the *Harare Declaration*. Yet the approaches are different, in fact, at points, quite radically different. For example, whereas the NIR *Statement* calls for "power sharing" *The Harare Declaration* calls for "the transferring of power to the majority of the people".

The Kairos Document was produced largely by black ministers and theologians in the Johannesburg-Soweto area during the height of the social crisis in 1985. It was subsequently endorsed by others, both black and white, in different parts of the country. Since its publication it has sparked off wide-spread debate both in South Africa and overseas. Those who prepared it, the "Kairos theologians", do not regard it as a finished document, but as a statement *in via*. At the same time it is meant to be, not a balanced statement of faith, but a sharp and radical response to the present Kairos, "a moment of truth not only for apartheid but also for the church".

> The moment of truth has compelled us to analyze more carefully the different theologians in our Churches and to speak out more clearly and boldly about the real significance of these theologies. We have been able to isolate three theologies and we have chosen to call them 'State Theology', 'Church Theology' and 'Prophetic Theology'. In our thoroughgoing criticism of the first and second theologies we do not wish to mince our words. The situation is too critical for that.

Let us then compare the two different approaches, and ask, in the process, whether or not the NIR *Statement* falls into the category of 'Church Theology' as set forth by *The Kairos Document*.

Firstly and fundamentally, the *Statement* and *The Kairos Document* differ in their analyses of what is happening in South African society. This is a critical difference between them because it determines much of what follows by way of prescription for Christian involvement in social action and transformation. As Nicholas Lash has observed, "The struggle for the accurate 'description' of reality (thus) becomes an aspect of the struggle for social change."[9] Indeed, whereas *The Kairos Document* makes social analysis a priority and criticizes the churches for failing to engage adequately in it, the NIR *Statement* avoids any attempt to do so, possibly for fear of splitting its constituency. But even though it does not engage in social analysis, such analysis is implicit. It is evident in the underlying conviction that racism is the major problem.

The Kairos Document goes much further and speaks of a conflict between "oppressor" and the "oppressed". Clearly, racism is regarded as only part of the problem which is, at root, one of economics and material interests, of poverty and power. The primary problem is not simply that of racism but of conflict between "an oppressor and the oppressed...between two irreconcilable *causes* or *interests* in which the one is just and the other is unjust." This understanding of the problem is absent from the NIR *Statement*.

Secondly, *The Kairos Document* is a radical and sharp critique which seeks to confront both what it calls 'State Theology', that kind of theology which seeks to justify the present *status quo* "with its racism, capitalism and totalitarianism"; and 'Church Theology' that is, the theology of the leadership of the so-called English-speaking churches whose criticism of apartheid "is superficial and counter-productive because instead of engaging in an in-depth analysis of the signs of the times, it relies upon a few stock ideas derived from Christian tradition and then uncritically and repeatedly applies them to our situation." Specifically mentioned and examined are: reconciliation (or peace), justice and non-violence. The point of the critique is that such 'Church Theology', while it appears to challenge and reject apartheid, actually ends up by preventing the churches from engaging in concrete action which will bring about change. In the process, these central Christian themes are debased. For example, while *The Kairos Document* does not explicitly support violence in the struggle for justice, it is very critical of the way in which non-violence has been absolutized by the churches.

> Non-violence has been made into an absolute principle that applies to anything anyone *calls* violence without regard for who is using it, which side they are on or what purpose they have in mind.

What happens, in fact, is that "violence" becomes part of state propaganda. It refers to the actions of those who seek to overthrow unjust structures, but not to the violence of the structures nor to the violence used by the State in maintaining such structures.

In contrast, the NIR *Statement* offers no critique, except by way of implication, of either the state ideology or the churches, and its very name is indicative of the centrality which the idea of reconciliation plays in its understanding and programme. There is, of course, a clear rejection of apartheid, and its concluding recommedations express rejection of the way in which the state has responded to the crisis in South Africa. But there is no attempt to uncover and judge the ideology which lies behind it. With regard to the churches, the *Statement* seeks to be as conciliatory, balanced and inclusive as possible given its rejection of apartheid and the proposals it makes. *The Kairos Document,* on the other hand, rejects any attempt to be balanced and is especially sharp in its criticism of what it regards as a message of "cheap reconciliation"; it seeks to be as exclusive as is necessary to

confront the system totally. White repentance and a clear commitment to fundamental, non-racial change, must precede negotiation
and reconciliation.

Thirdly, over against 'Church Theology' the *The Kairos Document*
propounds what it calls 'Prophetic Theology', a theology which recognizes that the root problem is oppression, and that God is on the
side of the oppressed in their struggle for liberation. This requires
recognition that the present government has lost its moral legitimacy
and, in accordance with Christian tradition, may be called tyrannical,
that is, an "enemy of the common good" which has to resort to terror
in order to maintain its power and privilege. It is incapable of change.

The NIR *Statement,* on the other hand, assumes that the Government can change, and that it can bring about the changes needed to
prevent catastrophe. Thus, whereas *The Kairos Document* categorically rejects negotiation at this stage in the struggle, the NIR sent a
delegation to the State President to present its vision for change and
the steps that need to be taken to achieve it. *The Kairos Document*
maintains that only the people acting "from below" can bring about
the changes that are necessary. Therefore the churches, instead of
trying to convince those in power to change should commit themselves to the struggle of the poor and oppressed. The Christian response to those in power must be one of confrontation until they
indicate they are willing to undergo fundamental change. It is argued
that the *justice* which 'Church Theology' seeks is the "justice of reform, that is to say, a justice that is determined by the oppressor, by
the white minority and that is offered to the people as a kind of con-
cession." In other words, it is justice on the terms of those in power
which leaves relatively untouched the basic structural injustices of
apartheid. 'Church Theology' addresses those in power, those on the
top, calling upon them to act justly. But what is required is church
support for those who are below, the oppressed, in their struggle to
get rid of unjust structures.

Fourthly, whereas the NIR *Statement* sets out a programme of
action for Christians and the churches, which is along the lines of the
church being an "alternative community" or a Third Force working
for reconciliation, *The Kairos Document* explicitly rejects such an approach in the interests of liberation. On the contrary , the church and
Christians have to identify and participate, albeit critically, with those
engaged in the struggle for justice, and therefore in their organizations. Whereas the strategy envisaged by the *Statement* is at the level
of proclamation and witness, prayer and fasting, the creation of opportunities for non-racial worship, fellowship and discussion, education for change, the sharing of suffering, the strategy of *The Kairos*

Document, while accepting these, goes much further in encouraging direct political action. Indeed, acts of civil disobedience are specifically stated. Indeed, tacitly, *The Kairos Document* gives legitimacy to the use of violence if this becomes necessary in the struggle for liberation. In the Christian tradition of the just war, it supports, as many Christians have in the past, the just revolution.

This short comparison highlights two very different approaches of Christians in South Africa to the present political struggle, even though they both agree that apartheid must be ended. They differ in their prognosis because they differ in their social analysis, in their attitude towards the present government, and in their understanding of the task of the church. A large part of the reason for their different approaches is, however, the fact that the NIR *Statement* was drafted by church leaders who were concerned to take their constituency with them, especially the white, more conservative evangelical component, whereas *The Kairos Document*, a product largely of black theologians, was addressed primarily to black Christians involved in the liberation struggle.

For many of those involved in the NIR, *The Kairos Document* exceeds the boundaries of legitimate church action, the "church should be the church". For the "Kairos theologians", the NIR *Statement* would be regarded as an example of 'Church Theology', and it is, undoubtedly, where much of the church leadership opposed to apartheid would place themselves. *The Kairos Document* is meant to be a prophetic challenge to them to move faster and to commit themselves more unequivocally to the struggle for liberation. At the same time it is not primarily an attempt to address church leaders, but an attempt to provide a theological basis for those Christians who are already committed to the struggle. Thus it radically redefines the nature of the church struggle in South Africa.

Non-Violent Social Transformation

In concluding, I would like to propose several of these which should guide the church in its participation in the struggle for a liberated and just South Africa. As a signatory of *The Kairos Document* I agree with its criticism of the misuse of "non-violence" by the state and often by the churches, and I acknowledge that the Reformed tradition in which I stand has, in the past, supported the idea of a just revolutions and may with good reason do so again. Nevertheless, I still believe that non-violent strategies for social transformation remain the church's primary responsibility, and, that given the spiral of violence in South Africa, everything must be done to prevent its escalation to the point of mutual self-destruction.

(1) In the struggle for a just society the church cannot be neutral, but there are different, complementary strategies.

The two approaches represented by the NIR *Statement* and *The Kairos Document* are not necessarily antithetical or exclusive of each other, though both can be interpreted in that way. If I had been present at the NIR conference, I would undoubtedly have signed its *Statement* even though critical of some aspects of it, just as I signed *The Kairos Document* despite some reservations. In some respects the NIR *Statement* is a far-reaching document which could have important ramifications throughout the country amongst groups of Christians who have generally been cautious about socio-political involvement. For many of them the NIR was a major step forward, a catalyst for change, and the *Statement* a challenge for action. Such transforming encounters are necessary, and the programme of witness and worship which they promote are essential.

But complementary strategies are not an excuse for neutrality or ambiguous commitment. And this is the strength of *The Kairos Document:* it is unequivocal in its stance. *The Kairos Document* is by no means perfect, and many of those who signed it have expressed criticisms of it. It is a document that was developed in the heat of crisis. Yet it is also a document which seeks to grapple seriously with the biblical, prophetic tradition in relation to the context; not one which surrenders Christian faith and tradition, but which retrieves and restates it for today. Its sharp analysis and concrete proposals, developed further in *The Harare Document,* are precisely what the churches need to hear if they are not to become irrelevant to the struggle for the future of South Africa. Moreover, its message is one which speaks directly and positively to those involved in the struggle who no longer believe that the Christian faith has anything to say to them.

(2) The church must be the church, but this does not mean that it has its own political programme alongside that of the struggle for liberation. It must participate in critical solidarity.

One problem that I have with *The Kairos Document* is that the line between the church and political movements gets blurred; the problem that I have with NIR *Statement* is that no connection between them is made. The slogan "Let the church be the church" is often used as a way of escape from political commitment into neutrality. Similarly, the idea of the church as an "alternative community" or "third force" is sometimes interpreted in this way. *The Kairos Document* will not allow this. The church has to identify with those who are struggling for justice and not start its own political programme. Indeed, many of those involved in liberation movements are members of the church. Yet *The Kairos Document* also recognizes that Christians have to participate in "critical solidarity" with movements for social change.

Critical solidarity, if it means anything, means that the church has a unique contribution to make in the struggle for liberation, a contribution that will remain necessary in the new society. Central to this contribution is its spiritual resources, the resources of the biblical tradition to which it seeks to bear witness. To deny this contribution is fatal for both the church and the struggle for liberation. Thus the church, when true to its vocation, will always be in a critical relationship both to those in power, and those who take power. The church is not the servant of a political movement but the servant of the kingdom of God, and therefore of *people* struggling for justice. It is always critical of that which dehumanizes and destroys people and communities, and especially people and communities which are powerless, disadvantaged and poor. "The only 'permanent allies' of Christianity are, or should be, the weak and dispossessed: and their identity changes."[10] Critical solidarity also means that Christians should not absolutize political conflict, or arrogantly come to regard themselves and their party in the conflict as doing the will of God, whether it is in defense of the *status quo* or in seeking to change it. This leads us to our third thesis.

(3)   *The gospel of reconciliation and liberation, as well as the political strategies of negotiation and confrontation, are not antithetical but two sides of the same coin.*

The good news that God has reconciled the world to himself in Jesus Christ is the foundation of Christian faith and action. Reconciliation is an act of God in Jesus Christ, it is something which is given. At the same time, Christians are called to be reconciled to their neighbours and their enemies through suffering love and forgiveness. Reconciliation to God is inseparable from reconciliation with one's fellows. Such reconcilation requires repentance and change, not just a change of attitude, but fundamental change which affects the very structures of existence. In South Africa it is possible for individuals of different races to discover the deep significance of Christian reconciliation. But as long as apartheid structures continue, the genuine reconciliation of social groups remains elusive, and therefore peace remains elusive. Both whites and blacks are chained, and the liberation of the one is necessary for the freedom of all. "Cheap reconciliation", and therefore negotiation prior to a genuine commitment to change, only prolongs the bondage.

In this regard something needs to be said about the tyrannical nature of the state. I affirm with *The Kairos Document* that the South African government has acted in a tyrannical way and should be replaced by another. However, the Christian must always be open to the possiblity of change, the "possible impossibility" (Barth), and should not regard the state in a static way. Negotiation and confrontation are not necessarily exclusive of one another, indeed, as Moses in his encounters with Pharoah demonstrated, they may need each other in order to achieve the desired goal of freedom. Ronald Preston, the British theologian has some wise words to offer us here, he writes specifically with South Africa in mind:

> If Christians find themselves genuinely on opposite sides of it (i.e. conflict) they must take part in fear of the Lord, but never let go the possiblity of reconciliation through the conflict, but not avoiding it. This is a desperate situation, so we must work to avoid polarization at all costs. But if it occurs, the attitude I have mentioned demands great spiritual resources but it is not impossible.[11]

There is an alternative to "cheap reconciliation", it is reconciliation through the suffering witness of the cross.

(4) *The suffering witness of the cross, and therefore non-violent redemptive action, remains the paradigm for the Christian, even though there is an honoured Christian tradition which supports the idea of a just revolution.*

It should already be clear that the problem of violence in South Africa is a complex one. I stand by *The Kairos Document* in its strong criticism of the way in which "non-violence" and "violence" have both been misused as part of state propaganda. The church in South Africa needs to be very clear about the nature of the violence which is endemic in our society, and why it is that others have been forced to use violence in order to bring about change. Tragically, it would appear that the authorities only begin to respond significantly when they are forced to do so in this way. But ultimately the spiral of violence will destroy society unless it is first of all limited, and then brought to an end. Hence the need for Christians to struggle for justice and liberation in a way which both serves that end and yet, in doing so, breaks the spiral. It is in this regard that we have to understand the call for disinvestment and other acts of civil disobedience, together with the those forms of pressure called for in *Harare Declaration*. In one of the best articles I have read on disinvestment, Sheena Duncan, the past president of the Black Sash in South Africa, an organization of white women committed to non-violent social change, concludes: "It is for these reasons that I am in favour of strategic, economic pressures, carefully thought out, carefully monitored, and adjusted according to the observed effects. It seems to me," she continues, and I agree, "that these may be our last hope for avoiding a long-drawn-out civil war which would result in total economic collapse."[12] Actions such as these are crucial in this point that the church universal can participate in the struggle for the future of South Africa.

REFERENCE NOTES

1. John W. de Gruchy, *The Church Struggle in South Africa*, Grand Rapids, Eerdmans; Cape Town, David Philip, 1979.
2. Ian Linden, *The Catholic Church and the Struggle for Zimbabwe*, London, Longman, 1979.
3. See my essay, "Christians in Conflict: the Social Reality of the South African Church", in *Journal of Theology for Southern Africa*, No. 51, June 1985.
4. See my essay, "Theologies in Conflict: the South African Debate", in Charles Villa-Vicencio and John W. de Gruchy, *Resistance and Hope*, Grand Rapids, Eerdmans, 1985.
5. See John W. de Gruchy and Charles Villa-Vicencio, *Apartheid is a Heresy*, Grand Rapids, Eerdmans, 1983.
6. Published in the *Journal of Theology for Southern Africa*, No. 52, September, 1985, p. 58.
7. The full text of the NIR *Statement of Affirmation* was published in the *Journal of Theology for Southern Africa*. No. 54, March 1986.
8. *The Kairos Document* was reproduced in full in the *Journal of Theology for Southern Africa*, No. 53, December 1985.
9. Nicholas Lash, *A Matter of Hope*, University of Notre Dame Press, 1982, p. 132.
10. Nicholas Lash, *A Matter of Hope*, University of Notre Dame Press, 1982, p. 289.
11. Ronald H. Preston, *Church and Society in the Late Twentieth Century: The Economic and Political Task*, London, SCM, p. 112.
12. Sheena Duncan, "Some Personal Observations on the Disinvestment Campaign", *Sash*, Vol. 28, No. 4, February 1986, p. 21.

MILLARD W. ARNOLD

With Respect to Morality, Justice and Law In South Africa

> *"I don't say the law is the whole answer, but I'm not the first to say a society may be worse than its laws, but hardly any better."*
> — A. Leon Higginbotham

In the evolution of a state — in its progression from a collection of varied ideologies and customs to cohesive community embodying the spirit of a nation — nothing may be more important in that transformation than the concept of law and the related principles of justice and morality.

Every state, regardless of ideology, exists on the basis of a legal order. Legality is a rationalization for order, and order is the primary function of a state. The nature of law is to establish the state, provide proper channels for conflict resolution, serve notice of the occasions and circumstances upon which the state will exercise its policy authority and codify the essence of the accepted social morality.

Under international law, a state is defined as any entity that has a permanent population, a defined territory, a government, and the capacity to enter into relations with other states.[1] It is of necessity a rather narrow, nearly simplistic delineation of a state. It is a definition that is useful legalistically, but hardly of value in capturing the range of complexities that constitute the nature of a state. Politically, a state is defined as a collection of individuals organized in a single system of political order under a government with the power to exercise sovereignty or supreme authority over a given territory.[2]

The state then, is a combination of individuals and territory governed by law. The essence of sovereignty is the right of the state to enact laws that ensure order. In turn, the laws enacted reflect the underlying virtues of the individuals that make the state possible.[3] As such, the state is a kind of social institution intended to establish and enforce a sense of collective morality. That morality in turn, is the genesis of the state's civil law and police authority. The distinction then, between the legal and political definition of a state is the concept of morality.

The individual ranks as the minimum, irreducible element in the composition of the state. As an individual, his/her needs are simply those of immediate survival.[4] Through family, friends and finally the state, this need of immediate survival is replaced with that of a greater need, one of the perpetuation of self. To insure his/her survival, and guarantee his/her immortality, the individual seeks the absolute domination of his/her environment. Alone, the individual is limited in assuring him/herself the necessary control over his/her surroundings that would insure his/her survival. Consequently, whether willingly or unwillingly, individuals organize themselves into states to obtain mutual protection and cooperation in the continuing struggle for survival and immortality. The state then becomes the institution or vehicle for the domination of the environment. To do so effectively, some form of societal order is necessary, hence the concept of the "Rule of Law".

In South Africa, the Afrikaners, a collection of individuals concerned with their immediate and ultimate survival, have acquired control of the state and have manipulated its institutions in their own interest. They ruthlessly pursue not wealth or even individual power, but the collective control of themselves. Guided by a belief that God had deemed that only a portion of humanity can be saved, and persuaded that through faith and their peculiar circumstances — white people on a black continent — that they are a chosen people, the Afrikaners conduct their life on the basis of a rigid discipline designed to thwart temptation. The failure of any Afrikaner to believe totally is seen as insufficient faith and hence imperfect grace.[6]

As a result of the unshakeable belief that their presence in South Africa represents God's will, and convinced that their lifestyle and beliefs will lead them to a destiny which they have been assured was theirs from eternity, the Afrikaners have structured the state not only to ensure their survival, but the survival of their beliefs as well.

The aims of a state, indeed its strength, should be to aid the individual in achieving his/her wants, whether they are immediate wants which contribute to his/her material welfare or long-term wants which provide for his/her spiritual well-being. Whether a state is to be considered successful depends, to a large extent, on its ability to assure the individual that it can provide for his/her wants despite conflicting or competing interests. To do so effectively, particularly if the state is of diverse composition, requires a certain degree of flexibility.

The mandate of a state is constituted on the implicit or explicit consent of the individual.[7] It is in turn a consent between state and individual that reflects a shared sense of morality. The stability, indeed the very duration of a state is founded on the belief of those governed that the state's concept of morality continues to be consonant with their own. The state, as the highest political authority, is imbued with the responsibility of determining, legislating and enforcing the prevailing sense of morality. From morality springs legality. Morality is concerned with questions of good and evil; legality addresses only the differences between right and wrong. Of the two, morality is the higher principle. In the context of the state, morality is the ongoing acceptance of the collective societal values — the consensus of the governed. Justice is the achievement of morality, the conformity of life to the realization of man's highest ideals and noblest aspirations.

Law is the attempt to approximate justice. Justice represents the nirvana of man's relationship with man, and as such, it therefore implies the true equality of man.

To the Afrikaner, questions of law, justice and morality can only have meaning within the grand design of God's will.[8] To apply human standards of justice and morality to God's will is to insult his judgment and question His omnipotence. To the Afrikaners, the state exists for but one purpose and that is the glorification of God.[9] That being the purpose of the state, the Afrikaners' duty is to increase the glory of God by organizing the state in accordance with God's commandments. The Afrikaners' profession of faith emanates from the teachings of John Calvin which demanded that true believers actively involve themselves in the affairs of state so as to bring those doomed by God under the laws of the Church.[10] Those who were not chosen, and who faced eternal damnation, should nonetheless be subject to the discipline of the church, not in order to attain salvation, but for the glory of God.[11] Indeed, while the Afrikaners's fatalist philosophy guarantees them salvation, it also demands that they prove their faith through positive acts of goodness.[12] In turn, faith dispenses religious doubts and insures certainty of grace. For the Afrikaners, the need to order society to conform to the wishes of God, and the compulsion to prove their faith through acts of positive goodness has resulted in the establishment of "homelands" and separate development for the vast majority of the people of South Africa. This goodness, this manifestation of faith has, however, meant that the Afrikaner has been psychologically burdened with a tremendous sense of physical insecurity. For while the Afrikaners are convinced of their ultimate destiny, their daily existence is an active, fearful struggle against wickedness as personified by the African. To the Afrikaners, the sensuous and emotional aspects of the Africans' culture and religion are wicked and sinful. The tempting, seductive appeal of the African's way of life, its joyful oneness with nature, has had to be resisted at all cost if the Afrikaners are to achieve their expected destiny.[13] It is clear to the Afrikaners that God has placed them amongst blacks — amongst temptation — to test their strength and will. Afloat in a sea of blackness, straining to be good while surrounded by evil, the Afrikaners existence is one of continuous fearfulness, alienation and anxiety. Rigid societal discipline and the repression of anything of an epicurean nature, has lead the Afrikaners to structure the state along lines that would help them overcome their acute sense of chaos and disorder.[15] Law, justice and morality are subjugated to the Afrikaners' belief that their survival is at stake and the debasement of those virtues is necessary if the Afrikaners are to dominate their environment, and have meaning as a people.

Justice and morality are utopian, chimerical virtues; Law is an exacting and tangible principle. A state may have justice and morality absent but the absence of law plunges the state into chaos and anarchy. The survival of the state is predicated on order, and order without law is a contradiction in terms. The individual is by nature violent. Living outside the concept of the state, the individual is only assured his/her survival through violence. Upon the acceptance of his/her need for the state, the individual also accepts the need of the state for order. The individual thus exchanges his/her personal violence for the security of the state. In consenting to the need for a state, and by submitting his/her individual morality to the cauldron of the collective morality, the individual tacitly accepts the authority of the state to issue laws which preserve and protect the order necessary for his/her and the state's survival.[16]

Laws are enacted first and foremost for the continuance of the state and the limitation of personal violence. The state, through the authority vested in it by its inhabitants, is recognized as the only entity permitted to use violence to enforce its will.[17] The moral fibre of the state will sustain the use of violence provided that its use is not arbitrary or capricious. Violence, which, if used by the individuals would be immoral, is acceptable for use by the state if such violence is used to enforce the Rule of Law. Indeed, the failure to support law with force results in contempt for the law and contempt for the state.[18] Yet, the strength of law, rests not in violence but in justice — in the attempts to conform law to the accepted morality. In serving the state and facilitating harmonious relations between individuals, the law acquires a degree of definiteness and authority that elevates law above detraction. In a state where law is respected, it serves both as a guardian of order and an advocate for change.[19]

Law reflects the morality of the state and conversely the morality of the state is reflected in its law. According to the law in South Africa, it is therefore immoral for people of different races to love and marry;[20] immoral for a black to travel freely and without restriction in the country of his birth;[21] immoral for people of colour to wish to participate in government;[22] immoral for a black to work in jobs classified as "skilled";[23] immoral for a black to be in certain areas more than 72 hours;[24] immoral for an urban black to have his wife and children with him as a matter of right;[25] immoral for a black to be "idle", "redundant" or "superfluous";[26] immoral for a black to live in an area designated as white;[27] immoral for blacks to have rights outside their specific ethnic homeland;[28] immoral for blacks and whites to participate in the same political party[29] and immoral for blacks to think of themselves as human beings blessed with certain inalienable human rights and dignities.[30] Indeed, given that the Afrikaners view themselves as God's chosen people, it is only natural that such a belief would negate the concept of the basic equality of man, resulting in the immorality of the South African legal system.

In a state in which the vast majority of the population has had no input in the collective morality which governs them, law soon ceases to be the binding force which assures the stability of the state. Laws are enacted to be respected. But laws that do not emit the collective values of the individuals who comprise the state cannot and will not be respected. If it is demonstrated that the law does not reflect the accepted will of the people, or if the individual has objections to the law as enacted, there ought to be, within the political process, avenues whereby the law can be modified or changed. In South Africa, this is not the case. Opposition to the law is routinely met with force, despite the obvious caveat that no state can afford to use force on every occasion.[30] Paradoxically, the more force used to impose the state's will, the weaker the state becomes.[32] The failure of a state to afford channels of political dissent or methods for seeking change guarantees the certainty that change, when it does come about, will be violent. Violence, the ultimate weapon of the individual against the state, is resorted to when all else fails and the individual becomes convinced that his/her aspirations can never be met within the framework in which he/she exists.

There is a basic, unresolvable tension at work in present-day South Africa. A tension between the desires of the Afrikaners for the maintenance of their way of life, and the desires of the vast majority of the people of South Africa for a way of life which speaks of their dignity as human beings. The promise of South Africa is enormous, but it is a promise that may never be realized. The failure of South Africa is the failure of the Afrikaner to structure a society that attempts to satisfy the aspirations of all its inhabitants. It is tragically, the failure to understand the dynamic nature of the state. Rather than build a state around the strengths of all its people, the Afrikaner has built a state based on fear of those strengths. Rather than seek the consensus of the many, it has imposed the will of the few.

South Africa is in a futile, but mad race against the inevitable violent change that has to occur. A change that is dictated by the failure of the South African government to enact laws reflective of morality instead of repression; decency instead of degradation; justice instead of inequality.

And yet, without morality, without decency, without justice, no state can long endure.

REFERENCE NOTES
1. Convention on Rights and Duties of States, 1933, 49 Statutes 3097, T.S. No. 881.
2. See generally: W.W. Kulski, *International Politics in a Revolutionary Age* (New York: J.B. Lippincott Company, 1968).
3. James Marshall, *Swords and Symbols* (New York: Funk and Wagnalls, 1939), p. 165.
4. James Feibelman, *The Reach of Politics* (New York: Horizon Press, 1969), p. 25.
5. *Ibid.*
6. For a more complete study of the religious evolution of the Afrikaner, see generally: W.A. de Klerk, *Puritans in Africa: A Story of Afrikanerdom* (London:

Rex Collins, 1975). Much of the analysis of the Afrikaner and his religion found in this article is derived from Mr. de Klerk's work.

7. See generally: Willmoore Kendall, *John Locke and the Doctrine of Majority Rule* (Urbanna, Ill.: University of Illinois Press, 1959) pp. 90:123.
8. W.A. de Klerk, op. cit.
9. *Ibid.*
10. See generally: Max Weber, *The Protestant Ethic and the Spirit of Capitalism* (New York: Charles Scribner's Sons, 1958) pp. 98-139.
11. *Ibid.*
12. *Ibid.*
13. See generally: Michael Walzer, "Puritanism as a Revolutionary Idealogy," in *History and Theory: Studies in the Philosophy of History, Vol. 111* ('S-Gravenhage, Netherlands: Monto 1961), pp. 75-90.
14. *Ibid.*
15. *Ibid.*
16. Feibleman, op. cit., p. 165.
17. Feibleman, op. cit., p. 165.
18. Marshall, op. cit., p. 59.
19. Marshall, op. cit., p. 66.
20. Prohibition of Mixed Marriages Act, No. 55 of 1949, §1.
21. Bantu (Abolition of Passes and Co-ordination of Documents) Act, No. 67 of 1952, §15.
22. Promotion of Bantu Self- Government Act, No. 46 of 1959.
23. Bantu Building Workers Act, No. 27 of 1951, §15.
24. Bantu (Urban Areas) Consolidation Act, No. 25 of 1945, as amended, § 10.
25. *Ibid.*
26. *Ibid,* §8.
27. Population Registration Act, No. 36 of 1966, §S12.
28. Promotion of Bantu Self-Government Act, No. 46 of 1959. See also Bantu Homelands Citizenship Act, No. 26 of 1970 and Bantu Homelands Constitution Act, No. 21 of 1971.
29. Prohibition of Political Interference Act, No. 51 of 1968.
30. See generally: Muriel Horrell, ed., *Laws Affecting Race Relations in South Africa (To the End of 1976)* (Johannesburg, South Africa: South Africa Institute of Race Relations, 1978).
31. Marshall, op. cit., p. 62.
32. Marshall, op. cit., p. 60.

PAULUS ZULU

Black Political Movements. Organization and Strategies — A Theoretical Overview

Introduction

There is general consensus among political scientists that conflict is central to political activity. Differences arise on the nature and causes of the conflict. Black politics in South Africa adds an additional dimension to the debate in that it is mainly the politics of exclusion. It is a fight by the majority of the population to gain entry into the arena of regulated conflict. However, because of the white resistance to blacks entering the arena, the latter have waged a fight for the transformation of the fundamentals of the socio-political system in the country.

Both classical democratic and Marxist theories believe that in a situation of gross inequalities the "actions of the dispossessed will serve to counter social inequities."[1] This implies that political movements which oppose the *status quo* arise out of the resolve, by the subordinates, to assert their claims to equality and human dignity. I shall come to this point in dealing with the various black political mobilization movements below.

The Situation in South Africa.

In terms of the distribution of power and authority within the social, political and economic spheres in the country, whites command total control over blacks. Politically, the creation of the Houses of Representatives (Coloureds), and Delegates (Indians) as well as the homeland administrations, has not diminished the power of the white parliament whose sovereignty resides in the fact that it alone defines the framework of power for all others. Economically, the ownership of the means of production in what the white parliament regards as "white South Africa" is in white hands. Within the social sphere, whites command total hegemony in the areas of education, art and material possessions. Further, the government as a representative of the ruling white power bloc, does not hesitate to use naked force should this *status quo* be seriously challenged.

The State's Mechanisms of Control
Given the glaring inequalities mentioned above, one might enquire why the disadvantaged have tolerated this relationship for so long. Conventional political theory assumes that "... victims of injustice in an 'open system' are free to take action upon their concerns ..."[2]. The arguments in this paper are:
  i) that the South African system is not open;
  ii) that since it is not open, victims of injustice are not free to take action upon their concerns; and
  iii) because they are not free to take actions upon their concerns this has created strains among and within their specific mechanisms of resistance to both domination and exploitation.

This leads us to an examination of the state's mechanism of control so as to maintain its domination and exploitative roles, since what is taken either as compliance with or resistance to domination is premised on these mechanisms.

The State's Mobilization of Bias
In this context the state is used to include not only the legislative and administrative regime, but also those groups that participate in the definition of the rules upon which governance functions.

In political parlance this refers to the "ruling elite" i.e.: those who have the opportunity to constitute the legislative and administrative regime in the country. The South African state mobilizes bias in two ways:
  i) by excluding from the agenda, or manipulating the issues which pertain to the powerless i.e.: the black population; and,
  ii) by influencing, shaping or even determining the way in which the subordinate group reacts to their inferior status. This entails the employment of the ideological state apparatus which may even include the use of blatant force.

The formation of black political mobilization and worker movements is a response to the state's mobilization of bias. I shall proceed to analyze these movements within this framework. Before going into detail, I wish to point out that domination and exploitation have polarized South African society, and that there are two forces which control the poles. The Nationalist Party defines the control pole, whilst the African National Congress defines the resistance pole. Black organizations, in particular, are judged by their distance from either pole, and this judgement is more in terms of their fundamental philosophies than in terms of strategy.

Black Political Organizations and Resistance to Domination

In practice, black political organizations mobilize on the ticket of resistance to domination. Differences exist with regard to their definition of the social and political situations, and this leads to differences in strategies. To infer that they all share a common goal and only differ on political strategies, is perhaps to oversimplify the issue. In the context of the mobilization of bias, these differences are fundamental; hence the state accords them different treatments. This is more evident in the present turmoil caused by the crises in townships' administration as well as in education.

Co-optation and Black Political Organizations

Co-optation is a subtle and manipulative strategy that the state employs in order to create social and political stability. Erwin and Webster define co-optation as " ... a process whereby the leadership of a conflict group is absorbed into the dominant group's institutions in such a way that no shift in the balance of power takes place. The opposition conflict group is given a platform without an independent power base, and so effective opposition is stifled without having to alter the distribution of power..."[3]. The foregoing definition limits co-optation to the machinations by the super-ordinate or ruling group, and leaves the subordinate or conflict group without any independent source of power.

In the analysis of black political organizations operating within the state's framework, the definition of co-optation will be extended. It will be argued that it does not only envisage a unilateral shift in the power positions, but that it is a dialectical process where the state as well as the co-opted elites make shifts in order to accommodate each other even though from positions of unequal power.

In supporting the institutions which prop up the leadership of the conflict group, the dominant group makes shifts which may eventually undermine its position. It is this shift which is perceived as gain by the beneficiaries from within the subordinate group, and this acts as the sustaining cord in this uneven dialectical process since the dominant group decides upon the framework of operation.

Co-optation is therefore more functional than disfunctional to domination since

i) domination is unevenly felt by the subordinate groups as the state accords favours to the co-opted elites. This drives a wedge between the various black groupings; consequently they engage in various forms of in-fighting. In this context, one would therefore argue that the apparent black on black violence which has dominated the political scene over the last two years is fundamentally a manifestation of black anger against the state.

ii) total transformations seldom, if ever, come from above, hence the dominant group can never define a framework that has the capacity to challenge the basic relations of power since that would be suicidal. To operate within the state's defined framework is thus to accept failure by definition.

However, the above arguments do not necessarily entail a summary dismissal of organizations which operate within the state's defined framework. Politics is a game about power, and to the extent that power both determines and influences the lives of millions of individuals, one cannot ignore the effects of the gains made in the tactical shifts in the process of co-optation. Hence, co-optation into the Tricameral parliament has given power to the various coloured and Indian ministries to distribute resources albeit on a limited scale. They are responsible for the portfolios of education, housing, health, etc. within their own affairs and employ massive bureaucracies. Similarly, homeland administrations fare equally well within their geo-political territories. Admittedly, this is far from meeting the aspirations of the people, and judging by the current turmoil in the country the demise of co-optation is at hand. However, there is no denial that the co-opted structures have enhanced their standing in some quarters especially among some sections of the aspirant petty bourgeoisie; some professional and managerial elites whose positions depend upon the existence of such structures, or among the masses in need of social services such as pensioners and workers caught up in the vicious circle of poverty and the absence of shelter.

However, co-opted or "within establishment" organizations have failed to usher in the expected stability in the black communities for numerous reasons:

i) Black people, especially the youth and the more educated blacks, perceive them as the brain child of white power and intrigue. What bedevils their negative image is the apparent favouritism towards these organizations and their leadership by the state and other control institutions such as employers and the press, including the liberal press. Official and editorial references to individuals or organizations falling within the co-operation tradition as "moderates" imply that others are extremists. This has alienated many, especially the intellectual elements, from these organizations, since they perceive them as moving closer to the Afrikaner Nationalist control pole and further from the resistance pole as defined by the African National Congress.

ii) On numerous occasions the leadership from these organizations has come out in opposition to the strategies of liberation as defined by the mass of the subordinate people. Such strategies include consumer boycotts, disinvestment, work stayaways and school boycotts. What has aggravated the internal conflicts is not that the leadership from within the establishment organizations has condemned such strategies, but that it has mobilized the same organizations to physically combat the mass of protesters, students and workers alike. In this regard these organizations have aligned themselves more with the state than with the people.

iii) Structurally, organizations which function within the establishment are riddled with contradictions. For instance, the homeland administrations as well as the Houses of Delegates and Representatives control departments such as education etc, (even though absolute control rests with the white parliament). School boycotts are thus, in essence, boycotts against these bodies. It would, therefore, be impossible for them to bring to a halt an apartheid education in practice without bringing themselves to a halt. Hence they perceive the revolt against authority as a revolt against themselves. It is, therefore, logical that these bodies and organizations have been active in the formation of vigilantes and have been seen to combat black resistance in the townships as well as in rural areas. However, this has had serious implications.

Admittedly, black people abhor the destruction of property and the loss of lives, but to be seen to be siding with the army and the police in fighting protestors against what is regarded nationally and internationally as an unjust system, shifts the debate away from the immediate scene of action into the ideological terrain. The consequences are that the victims of state power have perceived intra-establishment organizations and bodies as fulfilling the "dirty-work" of Afrikaner Nationalism.

Extra-Establishment Politics and Resistance to Domination

Up to now this paper has dealt with organizations and bodies which act with the government's blessing. The argument has been that even though some of them might be apparently working against government policy, in the final analysis, they are functional to the furtherance of that policy, since structurally it is very difficult, if not impossible, to perform contrary to the policy that nurtures them. The second part of this paper is an attempt at an analysis of those organizations which function outside of the state's created machinery.

Tom Lodge takes 1976 as a watershed in black politics and refers to the subsequent period as "... a political renaissance in the townships of South Africa"[4]. He attributes this renaissance to the development of "... a popular political culture of a highly organized variety" and declares that, "today in 1985, every sizeable urban settlement accommodates a civic organization, a student and scholar association and usually a trade union as well." According to Lodge these organizations reflect the particular concerns of their respective constituencies and "collectively they constitute a radical opposition to the *status quo.*"

Basic Philosophical Issues

All extra-establishment organizations share a common social definition of South African society which they perceive in terms of either racial domination or capitalist exploitation or both. Also, extra-establishment organizations to a large extent share a common policy of resistance to domination and exploitation. According to these organizations, social relations in South Africa are predicated, in the first instance, on racial domination which ultimately determines the position of blacks in the economic order. Official reforms are perceived by these groupings as manipulative and not designed to effect the basic changes in the nature of South African society; hence the principle of non-cooperation with officially sponsored political and administrative institutions at every level.

Strategies of Resistance to Domination and Exploitation

Extra-establishment organizations are central in most actions of resistance to white domination and exploitation. In the words of Lodge "... not because of any intentional strategic master-plan"[6] of the leadership but simply because the rationale for their existencce is, in the first instance, derived from the oppressive conditions confronting black society in the schools, the townships, and at work.

Until recently, extra-establishment organizations like the National Forum and the United Democratic Front have been criticized for being reactive and lacking a programme of action. However, recent developments, the protracted unrest in the townships, the consumer boycott instituted by civic organizations and trade unions, as well as the crisis in education, have had serious implications in the country's politics and economy. The recent shuffling and re-arrangement of chairs by the government is a response to the politics of confrontation rather than cooperation. The legitimacy crisis in local government has left only three out of 34 local authorities still operating in 1985, despite the fact the the government had envisaged that by the end of 1984, 104 would be fully operative.[7]

Problems

Extra-establishment organizations have faced mounting obstacles both from the state, as well as from organizations and bodies which function from within the establishment. The state has used the power at its disposal to cripple and maim the leadership of these organizations through detentions, bannings and adverse propaganda in the news media. In addition, the formation of vigilante groups, mostly by bodies which function within the establishment, has resulted in serious clashes involving the destruction of property and loss of lives. What has been disturbing is the allegations from the various communities that where vigilante groups have attacked protesting bands of blacks, or destroyed the property of individuals allegedly belonging to extra-establishment organizations, the police or the army have stood by and watched without taking any action. On the contrary, where protesters have attacked incumbents within government institutions or their property, the police and the army have retaliated with full force. In numerous instances, the police and soldiers have guarded these officials and their property for long and varying periods of time.

In-Fighting Within Extra-Establishment Groupings

During the latter half of 1985, the press and the electronic media reported numerous incidents of in-fighting among extra-establishment groupings particularly the United Democratic Front and the National Forum, especially the Azanian People's Organization.

A look at the basic philosophies of these two organizations reveals the following:

i) Because of its heterogeneous formation and a heterodox leadership the United Democratic Front adopts a flexible political philosophy and has used the Freedom Charter as the basis of its ideological development. On the other hand, the National Forum adheres to an orthodox black consciousness philosophy and dismisses the role of whites as irrelevant in the struggle for black liberation.

ii) While the United Democratic Front believes in gradualist socialism the National Forum's programme calls for "The establishment of a democratic anti-racist, worker republic in Azania."[8]

iii) A look at these principles shows that while there are differences, these are not irreconcilable, especially since both movements accept the unity of South Africa as one country for all who live in it.

Reasons for the outbreak of violence between the two organizations must therefore be sought elsewhere.

i) Organizational structure: The United Democratic Front, in particular, is a heterogeneous organization comprising some 600 affiliates ranging from students, community organizations, professional associations to trade unions. Such a structure is riddled with problems of control, discipline and accountability.

ii) There have been allegations from some quarters that there may be plants within both organizations and that the former have exacerbated the differences between the two, in an attempt to discredit both organizations and in the process fragment black resistance as crystallized in the current unrest in the townships.

iii) The state has constantly harassed, detained and immobilized the leadership of both organizations. This has had detrimental implications for both the strategy and day to day operations of both organizations. It is, therefore, not far-fetched to infer that it is the fringe elements, rather than the leadership, who have been responsible for the periodic outbursts of violence which have claimed some lives.

iv) The structural violence on the part of the state has triggered a counter reaction to respond with violence. However, this has changed direction, and instead some elements from within the organizations have chosen their relatively powerless counterparts as the targets of their anger and frustration.

Black Political Movements and the Future

While blacks have a history of resistance to both domination and exploitation, the eighties have ushered in an unprecedented epoch. Lodge claims "what distinguishes present day black 'resistance politics' from its forebears is that it is a politics of power."[9] One does not have to go too far to seek for explanations:

   i) The level of mass organization and conscientization is much higher than at any previous time. The rapid development of a powerful worker constituency has broadened the terrain of the "struggle" from the communities to the factory floor. The current political language in the townships has moved from "domination" to "oppression and exploitation".

   ii) The emergence of a "progressive" union movement has not only consolidated black power but has also brought with it immediately realizable gains. This has had positive psychological implication as blacks have moved away from quiescence to challenge. Also, blacks have learnt to adopt varying strategies such as employing consumer and worker power. This has made them less vulnerable to the state's power.

   iii) The re-emergence of the African National Congress on the political scene has not only boosted black morale internally, it has resurfaced the international nature of the conflict in South Africa. Further, white pressure groups including big capital, have had a rethink on the role of the ANC in South African politics.

Conclusion

In conclusion, two points need to be stated unequivocally:

   1. The present crisis in the country is ample demonstation of the bankruptcy of the politics of co-optation and reform from above. The proclamation of the state of emergency in July 1985 was followed by an escalation of violence in Natal and later the Western Cape; both had been relatively quiet till then. Admittedly, the detention of the leadership in the civic and student extra-establishment organizations has had a crippling effect, but as Lodge states "the movement may become less easy to identify and anticipate as its more violent fringes assume a central role", and "by the time the authorities are ready to negotiate it may be difficult to find anyone to negotiate with."[10]

   2. It is the extra-establishment and not the within-establishment organizations that have extracted meaningful concessions which have amounted to reforms in the country. For instance, almost all reforms in education have emanated from Soweto '76 and the subsequent students' protests; reforms in the labour movement were a sequel to the 1973 strikes and finally, the granting of the 99 year lease and the recent announcement of freehold rights for "urban" Africans are in response to pressure exerted by extra-establishment civic organizations in the townships.

3. Finally, extra-establishment organizations such as the National Forum, the United Democratic Front, Progressive Unions and the New Unity Movement will always have an advantage over any structures that emerge from the state's co-optive programme. They will always be the peoples' organizations and as such respond to the peoples' and not the state's needs. Their growth might perhaps vindicate both classical democratic and Marxist theories, that "the action of the dispossessed will serve to counter social inequities".

REFERENCE NOTES
1.   Gaventa, J. *Power and Powerlessness. Quiescence and Rebellion in an Apala-chian Valley,* Clarendon Press, Oxford, 1980.
2.   Gaventa, J. *ibid.,* p V
3.   Erwin, A. and Webster, E. "Ideology and Capitalism in South Africa" in Schlemmer, L and Webster, E. *Change, Reform and Economic Growth in South Africa,* Ravan Press, Johannesburg, 1978
4.   Lodge, T. "Contemporary Black South African Organizations", paper presented at the Labour Horizons Conference — Andrew Lewis Associates, 1985, p 1.
5.   Lodge, T. *ibid.*
6.   Lodge, T. *ibid.,* p 17
7.   Gelb, S., Lewis, J., Swilling, M. and Wester, E. *Working Class Politics and National Liberation in South Africa. Old Tactics, New Forces,* Forthcoming, 1986.
8.   Lodge, T. *op.cit.,* p 18.
9.   Lodge, T. *op.cit.,* p 20.
10. Lodge, T. *op.cit.,* p 23.

ESSY LETSOALO

The Changing Role of Women in Employment

Introduction

Women have increasingly become the subject of debate in various circles, ranging from feminists to professional and international organizations. This subject is not only debated at various levels, but it is also debated for reasons that vary from concern with the domination and exploitation by the other sex to concern with the neglect of this important human resource for economic social and political advancement. Both these factors revolve around attitudes towards women in paid and unpaid employment. We deliberately focus upon black women here, not because we live in apartheid South Africa, but because black women differ significantly from women of other races in matters of employment. In còuntry after country women have gained the right to vote, to enter all forms of paid employment and to seek educational qualifications on equal terms with men — black women still have to fight for these rights.

Sexual Division of Labour

In the traditional African society there was a marked distinction in the roles of sexes. Men performed tasks such as hunting, livestock rearing and ploughing. Women's responsibilities included weeding, harvesting and threshing. In addition to their contribution to the production of food, women were responsible for the bulk of the so-called domestic work, that is food preparation, wood and water gathering, and child rearing. This points out the obvious disproportionate division of labour in the traditional African society. Women performing 60-80 percent of the agricultural labour

(United Nations, 1972) and domestic work means that their predominant role in the satisfaction of basic human needs and services antedates recorded history. Long before the "basic needs" concept became fashionable in the literature on development, African women were already engaged in what is now debated by social scientists planners and governments: They produced food; provided water and clean clothing; taught children language, healthy habits and to perform certain tasks; and they even participated in the decision making: The familiar tendency of men to 'sleep over' any matter before taking decisions.

International Division of Labour

The above-mentioned important role of women in the productive rural labour force was (unfortunately) changed by circumstances of an international nature. Whereas European women became increasingly engaged in paid employment because of the shortage of men during and in the immediate post World War II years, African women changed their productive role because of colonization and the establishment of industrial capitalism. With colonization came the reduction of land for rural pursuits, leading to the majority of families being without this source of employment and survival. With industrialization comes forced employment of African men in mines and industries, thus turning many women into household heads (Essy Letsoalo, 1982 and Bellina Leseme, 1983) who must find ways of supplementing their husbands' migratory remittances for their families to survive; and, who must take decisions independent of men. Thus we find former farmers now engaged in the informal sector, petty commodity production or casual work.

The modern black woman in South Africa is found in two settings. The one group is found in the rural tribal enclaves, where they are confined by the apartheid legislation. Nothing could be more of a limitation on women's rights than this denial of the right of black women to be with their legal husbands. The other group is found in the so-called black urban areas, in the backyards of their white madams and even in hostels/compounds. Although the roles of these two groups of women in employment differ, they have one thing in common. They suffer triple oppression, as blacks, females, working class or all three. Women in the tribal enclaves, like women in peripheral capitalist societies throughout the Third World countries, lag far behind men in access to the benefits of development. These women suffer from illiteracy. Research by Bellina Leseme in the Northern Transvaal shows that only five percent of the women are literate, having secondary education. The myth that women are essentially domestic workers, whose primary responsibility should be in the home, has contributed to the neglect of education for women. In addition, black women's access to education has been hampered by the apartheid policy of racial discrimination. As a result of lack of education, the modern rural woman has to work very hard in the fields and yet watch her kids die of malnutrition. The lack of basic employment opportunities forces her to spend a whole day working for as little as R3 in the government rural works programmes, on white farms or in apartheid-directed Bantustan industries. The modern urban black woman is no less a victim of apartheid. After all, these women find themselves in urban areas because their villages were impoverished by white settlement in South Africa and all its consequences. These are the women whose changing role in employment has been generated by the systems of sexual and racial domination. Research by Veronica Martin and Chris Rogerson (1984) shows that the geography of women's work in South Africa is a reflection of the history of black proletarianization. Black women are, for example, late-comers in the manufacturing sector, being absent from the industrial workforce until the 1960's. The same research shows the over-representation of black women in food and textile industries, the so-called 'female ghettos' where women are generally the vast majority of employees.

Black women also dominate the urban informal sector. Initially, this was their only opportunity to make a living because they had less of a chance in the regularized wage employment sector. Within the informal sector, also, the role of women has changed over time as demonstrated by the research by Keith Beavon and Chris Rogerson (1984). This changing role has been the result of the advancement of men to 'better' jobs. The only exception to this rule is the domination of women in the informal sale of liquor, from the days of home-brew to the present prestige shebeen, and their monopoly in prostitution.

Research by Jacklyn Cock (1980) shows that the majority of urban women are employed as maids/domestic workers. Most of these women work for almost 12 hours a day, seven days a week. Their conditions of employment are terrible — extremely low wages and no security. Separated from their families, these women take care of their madams' children, while theirs are left in the care of relatives or other children. They see their own children only once or twice a year.

Last, but not least, we have the black women intellectuals. The small proportion of these women in the labour force is the result of the neglect of womanpower in development. Most of them are found in professions such as teaching and nursing, the so-called "female" areas. Women are least represented in politics, highly technical and managerial positions. The irrelevant education-system of South Africa is to blame for the limited impact of this group of women in employment. They are simply not prepared for the poor black community that they serve.

Attitudes towards Women in Employment

Having established that the role of women in employment has changed remarkably during the last fifty years, it is important to analyze those attitudes that have influenced their role. It is common among feminists and anti-sexists to argue that although women spend all their time and energy in employment, their contribution is negligent. This is to a large extent true for the modern woman. In the traditional African society the socio-economic role of women has never been undervalued. Indeed, attitudes towards women reflected respect for family roles. Woman's capacity for child bearing was considered the production of new human capital, no less important than their rural production work. It is, therefore, very much according to traditional values that in the post-independence era, African countries have women cabinet ministers. Non-African states are far behind in this respect.

The negative attitudes that affect women in employment today are the result of the neglected fact that the role of the black woman has often been quite different from that in the West — the male "breadwinner" concept and the woman's "place in the kitchen". It is towards the prevailing negative attitudes of men as employers and men as husbands that attention now turns. It has already been pointed out that women have traditionally constituted an important portion of the productive rural labour force. Yet, their inclusion in agricultural training programmes has been very limited. The attitude of governments and development agents is that female agricultural producers are ignorant, passive and tradition-bound. No wonder almost all rural development projects are failures (Uma Lele, 1975).

Women are generally considered to be cheap sources of labour. Consequently they are employed in situations where they are easily exploited through low wages, long working hours and miserable work environments. Even when they occupy high positions, "man-made" laws still see to it that there is sexual discrimination in remuneration — to the disadvantage of women, who earn as little as two-thirds of a man's salary for equal work. This attitude cannot be divorced from the view of women's vocation as wives and mothers. This attitude is particularly abhorrent when one considers that women, because of their demanding family commitments, mostly enter wage employment out of economic necessity. Furthermore, an unemployed woman is considered to have made this choice, or not to bother with employment. In contrast her male counterpart is pitied, gets sympathy and even evokes guilt feelings.

The legal status of black women as minors means that their relationship with men is one of subordinates towards superiors i.e. it is like the relationship between those who own capital and means of production and those who own nothing but their labour power. The women are the pillars of capitalist exploitation. They are the 'silent majority', just like the undeveloped countries against the industrial countries. It is not true that the women are not working. They are unpaid, but must work harder than the employed in order to survive.

Women's maternal duties are used to discriminate against them. Women tend to be considered temporary employees, who are a burden in employment because they are less willing to be transferred; or have less time for part-time studies or overtime. Of particular importance, however, is that women are refused employment because they may marry or fall pregnant.

The sexual exploitation of women by their male employers has a negative effect on women in employment. Some employers expect women to play mothers and wives at work. If a woman does not do that in addition to her regular duties, she is considered uncooperative and therefore unpromotable. Some men prefer their women to be unemployed. According to them, women belong at home or worse still, they assert that women cannot reason as well as men. The women, who are denied womankind by mankind in this fashion, form the unhappiest group of adults.

Feminism : The Black Version

The above attitudes of men towards women in employment indicate that virtues such as democracy, human rights, equality, and freedom are non-issues for women. For them the opposite is the norm — low wages, temporary employment, long working hours, monotonous work, unorganized labour, lack of qualifications, no advancement and no security. Indeed, the more racist a country, the more sexist the attitudes. Attention now turns to the attitude of women themselves to their ways of adapting in the so-called male spheres and their reaction towards negative, sexist attitudes.

Opinions differ as to why, despite their poverty, women are not advanced in employment. There are women, evidently those conservatives who have made it into the 'male' world, who think that women's inferiority complex and their failure to assert themselves sufficiently on serious issues place them at a disadvantage in employment. The second opinion, influenced by both political economy and feminism, asserts that the systematic exclusion of women politically, socially and professionally is an integral part of national and international structures of economic relationships in which the weak and powerless are marginalized (Louise Fortmann, 1979).

Whereas feminism in the West deals with the problems of male/female equity, it is argued here that black women in South Africa are confronted by problems of a different nature. Quintessentially, their attitudes towards women's role in employment are different. For instance, it is obvious that the liberation of rural women and their assumption of a fuller role in national development require substantive changes in both national and international economic relationships. The attitude of black women towards employment is certainly not that of inferiority. In the words of Marva Styles, these women "have asserted themselves as surviving force throughout history" *(Rand Daily Mail 3/7/84)*. Ellen Kuzwayo's analysis of these women as "downtrodden but determined" cannot be improved upon. *(The Star 23/7/84)*.

Black women do not work or struggle on because they want to be independent of men. They do so because they are determined to bridge the gap in the provision of basic human needs and services. The proliferation of women's associations, clubs and selfhelp groups testifies to this. The women are growing vegetables, erecting and running children's day-care centres, conscientizing communities — one can go on and on. Black women's commitment to community work is especially remarkable in the face of harassment in terms of apartheid legislation.

Conclusion
The changing role of women in employment has been referred to as a social revolution by Margaret de Vries (1971). However, the struggle is not yet over. It is true that there have been reforms; that the advantages of using womanpower more fully are becoming recognized by developing countries; and that laws have been passed to remove official sexual discrimination relating to labour and income. But, despite all these, abuses continue, showing that laws cannot change attitudes. Legal rights are a necessary step, but they are meaningless, unless the structures of discrimination and oppression are changed. If the concept of modernization has ever failed mankind (womankind too), then it is in the failure of negative attitudes towards women in employment to die out with the passing of the older generation. Women's issues remain matters to which lip-service is paid during election campaigns with no effort

to change these structures which tend to perpetuate negative attitudes. I wish to echo the words of the Zimbabwean Minister of Community Development and Women's Affairs. She said, "It must always be remembered that the attainment of equality for women is the task of society as a whole. It can only be achieved through a joint struggle by all social forces, as part of the general struggle for a society in which men, women and children can live in equality, freedom and prosperity. Outdated prejudices regarding the role of women must be elliminated." *(The Star 10/03/86)*. This is a prerequisite for South African women's full participation in employment.

BIBLIOGRAPHY

Beavon, K.S.O. and C.M. Rogerson: "The Changing Role of Women in the Urban Informal Sector of Johannesburg," S.A., Paper presented at the Working Group on Urbanization in Developing Countries, I.G.U. 1984. Lille.

Cock, J.: *Maids and Madams: A Study in the Politics of Exploitation,* Ravan 1980, Johannesburg.

de Vries, M.G. 1971: Women, Jobs and Development, *Finance and Development,* page 2 - 9.

Fortman, L.: Women and Tanzania agricultural Development, in Kim, K.S. et al, *Papers on the Political Economy of Tanzania,* Heinemann Educational Books Ltd, 1979 page 278 - 287.

United Nations: Women: The Neglected Human Resources for African Development, *Canadian Journal of African Studies,* 6(2), 1972.

Lele, U.: *The Design of Rural Development: Lessons from Africa,* World Bank, 1975, London.

Letsoalo, E.M.: "Survival Strategies in Rural Lebowa: A Study in the Geography of Poverty," M.A. dissertation, University of the Witwatersrand, 1982, Johannesburg.

Leseme, B.M.: "The Role of Women in Rural Development in Lebowa," M.A. dissertation, University of the North, 1983, Turfloop.

Martin, V.M. and C.M. Rogerson: "Women and Industrial Change: The South African Experience," *The South African Geographical Journal,* 66 (1), 1984, page 32 -46.

Rand Daily Mail, Johannesburg.

The Star, Johannesburg.

JOHN LAMOLA

Debate on Violence

The word violence is a loaded term. Violence itself is multi-dimensional in its manifestation. We can trace it through a wide spectrum which may range from the coercive and aggressive capitalistic commercial advertising practice, to corporal punishment, capital punishment, denigrating and dehumanizing living conditions, repression and of course the use of military force in political revolutions and international conflicts.

In an effort to delineate and categorize this phenomenon for sound academic tackling, Archbishop Don Helder Camara offered a typology of violence which identifies violence as three interrelated spiraling categories. The primary one being structural violence, which he calls stage one violence; revolutionary violence is the second stage, and institutionalized violence of the repression machinery of the ruling forces as corollary from the latter as being the third and final stage (op cit : 1971). Another analysis will demonstrate that the institutionalized violence of state repression is not the "final stage" as such, because it is customary of oppressive regimes to use the socio-economic factors as means of suppressing an oppressed mass. An example is a denial of full educational opportunities with the fear that the oppressed will intellectually and technologically rise to the level of their masters, and thus threaten their power position. The dehumanization of the underdog well serves the interests of the ruling classes. To use Camara's model then we note that the spiral is cyclic. P.H. Ballard adds to this typology criminal violence, that is violence committed in common crime. This violence may also be committed by the state. A clear

example is the state's violation of these conventions of international law (op cit : 1971). All these manifestations of violence
intermesh so well that a simple categorization is but artificial.
What we need to note from the foregoing explication is that violence is a real fact of our life. We are always living in real or potential conditions of violence. Vicencio even asserts that since
violence is an inherent part of all human relationships it is a contemporary ethical problem which is central to all ethical problems
(Ibid : 1980:1).

Notwithstanding the foregoing elaborate introduction, however,
the debate we are to assess is specifically the exchanging of views
by Christians across the world, and particularly in South Africa, on
the specified issue of the use of violence as a means of effecting a
change of an unjust socio-political order within a nation-state. Of
paramount importance to note is the fact that the issue of violence
and non-violence can never and should never be evaluated out of
context. Therefore, our context will be the debate as it ensues
within the ecumenical movement, and as it manifests itself in the
South African churches, particularly as since sparked by the foundation of the Special Fund of the Programme to Combat Racism
(PCR) of the World Council of Churches (WCC) in 1971.

In order to appreciate and to assess the debate factually within
the South African context, we are demanded to make a reflective
run-down of the South African church history. This is going to
take us through the 1960's — the period of confession against the
apartheid system, the tumultous years of the aftermath of the announcement of the PCR grants, the 1974 Conscientious Objection
Debate and the response of the church to the latent and current
black revolt, militarization of South African (SA) society and racial
polarization. Theologically speaking, the church in SA has at present entered a new era. This era was ushered in in September 1985
by the production of the Kairos Document — a theological response to the political Crisis in South Africa. The debate on violence and non-violence has been rekindled and is raging in
proportions reminiscent of the early 1970's when the news of the
PCR grants to the African National Congress of South Africa
(ANC) and Pan Africanist Congress of Azania (PAC) reached
South Africa.

Therefore in assessing the debate on violence and non-violence it
needs to be noted that we are actually attempting to assess a process which is still in motion. It is perhaps too early, contextually
speaking, to give a valid assessment of the debate in South Africa,
hence this work is cautious of being conclusive and closes with a

section on proposals for conducting the continuing debate.

An attempt is made to give a theological assessment from an ecumenical perspective. A general background is given, sketching the scenario of the causes and dynamics of the debate. Representative viewpoints on the debate, that is, contending options are then introduced and evaluated. In presenting these participant views on the debate it needs to be noted that they have been identified strictly on the basis of their theological character. There may be many other options on the violence/non-violence dilemma, but we are supremely interested on those that have been formulated by theological reasoning. Also on the thorny question of the objectivity of the presentation, we have provided as many theological facts as possible by exponents of a particular option as available to us according to their common use in general debates and discussions. An appraisal of the conduct of the debate together with theological ethical proposals has also appeared to be necessary.

Throughout the presentation of the debate an attempt has been made to relate all the points to the South African struggle. But still, the crucial SA situation has demanded a separate section. In the process of the analysis and assessment of the debate, a critical analysis of the theological themes which are raised during the debate, is also made.

Background to the Debate

(i) *From Confession to Praxis*

The violence/non-violence debate represents a matured and latter phase of the history of the church's struggle of theologically agonizing about the often ungodly economic and political structures of our world. It is a discussion which follows an analysis and perhaps a consensus that Christians are under a religious obligation to be actively involved in the human struggles of changing unjust political structures. The point of contention arises when we come to the "how" aspect of effecting this change.

Throughout the debate is it presumed that all the participants or participant-views are reacting from their conclusion that human oppression, repression, poverty and institutionalized racism stand to be combatted. The debate under assessment then, is a restricted one between Christians who are *convicted* on their active participation in the struggle against social, economic, political and legal injustice. An important fact which is raised or which precipitated the debate is Christian theology's understanding of the relationship between theory and ecclesiastic praxis, or rather between rhetoric and action. What ignited the debate to its present proportions was the WCC's decision to institute a programme to combat racism thus putting meat to the theological confessions against racism that the councils of the ecumenical movements have been formulating since its first assembly at Amsterdam in 1948. No member-church openly objected to the founding of the Programme to Combat Racism (PCR), since as per tradition, the PCR has been expected to be a mere forum to stimulate condemnation of racism through conferences and publications. The shock came when the PCR, within months of its foundation, established a Special Fund and issued grants to the liberation movements that have resorted to the armed struggle. This was in September 1970. By this time a majority of the constituent members of the South African Council of Churches (SACC) were direct member-churches of the WCC.

The church was challenged to review its theological understanding of the implications of the variation between theory and praxis, to re-evaluate its commitment to the liberation of the oppressed, and to morally and theologically investigate the methods used in the struggle for justice and peace.

A majority of Christians viewed the PCR grants as a logical consequence of the rejection of the racialism they have been professing. Others viewed it as a compromise of the Gospel. Many of these, ironically mainly SA churches, opted for an easy and traditional escape by advancing more theological arguments for debate, and used these as a justification for their refusal to support the PCR theology.

One important example of such new theological "controversies" brought up by the violence/non-violence debate is the topic of the Kingdom of God.

(ii) *The Kingdom of God*
The question of whether the kingdom or its standards can be ushered by human efforts became a theme of a number of WCC conferences such as the Melbourne Mission Conference in 1980 where the issue of participation in revolutionary struggles cropped up.

A common theological motivation of Christian involvement in reforming the evil structures of the world is the fact that Christians have an eschatological world-view. The present world is always viewed under the evaluating vision of the coming of the Kingdom of God which has been revealed in the apocalyptic writings of scripture as being the ushering in by God of universal conditions of peace, righteousness, justice, prosperity and abundance.

Apart from the scholarly debate on the existing presence or the futurity of the Kingdom (Deist, Du Plessis : 1981), the hottest issue is the role of the church in effecting the standards of this kingdom over against the present unrighteous world conditions. There are three views in this regard. The first holds that God Himself, unaided by any party, will bring about His kingdom. The second holds that God, through the agency of the church, His body, will and actually is already bringing about this kingdom. The church, as the first fruits of this coming era, is to uphold the signs of the Kingdom of God.

The third view extends the thesis of the latter view. It holds that not only the church will be and is being used by God in setting up the signs of the Kingdom. God also operates outside the church (extra ecclesium salum bonum!). Any institution which is struggling against the dehumanizing present world-conditions, working for peace and justice, is an instrument in God's hand at the service of the building of His kingdom. It therefore behoves the church to identify with such agencies and to seek a working relationship with them. This theological view sees the revolutionary organizations as expressions or people's quest for liberation and justice, as instruments of God's kingdom. In bringing about the signs of this kingdom the ultimate possible means of violent revolution may be used, just as God Himself will usher the ultimate Kingdom of Peace, through the violence of the Armegeddon and eternal condemnation of the enemy — the Devil — into a bottomless pit and the unrepentent to the lake burning with fire and brimstone.

The elaboration of the first mentioned view above, that is the view that the Kingdom of God will be ushered in by God Himself and that the Christians must diligently await this dawning of the kingdom by observing holy lifestyles and by not contaminating themselves with the affairs of this world, since this world may pass away at any moment, stands as a direct negation of the last mentioned view. Deist and Du Plessis argue that "growth of this kingdom must and can be left in God's hands" (ibid :1981:137).

Theological Views on Violence and Non Violence
Let us now proceed to introduce the participant-views in this violence/non-violence debate.

The three views introduced here are the ones that have appeared most dominant throughout the debate as it manifests itself within church-theological circles.

(3.1) *Pacifism (Non-violent Activism)*
Deriving from an absolute adherence to the New Testament (NT) ethic, it is maintained that non-violent political action is the only possibility consistent with obedience to Jesus Christ. It is argued that Jesus of Nazareth did not use violence in his ministry to the

poor and oppressed of His time, and actually violence in its varied manifestations is part of the evils that He came to overcome.

Coming to practicalities, exponents of ths view agree that this is not an easy option. It requires inner strength and discipline, and will often be unsuccessful. They can theologically explain why the obsession with quick success which is normally related to violence should not be used to play down the option of non-violence. Non-violent resistance is a witness to the transcendent power of God in Jesus Christ, a way of faith. The adherents of this view regard themselves as being engaged in some prophetic ministry of calling other Christians to the bygone standard of the Early Church, which they believe was pacifist, and which they maintain was betrayed during the Constantine Era.

In joint effort with other non-Christian (or non-religious pacifists) elaborate examples and models of non-violent action have been discovered and created. Gene Sharp, an American political scientist catalogues no less than one hundred and ninety eight (198) such methods (Hope & Young : 1981:232). In his classical book on this subject, "The Politics of Non-Violent Action" (Boston P.S : 1973), he maintains a corrective approach, putting into perspective most of the convictions, methods and goals of non-violent action. Primarily he explains that we need to differentiate between "passive pacifism of non-resistance" and non-violent direct action or "radical pacifism" (ibid :20 -23). In an article specifically devoted to the South African saga ("What Is Required to Uproot Repression? Strategic Problems Of The South African Resistance" in Sharp : 1980 :161 — 180) he argues that non-violent action can time-wise be more effective than violent methods. An example is taken up that the ANC and the PAC's resort to the armed struggle 23 years ago has failed to bring about the hoped-for speedy change of government in South Africa.

Next to Mahatma Gandhi, the most usually referred to doyen of non-violent resistance is the Rev Martin Luther King Jr. His philosophy can be summarily expressed in the following five points (Augsburger in Clouses (ed) : 1981:91) :

1. Non-violent resistance is not a method of cowards. It takes more strength to stand for love than to strike back.
2. Such resistance does not seek to defeat or humiliate the opponent, but to win friendship and understanding.
3. The attack is directed against forces of evil rather than against the people doing evil.
4. Non-violent resistance is a willingness to accept suffering without retaliation, to accept blows from the opponent with-

out striking back.
5. This resistance avoids not only external force, but also internal violence of the spirit.

The basic theological-ethical argument of the non-violence view is that the end does not justify the means. The means of a struggle for justice, humanity and freedom must be just, humane and free from the slavery of fear and hatred. Also, the goals of a revolution must be incorporated into the process of the revolution itself. If the goal is reconciliation, then only methods which do not exacerbate and entrench polarization must be employed. There is a general mistrust of a government which can come to power by military means. It is argued that once taken up, it is difficult to lay the guns down again. The result becomes a paranoic, totalitarian and authoritarian regime — the noble goals of the revolution are all lost.

3.1.1. *Critical Evaluation*

Without claiming to have said everything about this view, we now turn to evaluate it. First of all, we can point out the flaws of a hermeneutic which picks up Jesus of Nazareth, who lived in a different socio-political and historical context, as an absolute norm for contemporary ethical questions. Secondly, often pacifism is too universalized, there is little contextual construction of methods which will be appropriate for a specific situation. Much abuse of the examples of Mahatma Gandhi and Martin Luther King has been done.

The basic argument of the exponents of non-violent action — the fear of a replacement of one tyranny with the other, is in itself a relative political view. It may be a view which is based on an either incomplete (shallow) or biased analysis of a political struggle. It is wrong to set an operative norm from a relative and speculative proposition.

Real non-violent action cannot guarantee bloodlessness. A non-violent movement may produce peripheral violence. Conversely, it needs to be recognized that some violent action may also have a pervasive non-violent dimension. For example, an armed struggle may be accompanied with an educational campaign which is designed to persuade the enemy to surrender.

The growth of the non-violence movement owes much of its weakness from its adherents themselves. The majority of Christians within this camp view non-violence as being non-political. For them non-violent action is prayers "for those in authority" and the passing of church statements condemning the practices of "those in authority".

Religious pacifism is having the danger of giving the means too much priority (sacralization), over the end sought, leaving one more concerned about his "good" conscience than the good of the suffering.

3.2 Constructive Violence Theory

It is maintained that violence can have a positive value as well. Violence, like money, is amoral. It can either be used wrongly or rightly, destructively or constructively. Therefore, a final theological position on violence should be the one of "Christ-like" ambivalence.

There are Christians in conflict-areas who will passionately argue that they already and always find themselves in situations of open violence. They only find two options open to them, which are to either participate in the armed struggle in order to bring an end to the prevailing continuing *status quo* of violence, or to submit to the spectator-role while God's creation is being destroyed. The option of non-violence is not only viewed as impracticable and irrelevant in such situations; it is also tantamount to a disobedience of Jesus Christ — a neglect of Christian responsibility. To heckle for a consideration of non-violence in the midst of a violent conflict is to create confusion; and if the heckling is mainly directed to the less powerful victims of the conflict, it is to be homicidal.

In such situations the view propounded is that some form of a relatively just order must first be created before violence can cease. It is explained that, in this case the duty of Christian responsibility is then to attempt to humanize the means of conflict by ordering and controlling this violence.

Generally, this option has been recommended for two kinds of political situations. First, in situations where structural violence becomes increasingly reinforced by the violence of repression. Christians then engage in a violent struggle to bring an end to the recurrent violence of the *status quo*. The second kind of situation is in a case where it is realized that a more anarchical revolution is about to hijack or simply overtake the course of the struggle for liberation which is being waged. Then here whatever means that could help to bring the current struggle to its acceptable goals are being employed before a more violent wave starts.

Two ethical commitments are invoked by Christians engaged in this option, namely, the *love ethic* and the *Christian social responsibility ethic*. It is consented that an evil is used to stop an evil, albeit a lesser evil against a greater evil. This *reluctant* employment of evil is undertaken with an assuring meditation on the Grace of God.

The saint of this view is Dietrich Bonhoeffer (1906 — 1945) an eminent German theologian who participated in a conspiracy to assassinate Adolf Hitler from a motivation of a theological rationale that the murder of one man will avert the massacre of millions (Jews and the casualties of World War II). Bonhoeffer contextualizes the Doctrine of Grace on this matter : "Free responsibility ... is based on a God who demands the free venture in faith of responsible action and who promises forgiveness and consolation to the man who becomes a sinner by it" (quoted in Villa Vicencio : 1980:31). Again : "I believe that God can and will bring good out of evil, even out of the greatest evil. For that he needs men who make the best use of everything... I believe that even our mistakes and shortcomings are turned to good account" (quoted in De Gruchy :1984:47).

Another ethical motivation for the option of constructive violence is the so-called *balance-of-power-ethic*. Either the aggressor party must be weakened by destroying its power base (e.g economy) and by weakening the morale of its supporters to the end that it is bereft of all arrogance and self trust which makes it intransigent, or both parties in the conflict are supplied with equally sufficient combat power to the end that they realize that it would be to the interests of both of them to stop harassments, and would thus start to manipulate each other to a negotiated settlement.

The thinking on constructive violence has produced a welcome theological justification of YAHWEH — sanctioned bloody conquests of Israel's neighbours in the Old Testament (OT) accounts. It is explained that the nation of Israel was comparatively a minority, historically younger and militarily far less powerful than her neighbours. And with their alien culture and religion, her relations with her neighbours were tense and she was under constant threat of annihilation by them. Ontologically speaking, they were in a situation of violent conflict. In that situation they had only two options, viz, to subdue their hostile neighbours or to neglect all military engagement and be annihilated. They opted for the former, and God became their "commander-in-chief". They worshipped Him as "Yahweh-Nissi", the God of the armies of Israel (e.g Psa. 24). (ql) Interestingly, in line with the constructive violence theory, the Torah stipulated military conduct, checks that would ensure that the means of war are reasonable and "humane" (NB Deut 20:1 — 20).

When going to the N.T. as a source, this school of thought comes out with a realization which has been epicly verbalized by

Canon Burgess Carr at the All Africa Conference of Churches (AACC) 1974 annual conference that, "in accepting the violence of the Cross, God, in Jesus Christ, sanctified violence into a redemptive instrument for bringing into being a fuller life."

Adherents of this view differentiate between terrorism and constructive violence. Terrorism is adjudged as barbaric because of its overt or potential indiscriminate killing of non-combatants (civilians). It is negative, destructive violence since it generates feelings which will make reconciliation impossible. Constructive violence on the other hand, is a politically strategized interventionist counter-violence, which is directed at military targets, and is waged with the clear goals of instituting a more just, peaceful and acceptable society.

3.2.1 *Critical Evaluation*

The first obvious problem with this view is that generally, it seems to be taking lightly the issue of the taking of another human being's life. Christian anthropology holds that the offender does not degenerate to the level of being a non-divine-creature. Cardinal to Christianity is the doctrine that all human beings are created in the image of God for the purpose of having life in its fullness. The Grace of God which has been revealed through Christ has made the preaching and the appropriation of this abundant life possible. It is therefore contrary to the missionary *cantus firmus* of Christianity to destroy human life, since we must make sure as Christians that nobody dies without having experienced the forgiving and life-giving Grace of God. We are called to save and to give not to destroy.

Secondly, there can be no guarantee that the violent means used can never be kept from themselves becoming the instruments of dehumanization. It can also not be guaranteed that those participating in "constructive violence" can always maintain their supposed moralistic motivations and controls.

One other obvious problem with this option is that there has first to be a consensus that one is already in a violent conflict situation. Because of this phenominological diversity of violence and of human beings intellectual-ideological shortcomings, the element of error on this pivotal decision is present.

All said, the most serious danger about this thesis is that, all the arguments used here, can conversely be used by forces that are for the maintenance of the evil *status quo,* invoking noble ideas such as Law-and-Order and public safety. Note that the exposition given above on Yahweh's involvement in Israel's conquests, is the same one that was being used by the Voortrekker theologicans during the colonial conquest of South Africa (Azania).

3.3 *Just Revolution Theory*

There is already a well detailed theological-ethical belief that violent resistance to a tyrannical system can be justified, on proviso of a fulfilment of a set criteria. Today the recognized criteria might be :

1. All other possibilities of non-violent change must have been truly exhausted.
2. The cause fought for must be just.
3. The methods used must be minimally inhuman and just. No unneccessary, excessive, uncontrolled violence.
4. There must be reasonable prospects that the violent resistance will attain the ends desired.
5. There must be popular understanding and acceptance of the order which will be established after the violence succeeds.
6. The violent overthrowal of the existing power structures must be an act of obedience to God, and love toward men.

Exponents of this view locate its foundation from the theological reflection concerning the being of earthly governments. All human authorities are subject to God's divine sovereignty, and have a merely delegated power which they may strictly use for the common good of all their subjects. Any government which abuses this power to dehumanize any section of its inhabitants, forfeits its moral legitimary and poses itself as an enemy of the people. Christians then become under a moral obligation to withdraw their support from such a regime, thus working for its overthrowal. A number of persuasive means are used towards this end. The more the tyrannical regime becomes intransigent and brutally repressive, the more the methods of resistance become creatively intensified, with the ultimate recourse being the employment of open violence, after the check-listing of the provided provisions.

Here again, the means of violence are not uncritically justified. Violence is appealed to in obedience to God, as a last resort and with a code of conduct (cf : criteria). The main motivation is a vision of the order of justice. Thinly allied to the constructive violence, Christians opting for this view regard their participation in acts of violence as an interventional act to bring to an abrupt end a protracted institutionalized aggression against the people.

Appeal for theological-ethical justification is usually made to two ethical models : the *Grenzfall* ethic of Karl Barth, which holds that in border-line situations God, as Sovereign, commands that His law be broken in order that He might be obeyed; and Sipren Kierkegaard's ethic of the "theological suspension of the ethical", which holds that even though God's norms are absolute and eternal, at certain undefined moments in history God, who is the Alfa and Omega of history suspends (not annuls) these norms, and in that moment God-self through His word (rhema) and not his historically codified norm (logos) is to be obeyed.

Proponents of the Just Revolution theory maintain that each historical situation should be considered in its own right (social analysis) and that no biblical ethos should be applied uncut in every circumstance.

The Just Revolution concept has to be differentiated from the Just War Theory, since the latter restricts its arguments only in respect of the morality of a legitimate government to declare war against an external aggression.

Contrary to the claims of the critics of the Just Revolution theory that it is a conceptual legacy of the Constantinian Just War theory of the Crusades, upon a closer historical analysis it will be discovered that the just revolution theory as a product of theological reflection, emanated from the ecumenical movements' growing concern with the social contradictions found within nation-states such as South Africa. Challenged by the issues raised by the wars of decolonization, the violent struggles against racism and current North-South tension (Rich-Poor nations), the language of the theological debate on violence shifted since the post World War II era from the "Just War" to the "Just Revolution". The nuclear era has outruled any moralistic evaluation of the Just War theory. It is agreed that the conventional international war on which the Just War theory is based, may never be fought in the world. We are faced with the prospect of a cataclysmic nuclear war.

Underlining the development of this theological construction is the imminent rising of Liberation Theology with its reflection on God's character and mission as being in favour of the political, social and economic liberation of the oppressed. Just as the church has generally been engaged in the mission of "winning souls" (internal liberation?) through overt evangelistic techniques, so it has to be openly engaged in the newly discovered holistic liberation of man by employing demanded politico-military techniques.

3.3.1 *Critical Evaluation*

In evaluating this theory the same set of questions which were raised about the constructive violence option, are still relevant. Prime to them all, of course, is the issue of the sanctity of human life. Even though the evaluative questions seem generally identical, the author maintains that there is a difference between these two theories. It is a challenge of historico-theological analysis to fully distinguish between them.

The employment of Bonhoeffer's thesis on grace, which maintains that a Christian may engage in such questionable acts as murder if it is a lesser evil with the hope of God's forgiveness, opens up separate debate on the doctrine of grace. In his epistle to the church in Rome Paul polemicizes:

"What shall we say then ?

Shall we go on sinning so that Grace may abound

By no means!

For sin shall not be your master, because you are not under law, but under grace...

What then? Shall we sin because we are not under the law but under grace ?

By no means!

You have been set free from sin and have become slaves to righteousness"

(Romans 6: 1,2,14,16).

Lest we have an improper understanding of Bonhoeffer, let us explain that Bonhoeffer's theses which is used here is derived from his polemics against what he terms "cheap grace" — a kind of Christian lifestyle which calls for no transcedental moral obligations (Ibid :1959) His point is that if you have to do an evil to avoid a greater evil then you become more guilty if you do not do it.

The Debate Within the Context of South Africa

It is important and interesting to note that the current debate has been sparked by the formation of the Special Fund of the PCR, and that the PCR, even though its scope is international, was primarily motivated by the socio-political situation in South Africa. SA boasts the status of being the only country in the world where racism is entrenched in the Constitution and has modelled the order of society.

In 1961, the year of the Sharpeville massacre, the year in which Great Britain gave a blessing to the racist Republic of South Africa Act of 1961, and the year in which eventually the liberation movement in the country finally realized that no peaceful means is going to change the racist white minority regime, — the World Council of Churches called a consultation with its South African constituency (Cottesloe Consultation). At this Consultation the SA Church issued ecumenical statement condemning racism. This was followed in 1968 by the South African Council of Churches' (SACC) "Message To The People Of South Africa". The "Message" gave a lucid theological confession against the purported scriptural justification of apartheid and against the SA political system.

During the 1961 and post 1968 era, there seemed to be no serious controversy in the church on the theological-ecclesiastical stand vis-a-vis racism (except the Dutch Reformed Church and some white-ruled pentecostal churches).

The crunch came when that confession had to be made concrete in an actual obligation to remove the racist *status quo*. The crunch came on 6 September 1970 (Thomas : 1979:72) when the news of the PCR grants to the ANC, PAC and the Zimbabwean ZANU and ZAPU reached South Africa.

David Thomas in his "Councils In The Ecumenical Movement In South Africa 1904 — 75", gives a "newspaperman's" report of the SA Churches' reaction to the PCR grants. The Church was thrown into confusion.

Ironically, and quite embarrassing for the World Church, some member churches of the WCC in S.A castigated the PCR grants as being "implied support for violence" (Ibid :74). They could not understand how the WCC could support the "terrorist organizations". The immediate reaction had to come from the South African Council of Churches. Its executive committee released a statement disassociating the SACC from the WCC Action, and accused the PCR for taking the decision without first consulting the churches in SA. The government's reaction was : Prime Minister J B Vorster threateningly called on the SA Churches to withdraw their membership from the WCC (Ibid : 75).

The turmoil brought about by the PCR grants led the SA Churches or agonize over the issue of violence/non-violence for the first time. It also tested their commitment to political change in South Africa. Most significantly it precipitated or revealed for the first time the division in the churches, which was racially determined along ideological lines. For black Christians the WCC grants was God's answer to their prayers and an assurance of their righteous political liberation; to the majority of white Christians it was a betrayal of the Gospel and a threat to the *status quo* from which they have all along been benefitting.

For black theologians, it was hypocritical for the white dominated eccelstiastical forums to condemn violence whilst these churches were ordaining and supporting military chaplains — when they were blessing the guns of the forces of the iniquitous racist regime. A call was arising from the black church that the churches have to minister to both sides of the borders of SA. The grants from PCR were viewed as a legitimate and commendable ministry to the other side.

Echoing the sentiments of counless thousands of black Christians in South Africa, Rev Canaan Banana, wrote from Rhodesia's government's reaction was : Prime Minister J.B. Vorster threateningly called on the SA Churches to withdraw their membership from the WCC (Ibid : 75).

The turmoil brought about by the PCR grants led the SA Churches to agonize over the issue of violence non-violence for the first time. It also tested their commitment to political change in South Africa. Most significantly it precipitated or revealed for the first time the division in the churches, which was racially determined along ideological lines. For black Christians the WCC grants was God's answer to their prayers and an assurance of their righteous political liberation; to the majority of white Christians it was a betrayal of the Gospel and a threat to the *status quo* from which they have all along been benefitting.

For black theologians, it was hypocritical for the white dominated ecclesiastical forums to condemn violence whilst these churches were ordaining and supporting military chaplains — when they were blessing the guns of the forces of the iniquitous racist regime. A call was arising from the black church that the churches have to minister to both sides of the borders of SA. The grants from PCR were viewed as a legitimate and commendable ministry to the other side.

Echoing the sentiments of countless thousands of black Christians in South Africa, Rev Canaan Banana, wrote from Rhodesia's Wha Wha Detention Centre "The World Council of Churches is to be commended for its gesture of love, concern and compassion in coming to the aid of the struggling masses of our world. The WCC Programme to Combat Racism is a visible expression of Christian love." (In IRM, 1979:423).

Actually by this period (1970-72) there was already a filtration of Black Theology writings from North America into the black theological circles, particularly in the Christian student movements. Most of this Black American theology had an approach which seemed to have already concluded on the issue of violence — non-violence. One of the launching statements of the Black Theology movement, the statement by The National Committee Of Black Churchmen (1969) in introducing Black Theology concluded : "We commit ourselves to the risks of affirming the dignity of the black personhood... . This is the message of Black Theology. In the words of Eldridge Cleaver : We shall have our manhood. We shall have it or the earth will be levelled by our efforts to gain it." (in Cone and Wilmore :1979:102).

This new theological-philosophical thinking plummeted the SACC into another serious outbreak of debate when in 1974 it had to adopt a resolution on conscientious objection to conscription into the South African Defence Force (SADF). Unlike in 1970, when the church in SA was far behind the world church in theological development, the debate was now conducted in a matured way, and we can for the first time begin to resourcefully assess what took a form of a theological debate on violence and non-violence in ecclesiastic forums in South Africa.

True to the *modus vivendi* of the debate on violence, the debate in SA was more punctuated and at times overtaken by political events both within the country and in the Southern Africa region. All the presented views on the issue of violence are modelled by the proponents' own experiences of life in SA. On the one hand we have arguments coming from an experience of a sense of security and fear of change, and on the other hand those emanating from a sense of a constant experience of state harassment and a desire to change the *status quo*.

Since 1976 when SA entered a new political era which was preceded by a massive show of state intransigence and naked brutality, the debate on the ethics of violence/non-violence started to be more emotional. In fact in the black community ("church" implied) there ceased to be any debate on the issue. The option of violence was too obvious and natural. Black churches became empty as thousands of black young people fled the country to prepare themselves for the armed struggle.

Taking note of the events in SA in 1977, as if in despair, the WCC produced an article entitled "South Africa's hope — What Price Now", in December of that year. This article climaxed and brought together the points of debate on the PCR view of revolutionary violence that has also been raging in some overseas church circles. It marked a move towards the recommendation of the Just Revolution Theory as model of bringing about change in South Africa.

Also taking note of the development of a growing polarization of thinking on violence, the SACC resolved to establish a Commission on Violence and Non-Violence in 1978. Its mandate was to stimulate and conduct theological debate in the churches around the issue of violence/non-violence.

A Kairos came with the explosion of black revolts in September 1984. Once more the non-violent means of the struggle were

viewed to have produced nothing but the government's retreat into
the entrenchment of the apartheid system by coming up with the
Tricameral Parliamentary System. The Prime Minister's reform
rhetoric, which seemed to be extracted only by violent clashes between the police and the black repression of the dissidents of state
ideology. For the first time, the black communities developed
methods of simple military retaliation against state forces. The
church was overtaken.

The SACC Commission on Violence and Non-Violence asked to
be discharged in February 1985. Its role had become anarchronistic
and irrelevant; it had in fact achieved little during its seven years
of hard work.

A number of theologians conferred during 1985 and worked on
the production of a "theological response to the political crises in
South Africa". In September they released a document, named the
Kairos Document. Because of the Kairos's revolutionary analysis
of the South Africa state and its progressive views on violence, it
plummeted the SA church into an era reminiscent of the post
Special-Fund — announcement period. Some churches and leading
theologians disassociated themselves from the document.

The Kairos Document served as a catalyst, stimulating a debate
on violence which has been disappearing from SA theological
scene. It took a step further, the traditional churches' criticism of
apartheid by declaring the SA government a tyranny — and in line
with a theological corollary view — a tyranny which must be over-
thrown. It criticizes the churches' traditional view on violence, rais-
ing important points. The church is accused of only condemning
the violence of the oppressed victims all along whilst being soft on
the violence of the state. It subtly justifies the violence of the
oppressed. Since they are the victimized, they therefore ethically
have a right of defending themselves. The church's traditional non-
violent methods of protest are also criticized, but instead of calling
for a support of violence, the Kairos Document leaves the thesis at
a point of suggesting civil disobedience.

4.1 *Conclusion*
It is notable that in SA the adherents of a particular view on the
violence/non-violence debate are determined more by sociological
rather than theological factors. The debate has degenerated into a
black-view versus a white-view. Black theologians celebrate the
PCR theology and the theology of the Kairos Document. White
Christians (some) take them cautiously, instead they uphold a
"theology of reconciliation". The Kairos Document in fact deliber-

ately, and theologically, justifiably presents the thinking of the oppressed blacks.

The black church leaders who would refuse to be associated with an open violence option, opt for what they perceive to be the ultimate in the means of non-violent change of government in SA, namely, disinvestment and economic santions against SA. Unfortunately this has also opened a hornets nest.

The situation is causing those who are pacifist to retreat into silent careful comments on the situation. The black's view is the most audible. The debate is at the point of a tacit acceptance of the Just Revolution Theory or the constructive violence theory, but all this development is bereft of a clear theological motivation and direction.

5.1 An Ethical Appraisal of the Conduct of the Debate
Based on the belief that one of the roles of religious social ethics is to de-absolutize and analyze conflicting viewpoints in a debate with the hope of working for a fruitful communication between the rival positions, we proceed to appraise the conduct of the debate.

The first general point of criticism to be raised is that the debate is all reactionary. It is sparked off by certain events, and then the arguments advanced sometimes become too hinged on those events themselves. As an exercise of theological formulation aided at formulating a model which shall be used to influence the morality of society, basic dogmatic facts on the issue of violence are supposed to be always reflected upon with a view of positive discussion and dialogue in church, not to wait for an emotive situation to spark a debate.

Secondly, the debate has been influenced by self-interest — specifically, political self-interest and political ideology. This is more so in the case of SA. The debate becomes ideolȯgized. And as it happens in all ideological conflicts, people become blind to the concerns and interests of the other party. The issue of the relationship of the Gospel or theology to ideology is a debate in its own right. However, one needs to check if we are critical enough in our ideological affiliations in fear of them becoming so absolute that they end up determining our lifestyles to a point where they take a sovereign place in our lives, replacing the Gospel.

Linked to the foregoing fact on ideology is the way Scripture is being used. There is a propensity by both the pacifist and the violence option camps to use Scripture uncritically. People read their ideology into the Bible. Scripture is being manipulated to justify points of view.

Besides the violation of hermeneutical principles, there is a crucial dangerous tendency of not consulting the Bible at all. Philosophical ethics and scientific historical analysis seem to be the main formats of the views of the church in the debate.

The last but not least point to mention is the employment of emotionalism and sentimentalism. Emotionalism inhibits sound rationality. It does not permit sympathetic exchange of ideas. Sentimentalism inhibits pragmatism. People are prone not to be self-critical.

5.2 *Theological Ethical Proposals for the Conduct of the Debate*

With the foregoing appraisal in mind we should consider the following proposals :

5.2.1 The views of those who are faced by situations that prompt them to some action-decision on this issue, must be accorded priority. Particularly of those living under oppression and repression.

5.2.2 Those outside the conflict must be weary of paternalism. Aloof moral judgement is insulting to those who are caught up in the situation of a life and death struggle. The oppressed should be allowed their liberatory right to make their own decisions. Those outside should only learn and sympathetically advise, never condemn and order. This whole fact should be specifically addressed to those people who, for whatever reason, are associated with the oppressor class in a society, also those in foreign countries, and also to the church as well as academics. The institutional church and the academia like to play a detached self-delegated refereeing role in conflicts. The church should not provide raw moral instructions from a detached superior position, and academics should be reserved with their often cold (de-animated) and "double-talk" recommendations.

5.2.3 Moving beyond mere solidarity, we should aim at identification, which will mean putting ourselves into the boots of the victims of injustice, and "experiencially" attempt not only to understand but to be involved in their decision-making.

5.2.4 There should be open-mindedness, a willingness to listen and attempt to understand those holding views different from ours. Much of the attitudes of whites and some blacks in SA towards PCR is based on ignorance, ignorance which feeds on the prejudiced and malicious government media.

5.2.5 We should always sincerely identify and analyze the motivational factors of our arguments, investigating the reasons behind the opinions and particular point of view we hold. This will be an exercise toward subjecting our ideologies to the Gospel.

5.2.6 The respect of the catholicity of the church is imperative in the debate on violence and non-violence. Besides the need to subject one's views to theological-biblical criticism, it is required that this view be open to the judgement of the Christian community. Only in fellowship can the whole truth be discovered.

5.2.7 There is a need for a more self-giving reflection on the teaching of Christian tradition on violence. We must be free to be led by the Holy Spirit, even when He leads us to the formation of views that might be against those of our churches, political parties or the state.

BIBLIOGRAPHY

Ballard, P. 1979:
  A Christian Perspective On Violence. B.C.C, London.
Banana, C. 1979:
  The Biblical basis for liberation struggles. *International Review of Mission*, Vol 68, No 272, pp. 417 — 423.
Bonhoeffer, D. 1959:
  The Cost Of Discipleship. S.C.M, London.
Camara, D. 1971:
  Spiral Of Violence, Sheed & Ward, London.
Clouse, G. (ed.) 1981:
  War : Four Christian Views, Inter-varsity Press, Illinois.
Cone, J & Wilmore, G 1979:
  Black Theology : A documentary history, 1966 — 1979. Orbis, New York.
De Gruchy, J. 1980:
  Church Struggles in South Africa. D. Philip, Cape Town.
De Gruchy, J. 1984:
  Bonhoeffer And South Africa. Eerdemans, Michigan.
Deist, F & Du Plessis, I 1981:
  God And His Kingdom. Van Schaik, Pretoria.
Hope, M & Young, J. 1981:
  The South African Churches in a Revolutionary situation. Orbis, New York.
Sharp, G. 1973:
  The Politics of Non-Violent Action. Porter Sergeant, Boston.
Sharp, G. 1980:
  Social Power And Political Freedom. Porter Sergeant, Boston.
Thomas, D. 1979:
  Councils in the Ecumenical Movement South Africa 1904 — 1975. S.A.C.C, Johannesburg.
Villa Vicencio, C.:
  UNISA Guide TEA 301-C. UNISA, Pretoria.
Yoder, J. 1984:
  The Politics of Jesus. Eerdemans, Michigan.

LEBAMANG J. SEBIBI

Towards an Understanding of the Current Unrest in South Africa

The Uniqueness of the South African Problematic
People often wonder why black South Africans seem to be so fix-ated on the question of racism or apartheid. For black South Afri-cans, they say, any topic inevitably leads to endless and often torpid discussions of *racism, discrimination* as though this were the only problem in the whole wide world.

The thesis which says that the South African problematic is unique is supportable in two ways:
  (a) In South Africa one witnesses a situation where a miniscule *white minority* group (27%) practises racism against a vast *black majority* (73%).
  (b) Racism in South Africa is not only part of the customary arsenal of society, but it is also entrenched in the statute books of the legislature; in other words, these anti-social racial practices and attitudes are made to be part and parcel of the country's legis-lation and societal institutions.

Herein lies the *uniqueness* of the South African problematic.

Racism, of itself, is a heinous and horrendous societal evil because it leaves its victims hopelessly incapable of escaping from its dehuma-nizing practices. It is, indeed, in the incisive phrase of Frantz Fanon a "corporeal malediction", — a bodily curse about which one can do precious little. The highly revered President of Tanzania, Julius Nyerere, puts it in graphic terms when he says in substance:

- If a man discriminates against you because you have appalling table manners, it is bad — but not that bad because you may improve your table etiquette, and his discrimination against you will end.
- If a man discriminates against you because you are, say, a bad tennis player, it is bad — but not nearly that bad because one day you may improve your game and his discrimination against you will cease.
- If a man discriminates against you because you are a sloppy dresser, it is bad — but not nearly that bad because maybe one day you may acquire fancy apparel and his discrimination will certainly come to a welcome end.
- But, says Julius Nyerere, if a man discriminates against you because you are Black, then you have had it! This kind of discrimination leaves you with no way out. It leaves you with your back pressed hard against the wall because it is this type of ruthless discrimination that is aimed at the very foundations of your Being. In short, it is an ontological onslaught against the beingness of some people in society.

Indeed, it is this ontological dimension which intrudes a peculiar pungency to racism and to all its institutionalized forms.

And all this has a direct bearing on what is currently taking place in the South African townships — particularly since September 3rd, 1984.

The Nature of the South African Problematic: An Overview

South African townships are currently in flames. This is so because the ruling white minority, 27 per cent of the population, which wields almost all power in the country — political, economic and social — insists that it alone has the right to plan how South African society should be politically, socially and economically structured. This white minority is convinced that South Africa cannot be organized in any other way except in the apartheid way. The black majority, 73 per cent of the population, on the other hand is convinced that not only do they also have the right — the inalienable right — to participate in deciding how this country should be structured but also that the white minority's apartheid solution is morally unjust, economically disastrous and politically naive and untenable.

Thus the white minority's and the black majority's perceptions of how this beautiful and bountiful country should be structured and governed are poles apart. The polarization in perceptions could not be wider.

For a long time the combatants in this conflictual scenario were characterized by different types of power:

- Naked military and physical power — the instruments of coercion — have always been in the hands of the white minority since 1652. And the *ability* and *willingness,* on the part of the ruling minority, to exert physical coercion have in these days reached unprecedented heights.
- Numerical and moral power — the instruments of moral persuasion — have always been in the hands of the black majority. But the readiness and willingness of the black people to continue using the power of moral persuasion have in recent years been stretched to the limits.

These two states of mind, namely, the readiness of the South African minority group to defend their apartheid or racist policies with naked military force and the worn-out patience of the dominated and disenfranchized majority, create a formula and recipe for the combustion, smoke and fire, we witness in the streets of Soweto, the Vaal Triangle, Gugulethu, Langa, Duduza, Kwa-Thema — almost everywhere in the country.

But what accounts for this seemingly total loss of patience on the part of the black majority, especially at a time when many and various "steps in the right direction", seem to have been taken by the white Government? One could even say that, materially speaking, the lot of South African blacks has been bettered in recent years: school buildings, hospitals and clinics, playgrounds, tarred roads, better housing, etc., all these things have been bettered, upgraded and increased; and, to say the least, there is willingness on the part of the white Government to improve the quality of the black people's lives. What therefore, accounts for this apparent blindness — one could almost say ingratitude — on the part of South African blacks, foreigners to South Africa often ask in painful amazement.

I wish to submit that this hurtful puzzlement registered by our foreign friends is understandable because there are a couple of fundamental things about South Africa and its racial policies that invariably escape the foreign eye.

Allow me to touch on just two of these fundamentals:

(a) *The failure of the non-violent moral persuasion technique:*

Between 1652 and 1910 stand 258 stark years of struggle for the land between the indigenous people of this sub-continent and the Europeans (from Holland, France and Britain) who were determined to settle in South Africa and monopolistically hoard all meaningful power for themselves. The year 1910 is an important landmark in that it not only rounded up and completed the white man's conquest of this land, but it also witnessed the formal union of the two Boer Republics (the Transvaal and Orange Free State) with the two Southern English colonies (Natal and the Cape). This union of the four provinces was an all white affair: the union constitution completely ignored the existence of the indigenous people of this country. They became by and large a vote-less and landless majority in the land of their birth. The 1913 Land Act further institutionalized this landlessness by forbidding blacks to have ownership of land anywhere in South Africa except in the so-called "reserved" 13% of the land mass of South Africa — most of which is of course desert-like and arid.

The exclusion of blacks from the purview of the Union Constitution and their legislated landlessness prompted them, for the first time in the history of their long struggle, to form a black *national* organization with the sole aim of receiving recognition, acceptance into and participation in the newly established Union.

They formed the African National Congress (ANC) in 1912, all imbued with child-like optimism and faith in the universal brother-hood of man and the power of moral persuasion. Remember, most of these gentlemen were stalwart Christians, brought up and nurtured in Christian mission schools and therefore fired with the untameable idealism of the Christian Gospel. They believed if you taught and preached long enough, something was bound to happen in the hearts and minds of evil-doers and hard-hearted racists.

It is basically for this reason that the ANC, from 1912 to 1960, clung to the non-violent, pacificist, moral persuasion modes of challenge to a system which, in their perception, immorally excluded the indigenous black majority and treated them as non-persons. So for nearly half a century (1912-1960) the ANC pleaded, begged and preached — to no avail.

In 1959 the PAC joined the fray — and resorted to non-violent but direct action like the burning of discriminatory pass-books. The crack of guns at Sharpeville, Langa and Gugulethu reverberated throughout the world in March 1960. It was the Government's standard response to the non-violent challenge posed by the unarmed indigenous black majority.

In early 1961 both these non-violent national organizations (the ANC and PAC) were banned and wiped out of public circulation.

This was an untold tragedy because most people's faith in the use of non-violent means towards their God-given freedom got heavily dented.

In the interim a veritable barrage of racist laws came pouring out of the South African legislature. People often draw a distinction between how the natives of this coutry were handled before 1948 and how they were treated after that fateful year when the Afrikaner Nationalist Party gained ascendancy. Most blacks believe that the difference between the pre-1948 era and the post-1948 era lies in the fact that the regime of the National Party premiers after 1948 — D.F. Malan, Strydom, H.F. Verwoerd, John Vorster and finally P.W. Botha — is highly distinguished by the consistency, single-mindedness and fanatical ruthlessness with which they pursued and legislated in favour of the policy of *racial discrimination* — *apartheid*. Law after law was passed to apply to all spheres of South African life, for example:

In the Social Sphere

1949:	The Prohibition of the Mixed Marriage Act.
1950:	The Immorality Act.
1950:	The Population Registration Act (the Race Classification Board).

In the Residential Sphere

| 1950: | The Group Areas Act (to own land, live and trade in particular place one has to be of a particular race). |
| 1954: | The Native Resettlement Act (removal of "black spots"). |

In the Cultural Sphere

| 1953: | The Bantu Education Act (encouragement of ethnicity). |
| 1959: | The Extension of University Education Act (the creation of tribal, ethnic university colleges). |

In the Economic Sphere

| 1953: | The Native Labour Act (forbade "mixed" trade unions). |

In the Political Sphere

1951:	The Bantu Authorities Act (tribal, regional and territorial).
	Note: Admittedly, hind-sight tells us, that this was the first step towards the balkanization of the land into "homelands".
1959:	The Promotion of the Bantu Self-Government Act (an immediate preparation of the bogus independence of the "homelands".

This process of racist legislation took its course — inexorably —

despite of this fact the ANC and PAC were outlawed in 1961, the
indigenous people of this country were in many ways in a worse
state than they were in 1912. It is, however, important in this connection to remember that when the ANC was banned in 1961, its
Programme of Action and Defiance Campaign were anything but
violent. "Passive Resistance" is about the worst phrase one could
use, at the time, to describe the ANC's direct mode of action. Of
course the same "passive resistance" as a *modus operandi* applied
to the PAC. How can we forget that at the time of the banning of
these black people's organizations the President of the ANC, Chief
Albert Luthuli, was a Nobel Peace Prize Laureate, bearing eloquent testimony to the peaceful techniques hitherto adhered to by
these organizations.

But the Government literally pushed them underground and
turned their hands to instruments and weapons of war.

At this juncture one would have thought that the blacks would
completely shun the non-violent path to freedom. It was not so.
After a decade of almost complete quiescence — 1961 to 1968 —
the emergence of Black Consciousness organizations SASO, BPC
and others rekindled the dying embers of faith in the non-violent
means of the struggle. From roughly 1968 to 1977 the Black Consciousness organizations worked not only hard but non-violently to
exorcize the demon out of the black man's mind, the internalized
demon of the "white master" within the black man's mind and
heart. The 1976 students' flat refusal to learn the language of the
"white master" was indicative of the success of this exorcism. The
two or three year violence that erupted then was characterized by
the violence of the state and the counterviolence of the township
children. They preferred to die to being cowed into learning Afrikaans — the language of the "white master".

October 19, 1977 witnessed the banning of all black organizations despite their basic non-violent stance *vis-a-vis* the state.

The Azanian People's Organisation (AZAPO) emerged in 1979.
Its stance, too, was basically non-violent but bitterly anti-racist and
anti-discrimination.

1983 saw the formation of two black political fronts: the National Forum Committee (NFC) and the United Democratic Front
(UDF) both of them avowedly espousing an active but non-violent
stance against apartheid in general and the tricameral system in
particular.

However, their non-violent stance is being completely overlooked by the white regime as was the case with the ANC and
PAC's peaceful and negotiatory stances.

The point one wishes to make here is that the non-violent, moral persuasion technique adhered to systematically from 1912 to 1985 has failed lamentably to impress the South African white minority government.

I wish to submit that foreigners to South Africa often miss that point.

(b) *Apartheid: A two-fold concept*

This is another fundamental in our apartheid society that foreigners frequently miss to take cognizance of. Our non-South African friends invariably fail to distinguish the US-type of Afro-American struggle from the South African-type of black struggle. The former struggle is basically a "civil rights" struggle waged by a black minority within American society. But the South African black struggle is not primarily a "civil rights" one, it is a "human rights" struggle waged by a black majority within South African society.

This distinction is important; it is crucial because the current conflagration in South Africa somehow hinges on it. Let me try to explain.

When Dr. H.F. Verwoerd became Prime Minister in 1958, apartheid could still be understood as a single and simple social theoretical concept, whose basic ingredient was *"white supremacy"* in one unitary state, with the black majority under white tutelage. No other South African Prime Minister — from General Louis Botha, Jan Smuts, through to D.F. Malan and Strijdom ever suggested the policy of territorial separation of races, which would eventually develop into independent, self-governing enclaves — within the very confines of South Africa itself.

The architect of this concept was Dr H.F. Verwoerd — Prime Minister from 1958-1966. But even he had his initial periods of doubt and vacillation. It was obviously hard to deviate from conventional wisdom that whites were to be the guardians of blacks and that this would be the case almost *in aeternum*.

Many of us can still remember that in 1951, while Verwoerd was still Minister of Native Affairs, he flatly denied that granting self-government within a small Native territory would lead to dividing South Africa into a number of independent states (Muller 1969: 489). But when he became Prime Minister in 1958, he started to concede that his policy could in fact lead to the creation of a number of independent states in South Africa — leading to the eventual fragmentation of the country. With time Verwoerd openly admitted that he preferred a *small white South Africa* to a *large*

black South Africa. Indeed he preferred to remain poor and un-
mixed to being *rich and mixed.*

In 1959 Verwoerd stated in the House of Assembly:

"Then I say again that with an open mind and in the best interest of the white people of South Africa I choose an assured
white state — rather than to have my people absorbed in one
integrated state in which the Bantu must eventually dominate"
(Muller 1969: 489).

Thus the promotion of Bantu Self Government Act (No. 46 of
1959) was the first significant Verwoerdian step towards the addition of a major dimension to the South African apartheid policy.

Today we not only have the so-called ten "national states" or
"homelands", but in addition four of them have taken "independence" with the resultant six million black South Africans formally
and "legally" being de-nationalized and losing their citizenship.
And unless something drastic is done, and done soon — this horrifying *process of de-nationalization* would take its inexorable course
and cause irreparable damage to the black struggle in South
Africa.

The 73% of the population is being shunted away to their "right-
ful" 13% of the land while 87% of land is reserved to those who
are doing the shunting.

The point I wish to make is this. This Verwoerdian dimension
turned simple apartheid into a concept consisting of two concentric
circles: the inner circle of petty apartheid and the outer circle of
grand apartheid. While petty apartheid says "do not sit on this
park bench, sit on that one", "don't go to this cinema, go to that
one", "don't ride on this bus, ride on that one", — grand apartheid says *"you don't belong here".* In other words, petty apartheid
is the arena of civil rights, with issues like better working conditions, housing, roads, improved school buildings, hospitals and
clinics, etc., etc.

The white government *can* and *is* prepared to carry out most of
these issues. In fact most of the so-called "steps in the right direction" are steps taken within the arena of petty apartheid. No wonder blacks remain unimpressed by these "steps", because while
these praiseworthy improvements are taking place within the arena
of petty apartheid, the indigenous black people of this country are
losing their land through the process of de-nationalization within
grand apartheid. And unless this process is stopped no improvement will ever be good enough — not even the "Rubicon-
type" of improvement.

The black people — particularly the young — remain significantly unimpressed and dangerously angry.

I wish to suggest that the current unrest in South Africa is taking place within the context of the aforementioned two fundamentals:

(a) The failure of the non-violent moral pursuasion methods, and

(b) The perception, by blacks of apartheid as a two-fold concept, i.e. the two concentric circles concept of apartheid.

These two fundamentals form part of the essential ingredients of the current unrest.

In other words, there is a definite correlation between the present unrest in the country and these two fundamentals.

The Current Unrest: A Qualitative Leap Detectable

The history of the black struggle in South Africa has been long and checkered. It is a 333 year struggle for the land. As it was previously said, 1912 (formation of the ANC) only marks the formal and systematic nationalization of the black people's efforts to regain their birthright. It was a long struggle, characterized by waves — waxing and waning, and sometimes simmering under the surface for long periods at a time. The struggle came in high waves and low tides.

However, a couple of things characterize the present wave of the struggle.

This wave has lasted much longer than most waves associated with the history of our black struggle: it is a one year, two months old wave, which, instead of lessening in momentum, it is increasing in volume and velocity at a pace that leaves almost every protagonist in the drama breathless. When is it going to stop or wane, people ask? It is the one wave whose perdurance potential is unmistakably sensed by most people in South Africa — and it is this potential which scares the wits out of everybody's mind. People who are accustomed to dealing with "normality" in society, are suddenly faced with "ungovernable abnormality" having the potential of going on and on, on and on ... with no respite in sight.

And who are the protagonists in this unrest? In one sense it is true to say that it is all the disenfranchized black masses in South Africa. By saying so, one is saying that these black masses can and do identify with the potential for transformative power inherent in the unrest. But in the immediate and direct sense, the protagonists in this unrest are the angry, impatient young people — the high school population. They are the faceless, undaunted cadres wreaking havoc all across the country's black townships. Their facelessness has a way of striking holy terror in the hearts and minds of the unco-operative elements in the black communities. What they do to such elements is continually flashed in our daily newspapers across the country for everyone to see. The police, the army, the state of emergency — indeed all the coercive forces and might of the most powerful state in Africa have been rendered impotent by this undying waging of a *children's war.*

They are accountable only to their leaders — and their leaders are also faceless and underground. This is so because most of the accredited and community approved leaders are in gaol in terms of security legislation. The two high treason trials in Pietermaritzburg and Pretoria have robbed the black communities throughout the country of 38 of its most powerful and dedicated leaders. It is this factor and the repressive security laws which increase the need for the facelessness of the current leadership in the township. Faceless-ness goes with fearlessness. The young protagonists in this one year, two months' struggle are devoid of fear. I have seen them with my own eyes confronting police dogs and bullets with stones in their hands.

Their motto is quite shattering in its uncomplex and ingenious finality: *Freedom Now, Education Later.* It is on the basis of this motto that for months on end there has been no formal schooling to talk about in most black townships; as it is now, very few high school exams — especially matric exams, are going to be written this year.

Their demands span the spectrum of educational political, social and economic demands; the eradication of apartheid education which is responsible for shameful inequalities based on race. For instance, the 1983/84 per capita expenditure on school pupils was:

* White R1,184
* Asian .... R 997
* Coloured .... R 651
* Black.. R 213

The non-negotiable demand is one ministry of education, one educational system for every South African child.

Another demand of a political nature is the release of Nelson Mandela and other political leaders — and all the recently arrested student leaders, and negotiate a new South African constitution which will render the category of "race" irrelevant and criminal. Stop the de-nationalization process and the balkanization of the country.

Every South African must have the right to work and live wherever he/she wants: freedom of association, is yet another social demand.

In short, the demands come thick and fast — but all sharing one common denominator: *an end to all differential treatment based on race*. The young people are prepared to die — and are indeed dying — for this ideal. On the average five are buried every week as heroes and heroines of this struggle.

The area covered by this wave is not only the so called "emergency areas" but nearly the whole of South Africa. Recently Cape Town had to be included in the number of those "emergency areas" because of the high level of unrest reached in Athlone, Gugulethu and other Western Cape locations. The Orange Free State, for a long time known for its quiescence and docility, has also erupted in waves of anger in several unsuspected places: Parys, Bothaville, Odendaalsrus, Brandfort, etc. This is another special feature of the present unrest. It is literally almost country-wide.

What has this unrest achieved in real terms? It has played ducks and drakes with the country's economic climate. The South African Rand has hit an all-time low and it was not for his health that the president of the Reserve Bank had to go overseas cap in hand to negotiate a better deal with foreign banks and governments.

Also, a considerable dent has been made in the arena of grand apartheid: a couple of weeks after P. W. Botha's "Rubicon speech", he conceded and accepted the unheard of possibility that blacks could become "South African citizens, — and went on to mutter something on "dual citizenship" for independent "homeland blacks". Observers of South African politics believe that P. W. Botha could not have conceded this much in policy without considerable pressure. Is the *children's war* beginning to bite?

Be that as it may, the sacred walls of grand apartheid appear to have a serious crack ... and the road to Lusaka is becoming more popular by the hour.

These are the signs of the times, which form the silver lining in the dark cloud that at present covers our beloved country, South Africa.

BUTI TLHAGALE

Nazism, Stalinist Russia and Apartheid — A Comparison

This essay deals with a comparison between Nazi Germany, Stalinist Russia and the South African Apartheid Regime. It is a comparison between the present and the past. The essay submits right at the outset that the apartheid regime is not similar to Nazi Germany nor to Stalinist Russia, historically nor factually. In terms of numbers, South Africa has not experienced anything similar to the sadistic, cold-blooded mass murder of six million Jews under the Nazi regime (1933-44) nor to the senseless killings of 20,000 Soviet people during the Great Purge (1936-1938). And yet the horrors of the apartheid system, its pathological tendencies and its callous disregard for moral norms, compels one to see apartheid in the light of the politically criminal systems of Hitler and Stalin.

South Africa lives in the shadow of Nazism and Stalinism. Given the fact that the holocaust of the 1930's and the 1940's immobilized mankind by a grave sense of guilt, the horrors of the apartheid system are even more terrifying as they disclose mankind's forgetfulness. They reveal man's stubborn refusal to learn from the past. The underlying thesis of this essay is therefore the assumption that, though the crimes of Nazism and Stalinism differ from those of Verwoerdism in magnitude, qualitatively the difference is negligible. It is in the sense therefore that one cannot but compare the cumulative effect of the apartheid system with the terrors of Nazism and Stalinism.

266 *Hammering Swords into Ploughshares*

Historical Context: Brief Statements

Nazism

Nazism or the national socialist ideology fed on the rather ambivalent tendencies that prevailed within Germany in the 1930's and the 1940's. There was a negative attitude towards democracy, parliamentarianism, capitalism and even the modernization process in general. There prevailed a romantic yearning for the past and yet there was also a movement bent on creating a new society, the new Aryan race under the new leadership of Hitler. Hence the rejection of pluralism, of racial mixing. There was then a clearly anti-Western attitude, which generated a spirit of nationalism, a kind of a "mystical community" which strongly appealed to the German rank and file.

Stalinism

Whereas in the case of Hitler there is little or no attempt at rehabilitating or explaining away the gruesome mass murders that happened during his reign. Stalin, on the other hand, has had many apologists for the brutal existence in the Soviet Union during the 1930's. The context of the mass arrests, torture, arbitrary execution and mass deportation is generally depicted as emerging from the complex Soviet scenario of the 1930's.[1] First there was a looming threat of invasion from the Nazi-Japanese coalition (1937-1938). But prior to that, there were tensions generated by what was known as the "Cultural Revolution" (1928-1931). Enormous energy was concentrated on the rapid industrialization of the Soviet economy and the modernization of the agricultural sector. The mechanization of the agriculture led to a class struggle between the rich and the poor. The harsh "dekulakization" process (expropriation of property from the rich peasants) generated hostility and opposition. Then there were pressures generated by the advent of famine. Besides, the Soviet Union had embarked on "an historically unprecedented course", the establishment of a socialist revolution.[2] It is against this background then that one wishes to have a closer look at the Soviet holocaust. There are those who claim that the Stalinist terror was justifiable, hence the campaign to rehabilitate Stalin's memory.[3] On the other hand there is an attempt at the de-Stalinization of the Soviet Union, initiated by Nikita Kruchev in 1956.[4] Pro and contra arguments notwithstanding the cost, in terms of human lives, remains staggering.

Apartheid Regime

The general context of the South African System of racial domination and the ruthless suppression of any form of political resistance stems from the fear of the white minority of losing its privileged position cultivated over a period of three generations. The 4 million whites entrenched themselves as a privileged group at the expense of 25 million black people. Besides, South Africa has become a home for white South Africans. Their survival as a group will, therefore depend on their retention of political and economic power and, indeed, on their strength to control the oppressed majority.[5]

Race Mythology in Nazi Germany
Fleming in his book : *Hitler and the Final Solution,* points out that the racial doctrine of the National-Socialist worldview was based on three beliefs, namely (a) the fundamental inequality of mankind, determined by genetic traits; (b) the existence of different human types (races); (c) the existence of an irrevocably inferior race, a kind of anti-race, the Jews.[6] This doctrine was related to the Darwinian evolutionary theory that postulated the superior right of the stronger against the weak. From the viewpoint of the concept of the great chain of being, the Aryan races would then be at the top and the others at the bottom. This belief fuelled anti-Semitism by positing "the danger of extinction through over-alienation".[7]

The idea of a pure race, such as the Aryan-Germanic race, presented an alternative to the liberal humanitarian concept of civilization. At the beginning, the belief was that the inferior race — such as the Jews — would then serve the master race. But this belief degenerated into the desire to extinguish the "worthless" races. The Jews therefore became the scapegoats. They were accused of "imperialist designs on world hegemony", of plotting against the German nation, of embezzling funds. They were accused of practicing ritual murder etc. For these crimes and many others, Nazi Germany called for their disenfranchisement. They were to be boycotted and even expelled from public life. They were to be subjected to special laws. The pathological anti-Semitism served to unite the Nazi movement. They were hated and subsequently exterminated simply because they were Jews.

Race Mythology in South Africa
In the South African context, the racial mythology equally served to galvanize the dominant white groups. L. Thompson quotes sociologist G. Cronje as follows: "The more consistently the policy of apartheid could be applied, the greater would be the security for the purity of our blood and the surer our unadulterated European racial survival....total separation ..... is the most consistent application of the Afrikaner idea of racial apartheid".[8]

Quite clearly therefore given the socio-political conditions of the white minority amidst the threatening black majority, the racial factor was mobilized in order to facilitate white hegemony and to ensure its survival. Although the racial myth is wearing thin today, hence the abolition of the Act that prevents mixed marriages, most members of the white dominant groups compelled themselves to believe that Africans were a "sub-species of humanity". That belief still lingers on. It persists precisely because of its "suitability and expediency". It allows the Afrikaner nation to continue to arrogate political and economic control unto themselves. Whereas the Jews of Nazi Germany did not stand in the way of the Nazis, the majority of white South Africans seem to see the black people as a threat to their privileges, their monopoly to meaningful power (and not the sham of political power in the homelands) and to their Christian civilization. This, coupled with the irrational dislike for the black people, the dominant groups also perceive a real threat of being overwhelmed. Hence the fear of over-alienation through mixed marriages, or simple social intermingling. This explains the host of racial laws in the statute books virtually banning any form of racial intercourse in all public institutions and residential areas.

Mention must be made of the changing face of the apartheid system. But the changes represent a functionalist approach, a pragmatic response to the various pressures exerted upon the archaic political system. The system is still by and large informed by its own conveniently created political mythology. Like Nazi Germany of yesteryear the apartheid system continues its own version of discrimination e.g. the denial of citizenship rights, civil liberties, the right to free association, the right to political power sharing, the right to equal educational opportunities, the right to reside where one chooses etc. These denials are based on the survival instincts of the white minority and are conveniently reinforced by the racial mythology which in turn has found its way into the legal system of the country.

Like the Nazi-Germans it can be said that most white South Africans still believe that racial intermingling with "inferior races" will lead to the decline of the "superior white" civilized races. Hitler accused the Jews of conspiracy and subversion which accounted for the general decline of modern civilization. The fear of opening up the educational institutions and residential areas to all, irrespective of race — rests on the belief that the inferior black races will usher in the era of decline. And so the line of demarcation must remain intact. Reform will be possible so long as it does not threaten the tenets of the dogma of racialism.

Afrikaners as the "Herrenvolk"

In as much as the Nazis saw themselves as a different race, the Afrikaners have also belaboured under the belief that they are a different people. They even saw themselves as the chosen people, the "Herrenvolk", "a separate nation called by God to create a new humanity".[9] The major events in the history of the Afrikaners were seen in the context of God's guiding hand. These events welded the Afrikaners together in the face of the uncivilized world of the indigenous black people. There is of course a dissenting viewpoint, D.F. Malan, a one-time Afrikaner leader and Prime Minister, is quoted by historian H. Gillomee as saying that the Afrikaner sees God's hand in his personal fate and in that of his people. "But that he claims this as his exclusive right and thus raises his people above others as God's special favourite is a false and slanderous allegation".[10]

If it were to be accepted for argument's sake that at the level of belief, the Afrikaner did not claim to be a specially chosen people, such a viewpoint appears to contradict the practice of the Afrikaner religion which has always been exclusive, denying even those blacks of the reformed tradition, a common worship with the Afrikaners. Religious exclusivism and the practice of racialism reinforced the Afrikaner's idea of being a race set apart. Both the religious and racial mythologies contributed towards the maintenance of power control over the black races, hence the survival of the Afrikaner people.

"Judenfrei" Europe

In so much as the Nazis had no regard for the values of democracy namely, equality, the rule of law, the dignity of all people, civil rights and liberties — the apartheid society has been equally opposed to such values. Because of these denials, the apartheid regime lives in the shadow of Hitler's Nazi Germany. Aronson writes that "through conquest the German *Volk* would increase their daily bread, using swords as plough shares".[11]

Though the scale of violence under Hitler is hardly comparable to the violence of the apartheid regime, the South African government has not hesitated in using swords to suppress any form of resistance or challenge to its power, hence its restless pursuit of the African National Congress members in the countries surrounding South Africa.

The pathological hatred for the Jews by Hitler did not only stop at just depriving them of some basic human rights, it aimed at exterminating them as people. During 1939 the favourable solution for resolving the Jewish question was through emigration. The Jews were removed from the German territory and from the conquered territories. Fleming in his *Hitler and the Final Solution* states that after 1940 it was proposed by the German foreign office that all Jews should be removed from Europe as a whole and that the island of Madagascar be requested as a resettlement area for the Jews from France.[12] Himmler, one of the chief planners of the Jewish execution, is also quoted by Fleming as having hoped "to see the concept of Jew completely eradicated, through the large-scale deportation of the entire Jewish population to Africa, or else to some colony".[13] It was in 1941 that a new programme of solving the Jewish question was introduced. They were now to be "evacuated to the East". They were sent to labour camps. Those Jews who proved to be unfit for work in the camps were simply executed through gassing. Those Jews who resettled voluntarily were promised a paradise in the ghettos and provisions of potatoes and bread.[14]

It was at the Wannsee Conference of 1942 that the "Final Solution of the Jewish question" was agreed upon. Prior to this conference gassing had already been adopted as an execution method because execution through shootings was too burdensome on the executioners. And so Aushwitz, Riga, Libau, Treblinka etc are names that recall the brutal mass murders of the Jewish people. Hitler's lust for destruction cost the lives of six million Jews. But it was not only Hitler who was to blame, he had willing accomplices. Aronson asks a rhetorical question that "whether or not they (the accomplices) desired to exterminate the Jews, they certainly acted in the only way that mattered to bring that end about".[15]

The Myth of a White South Africa
In as much as Hitler wanted a "Judenfrei" Europe, the South African regime fantasized on the possibility of white South Africa without the black people. Black people will only be in white South Africa for the purpose of ministering to the master race. Foundations for the grandiose scheme had already been laid in the passing of the Land Act of 1913 which made the reserves the only areas where Africans could lawfully acquire land.

According to the recommendation of the Stalloard Commission "The Native should only be allowed to enter the urban areas, which are essentially a white man's creation, when he is willing to enter and minister to the need of the white man, and should depart thereafter when he ceases to minister".[16]

The restriction of land for purposes of occupation invariably forced Africans to work for the white people either on the farms or in the urban areas. This was the beginning of the process of land dispossession, turning the indigenous people into aliens in their own country. The South African towns were planned in accordance with the policy of racial segregation. People resided in different areas in accordance with their race classification. The passing of the Groups Areas Act led to mass removals of people. It became an effective tool of political control. It also became compulsory for blacks to carry passes at all times. This pass system restricted their freedom of movement. Seventeen and a quarter million Africans are reported to have been arrested between 1916 and 1981 for contravening pass law regulations.[17]

The movement of workers was further controlled by a network of labour bureaux. Workers were forced to register for work at the nearest labour office in the homelands. Migrants were granted a contract valid for one year only. Once they were registered they could not change to another category of work. They thus became prisoners of certain categories of work which were generally low income jobs.[18] Though the pass law system was recently abolished its legacy of pain and hardships will take decades to eradicate.

Resistance campaigns were organized against the pass system. The Sharpeville massacre (1960) was a direct result of the much hated pass system. Sixty-seven blacks were shot dead "the great majority being hit in the back as they ran".[19] The system of influx control has brought about social dislocation. The men were denied the right to be accompanied by their wives and children. Forced family separation has been in vogue since the creation of the pass system and influx control. The ubiquity of these bureaucratic controls has generated deep-seated feelings of discontent and frustration. The tightness of the system of control coupled with the threat of arrests if people step out of line likewise made people feel insecure. The lack of proper housing facilities, the absence of the freedom of movement, the forced separation of families, the severe restriction of job opportunities etc., constitute a serious infringement of fundamental human rights. The civil servants in charge of the state control mechanisms have generally carried out their orders with unparalleled harshness thus inflicting further humiliation on the victims of the apartheid system. Such hard-hearted behaviour is reminiscent of the insane recklessness of the Nazi accomplices who treated the Jews as nothing but "vermin".

Territorial Segregation as a Solution
The failure of Nazi Germany to get rid of the Jews through emi-

gration led to the so-called territorial solution. The Jews were "evacuated to the East" where they were eventually physically liquidated. South Africa's policy of segregating blacks from whites evolved in fits and starts. First there was the Land Act of 1913, which forbade Africans from purchasing land outside the designated reserves. This Act ensured a continued supply of labour for white farmers. The reserves were never intended as "a territorial base for future states".[20] The reserves did, however, become the basis of the policy of separate development. They were to become "reservoirs of cheap labour" and a place for the "redundant" and unemployed Africans.[21] Over the decades the government "relocated" people for various reasons.

Africans were moved from what was referred to as "Black Spots" because they occupied territory belonging to whites. Blacks were thus deprived of their freehold rights. Maré records that 88 000 people were relocated under the Black Spots category during the period 1970-1973 and a further 73 000 between 1973 and 1976.[22]

People were also removed because of the Group Areas Acts of "betterment" planning in the reserves, of the abolition of the labour tenant system and squatting on white-owned farms and because of the consolidation of the homelands. Between 1960 and 1982, 522,900 people are reported to have been moved. The Jews in the Third Reich were told that their new homes would be paradise, and the Black people of South Africa were also told the same story. The relocated people found themselves staying in tents or in corrugated iron houses, far away from places of employment. The Surplus People Report states that the forced removals...

> "are not merely examples of how inhuman and irrational the Nationalist government can be. The massive scale of the removals and the suffering that has been imposed on millions of people have not been incidental or accidental to the system of white domination that operates in South Africa. They have been essential to it — essential to the system of control over the black population that has been entrenched under apartheid"[23].

The government has invariably described the removals as "voluntary" or as "removals for development" and yet these removals have been forced upon people leaving them no choice but to go to their designated new homes.[24] The Bantu Homeland Citizenship Act of 1970 represents the "territorial final solution" of the Nationalist government. Archbishop Tutu, who insists that the apartheid system is "the most vicious system since Nazism"

observed that people starve in the resettlement camps:
"They are starving not because of an accident or a misfortune. No, they are starving because of a deliberate government policy made in the name of white Christian civilization. They are starving so that a little girl can tell you that when they cannot borrow food they drink water to fill their stomachs. This is the solution, the Nationalists have decided upon them".[25]

Short of liquidating the black people after the fashion of the Nazis, the Nationalist government has inflicted enormous suffering on the black people by systematically restricting them to the resettlement camps and imposing a tight control mechanism on their movement.

The Crimes of Stalin and Apartheid Compared

South Africa, like the Soviet Union under Stalin, is a totalitarian regime, though to a lesser degree. In 1938 a "cultural revolution" was initiated in Russia. This revolution emphasized the modernization of agriculture and rapid industrialization. The arts and the social sciences were given a Marxist interpretation. A proletarian culture was promoted amongst the working groups. A new set of values that would reflect a new Soviet people were also cultivated. In line with this general thrust there was also a programme aimed at collectivizing agriculture. The creation of collective farms coincided with the food crises in Russia. This led to the acceleration of collectivization. The agricultural sector was rapidly mechanized. Rich peasants were deprived of their excess property. Poor peasants were set against the rich ones. Those peasants who refused to co-operate were simply deprived of their property and exiled into distant locations.[26] Urban opposition (among the technical intelligensia) led to political repression. Between 1935 and 1939 there was a vigorous programme of membership screening an anti-bureaucracy campaign and ruthless elimination of traitors, spies and "wreckers" who sought to overthrow the regime.

In 1936 the political police were given extraordinary power to deal with the "enemies of the people". They could arrest and sentence without trial any person suspected of motives to overthrow the regime. Members of the top military personnel became the victims of the spy-mania. So too party members. The figure of those executed between 1936 and 1938 is estimated at between 20 000 and 100 000.[27] Stalin, like Hitler, is said to have elicited absolute obedience from his followers. According to Szymanski, the personality cult around Stalin "was invented to fulfil the need for an apparently worthwhile leadership and charismatic inspiration in a period of crisis and rapid transformation of institutions and values".[28] Accomplishments during his reign were phenomenal. An agrarian and literate society was transformed into an industrial and literate society. But as what cost? Cohen maintains that Stalin created a Holocaust greater than Hitler's.[29]

The Crimes of Apartheid
South Africa relocated not fewer than 3 million people in order to streamline its apartheid policy. Clearly the figures do not compare at all with Stalin's assault on 125 million peasants during collectivization between 1929 and 1933. What is at issue here is the ruthlessness of totalitarian regimes in pursuit of their goals. Stalin's regime reacted with merciless cruelty to those suspected of counter revolutionary intentions. The South African regime has been no exception. More than 25 000 people have fallen victim to the security legislation in the last three decades.[30] During the third State of Emergency in 1986 alone more than 8000 people were reported to have been detained. Those who were detained in the past three decades became victims of security laws such as the Suppression of Communism Act (1950). This law was deemed to be the "first step towards the creation of police-state in South Africa" [31]. It was later replaced by the Internal Security Act (1982). During the height of resistance in 1960, a State of Emergency was declared and the police were given extensive powers to arrest people without warrant and even hold them incommunicado.

The State of Emergency declared in 1985 and in 1986 revived the practices of granting enormous powers to the police. It thus became "clearer than before that the security police played a political role to keep the present power bloc in control"[32].

The apartheid regime, through its network of security laws, has been able to crush any opposition from the ranks of the oppressed majority. Through the Unlawful Organizations Act, the African National Congress and the Pan African Congress were outlawed in 1960. Some of the accused were given life sentences, others went into exile. Opposition organizations were again banned in 1977. Entrenched into the security laws are clauses allowing for the banning of persons, their deportation to the homelands, the banning of gatherings, the restriction of funerals of people who died of unnatural causes, either through police shooting or when blacks kill people seen as "collaborators". The increasing level of opposition has accelerated the pace of political violence. The police on the other hand are alleged to have shot people indiscriminately, during political upheavals.[33] In the 1978 Amnesty International Report

South Africa is charged with using torture. The report states that "All the evidence indicates that torture is extensively inflicted on political detainees and that the government sanctions its use".[34] Different methods of torture have been cited viz: application of electrical shocks to the body, physical attacks, solitary confinement, suspension from poles, being kept naked during interrogation etc.[35] Since the declaration of the State of Emergency the army patrols the township streets. Their very presence is seen as oppressive and provocative. The more opposition there is to the apartheid regime the more repressive the state becomes.

Is the Comparison Justifiable?
There are those who wish that a comparison between Nazism and Apartheid or between Stalinism and Apartheid should not be made at all. Take, for example, H. Adam who writes: "And yet it can be shown that contemporary South Africa hardly resembles fascist Germany, that the differences outweigh the similarities, and that the fascist analogy obscures a proper understanding of the South African System".[25]

Adam maintains that the South African regime is less totalitarian than Nazism and Stalinism because persecution is aimed at those who challenge it not those who merely abstain. Adam is conveniently oblivious of the fact that more than 3 million people have been forcibly relocated, most of them in desolate areas. The cost in terms of the quality of life is incalculable. More than eight million people have been deprived of their South African citizenship as a result of the Bantu Homelands Act of 1971. The pass system and the influx control system have facilitated the imprisonment of millions of innocent people. This is political persecution.

The Nationalist Party once upheld a pipedream of a "white" South Africa, a "negerfrei" South Africa like a "judenfrei" Europe of Hitler, whose white "volk" would not be polluted by the blood of other races. That political mythology has been shattered. Thus South Africa finds itself caught in the syndrome of the shifting goals. The dominant group therefore seeks to introduce "reforms" on condition that the power base, the political and economic control is retained in white lands.

Comparisons are made not so much with the intention of reliving the past or of recapturing the painful experience of those who have suffered in the past but rather with the intention of preventing the horrors of the past. A comparison between the figures of those who suffered during Nazi Germany and those of the victims of the apartheid regime can be informative but also misleading. Human beings are more than just numbers. Hence the insistence that the destruction of human life under any regime is reprehensible. The enormity of the crime of the apartheid system, its scandal, stems from the fact that mankind has experienced uncalled for pain at the hands of Nazism and Stalinism and yet the horrors of apartheid are allowed to continue. Elie Wiesel says that the Jews felt betrayed. "The world knew and kept silent and their solitude then was matched only by God's. Mankind let them suffer and agonize and perish alone. And yet they did not die alone, for something in all of us died with them."[37]

The above comparison is not necessarily a revision of the crimes of Hitler or Stalin. It is simply a statement of a claim that the oppressed black majority also belongs to the community of mankind. They too have a right to be protected from the insanity of the oppressive Nationalist Party, from their seemingly irrepressible lust for power. The above comparison seeks to challenge man's inhumanity to man. Complacency in the face of such naked oppression is criminal. Mankind cannot be allowed the luxury of forgetfulness. The horrors of the 1930's and the 1940's will continue to haunt mankind as long as man's inhumanity is allowed to flourish in the apartheid system. At any rate, this system generates violence which is bound to affect the relationships of the nations. The sanctions issue, a ray of hope for the oppressed, is a case in point. Alliances among the nations are gradually being determined by whether a nation supports sanctions against the apartheid regime or not.

Dietrich Bonhoeffer, the martyr of Nazism, once wrote that there were three ways in which the church could act towards the state. It could ask the state whether its actions are legitimate and in accordance with its character as a state. Secondly, it could assist the victims of state action. The third possibility is not merely to bondage the victims under the wheel, but to put a spoke in the wheel itself.[38] The issue of economic pressure on the apartheid regime, relentlessly championed by Archbishop Tutu and supported by local church, trade union and opposition political party leaders, is an application of Bonhoeffer's third possibility. Not only are sanctions an act of disapproval but they are also a resistance against human forgetfulness. The crimes of Nazism and Stalinism should not be allowed to re-emerge under the guise of the apartheid system.

REFERENCE NOTES
1. See for example, A. Szymanski, *Human Rights in the The Soviet Union*, Zed Books Ltd. London. 1984 p. 247.
2. Ibid p.248.
3. S. Cohen "The Stalin Question since Stalin" in Cohen S (ed) An End to Silence w.w. Norton & Co. N.Y. 1982. p. 24.

4. See also Herbert Adam and H. Gillomee, *The Rise and Crisis of the Afrikaner Power*, David Philip, Cape Town, 1979, pp. 128-144.
5. H. Adam *Modernizing Racial Domination*. University of California Press. Berkeley. 1971. p 10-17
. H. Adam H. Gillomee. *The Rise and Crisis of Afrikaner Power*. David Philip. Cape Town 1979
6. G. Fleming *Hitler and the Final Solution* Hamish Hamilton London 1985. p. 8
7. K.D. Bracher *The Age of Ideologies* Weidenfeld and Nicholson London 1984. p. 123
8. L. Thompson *The Political Mythology of Apartheid* Yale University Press. New Haven. 1985. p. 44
9. W.A. de Klerk *The Puritans in Africa* Harmondsworth. Penguin. 1975 quote in H. Adam & H. Gillomee *The Rise and Crises of Afrikaner Power* p. 17
10. H. Adam and H. Gillomee p. 114
11. R. Aronson. *The Dialectics of Disaster A Preface to Hope* Vesa London. 1983. p. 53.
12. See. Fleming G. op cit p. 43.
13. Ibid p. 44.
14. Aronson R. op cit. 23. See W. Lagueur. *The Terrible Secret*. Penguin Books 1980. p. 17 — 18.
15. Aronson R. op. cit. 43.
16. T.R.H. Davenport & K.S. Hunt (eds) *The Right to the Land* David Philip Cape Town 1974. p. 71.
17. H. Gillomee & L. Schlemmer (eds) *Up Against the Fences Poverty, Passes and Privilege in South Africa* David Philip. 1985. p. 1.
18. Ibid p. 4.
19. G. Gerhart *Black Power in South Africa*. The Evolution of an Idealogy. Univ. Press of California 1978. p. 238.
20. J. Bukler, R. Rotberg & J. Adams: *The Black Homelands of South Africa*. The Political & Economic Development of Bophuthatswana & Kwazulu Univ. of California Press 1977. p. 7
21. P. Lawrence. *The Transkei South Africa's Politics of Partition*. Ravan Press. 1976. p. 132.
22. G. Maré *African Population Relocation is South Africa* S.A. Institute of Race Relations. Johannesburg 1980.
23. L. Platzley & C. Walker. *The Surplus People Forced Removals in South Africa*. Ravan Press Johannesburg 1985. p. 67 See also J. Yawitch. *Betterment The Myth of Homeland Agriculture*. S.A. Institute of Race Reelations. 1981. p. 95; Maré's G. op cit. p. 44 — 45.
24. L. Platzley "Reprieves & Repression; Relocation in South Africa" in *South Africa Review* No. 3 1986. p. 383.
25. H. Gillomee & L. Schlemmer op. cit. p. 278 — 279.
26. A. Szymanski *Human Rights in The Soviet Union*. Zed Books London 1984. p. 212 — 224.
27. Ibid p. 243.
28. Ibid p. 256.
29. S. Cohen (ed). *An End to Silence* W.W. Norton & Co. New York 1982. p. 23.
30. M. Coleman & D. Webster "Repression and Detentions in South Africa" in *South African Review* No. 3 1986. p. 111.
31. *Political Imprisonment in South Africa*. Amnesty International Report 1978. p. 19
32. Coleman Webster. op.cit. p. 124.

33. See Southern Africa Catholic Bishops' Conference *Report on Police Conduct during Township Protests* Aug-Nov 1984 34.
34. Op. Cit. p. 56
35. *Ibid.* p.58; Coleman and Webster. op. cit. 121
36. H. Gillomee & H. Adam op. cit. p.25
37. E. Wiesel, L. Dawidowicz, D. Rabinowitz, R. Mcfee Brown *Dimensions of the Holocaust* Northwestern University Evanston Illinois. 1977 p. 7
38. D. Bonhoeffer, *No Rusty Swords,* Collins, The Fontana Library 1965. p. 221

Part 6

*Black Theology
in South Africa*

ALLAN BOESAK

If This is Treason, I am Guilty

I bring you greetings from the President and the people of Mocambique. I visited there recently and the most significant thing on that trip which was made clear to me is that the minds and the hearts of the people of Mocambique have not changed, and that in spite of what has happened, their own commitment to the struggle is clear; also, that they shall continue to seek ways and means to support, as much as possible, our own people in our struggle for liberation.

I think it is absolutely crucial for us to understand the meaning of this, given the difficulties that the people of Mocambique are facing right now. My visit to Mocambique and my discussions with government leaders there were really geared to this one fact, that we should all know; that nothing (so they say) has broken the solidarity that they feel with us. I have been there, and have *seen* the evidence of that solidarity. We should not allow the South African government, with whatever trick it may think up, to bring division between the people of South Africa and the people of Mocambique, or for that matter, between the people of South Africa and the people of any frontline country.

Now is a decisive phase in our struggle. Those of us who have warned that the South African government cannot be trusted, that the reforms that they are talking about are cosmetic, that apartheid and racism still reign supreme, and that the South African government still has only one goal, namely, absolute power for itself and for the white minority and continued control over the majority of our people in this country, were right. Subsequent events, since we have begun to make this clear, have shown that this government indeed cannot be trusted. While the South African government talked of reforms and while they were engaged in a massive effort to mislead the international community, they instituted a racist constitution. While they were talking about reform they continued the homelands policy. While they were talking about reform they continued the de-nationalization of South Africa's people, robbing our black people of their birthright and of their right to stay in this land. While they were talking about reforms they continued with their forced removals, with their policies of subtle genocide, by forcing our people from the lands where they had lived for so many years into those concentration camps the South African government calls relocation areas. While they were talking about reform and while they were signing peace treaties with countries like Mocambique, they detained us, they shot at our people, they tear-gassed us when we peacefully, but powerfully, demonstrated our own rejection of their policies and of their constitution. While they talked about peace with other nations they sent their police and their troops into our townships, they broke up our funeral services with violence, they threatened our unarmed people, and they murdered our children on the streets of the townships. While they were talking about reform, and while they were lying to the world saying that apartheid is dead, the unrest all over the country proved that the struggle for justice and our struggle for genuine liberation shall continue. The stayaway proved the discontent of our people but also proved the determination of our people. And these are the things that the South African government cannot even begin to understand or begin to stop. While they spouted their propaganda across the world we proved to the world and to the government that neither smear campaigns nor dogs or guns, nor tear gas can undermine the determination of our people to be free.

And so they are worried because they have this new constitution and with all the pomp and splendour they have opened the new Parliament, and they have their three "Parliaments", and they have the whites on one side, and they have the coloureds on one side, and they have the Indians on the other side. And the thing is not working and that is the problem of course. And so while they are there they are supposed — they are supposed — to govern this country. They are supposed to take note of what is happening, and they are supposed to think about this, and to make intelligent noises about what is happening. And they are supposed to see the problems of our country, and to try and find solutions because that is what they are there for — so they say. And indeed you know the problems facing South Africa. We have unrest in this land that has not stopped since it began in the

middle of 1984. There is a rising cost of living that cannot be stopped
by the government either, General Sales Tax will go up, essential
subsidies will be dropped, the salaries of the new MP's will have to be
paid, their new homes will have to be paid for, there is a tax relief for
the rich. I mean they were supposed to pay extra tax on all those
perks that they have; all those expensive cars, and homes and things
and the government said, "Oh no, Oh no, this is very difficult and we
can't to that — now we will have to wait a few years to implement this
policy." Who do you think is going to pay the 800 million Rand that
the South African government is losing because the rich are not going
to be taxed? You are going to pay for it, the people will have to pay
for it. And this is not something that is being discussed. Crossroads is
burning, eighteen people are dead, the war in Namibia continues,
three million Rand a day is spent on the government's illegal occupation of that country, and they should have been out of there long ago.
They are not discussing that.

Here in our own land there is a crisis in Education — our children
are not going to school and there are very good reasons for that —
they are not talking about that. What are they talking about? Well
you saw in the newspapers, the thing they are discussing is about
those white MP's who may or may not have had a Hottentot for some
grandfather some time. That is what they are talking about. And in
the middle of this bankruptcy, the State President makes an announcement. He says (and this is not for our consumption because we
know them and we don't believe them even when they say these
things, it is for the United States, for Britain, and it is for Mr Reagan
and for those people), "From now on the government will actually
recognize that there will be a permanent presence of black people in
the urban areas." We can now actually live in South Africa. That is
what they say. "And therefore there will be a cabinet committee who
will look into the possibilities of these black people being able to participate in the affairs of the government in the country within the
framework of the new constitution." That is a long sentence but it
comes from the State President.

I would want, publicly again, to ask the question — if the State
President makes the announcement that black people can actually
live in South Africa now, and the government will recognize them,
what does he expect us to think? They actually expect us to sit back
and be very happy and be very grateful and to say *"Ja, dankie baas...
ons het nou..."*[1] I mean, doesn't he know, that black people have
been here long before he came here, that black people belong in this

---

[1] Afrikaans for "Yes, thank you Boss, we now have..."

country, and that we will be here long after he goes back (if he chooses to), and doesn't he know that this land is not his to give us, that this land is ours and will one day again belong to us.

And so we are not grateful for these little concessions that they make. We are merely saying to the State President and to his government — do not fool yourselves now. Don't go around trying to fool the world either because even that will certainly not fool us — we know where we belong!

The problem that we have to face is how we can, in this situation, keep the initiative that we have gained. The fact that international pressure is growing, that in the United States in spite of constructive engagement, or maybe also because of constructive engagement, there is an unprecedented movement of protest against the South African government and its policies and against constructive engagement. Never before have people in the US been so engaged in solidarity with the people of South Africa. And this will happen again and again and again. And they are engaged in the struggle, not simply because they feel like it but because you, the people of South Africa, are engaged in the struggle and you have made them see that it is worthwhile for them to throw their weight behind us. And that is important.

All over Europe the movement against apartheid is growing. I have spoken not so long ago to a new organization called Western European Parliamentarians for Action Against Apartheid; and they have pledged themselves to try and put pressure on their own governments and through them put as much pressure as possible on the South African government so that fundamental change can take place. And again these people are doing that because in South Africa there are people who believe in the struggle and who fight for what we believe in, and who believe in justice and who believe in liberation, and who believe that we ought to be participating in that struggle. As long as you are involved, the people of the world, more and more, will become involved. And so to the chagrin of the South African government, President Kaunda goes around the world and asks for pressure on the South African government and he calls for disinvestment. And the Danish government has announced that it will no longer allow its companies to make new investments in South Africa. You see, the campaign is working... .

In response to this unprecedented international pressure the South African government is trying to show that it is really changing and so they say that Nelson Mandela can come out of jail. That Walter Sisulu can come out of jail. And while they say to

Walter Sisulu, "Please come out of jail," and Nelson Mandela, "please come out of jail", they take Sisulu's wife and they put her in prison. And they take fifteen other people and they put them in prison. What is the matter with this government?

But you see there is something that I noticed when Mandela was made the offer — there was a magazine in this country that wrote and said that Mandela should accept that offer because if he does it may not endear him — so they say — to the people who now want to claim him — like the United Democratic Front. But it will establish his credibility with all those peace-loving, thinking people in South Africa namely "they". I read that article and I thought — what a cheek! Who are they, to now claim Mandela for themselves? They are the ones who created policies which made it impossible for black people to live in this country like decent human beings. They are the ones, who, when we started to resist these policies, made laws that made it impossible for us even to make the first step in terms of saying; "This is our situation, this is our land. We want to live here as people recognized as citizens." And then they banned his organization, they drove him to violence, they locked him up for twenty-two years, they banned and banished his wife, they locked up in Robben Island and the prisons of this country the people who worked with him, they called him a terrorist, they called him a communist, and now — when they are in difficulty they want to offer him conditional release and they say then that we must not claim him because he must establish his credibility with them. Mandela does not need to establish his credibility with those people. Mandela does not need to establish his credibility with anyone but the people who are still in the struggle for justice and liberation in this country, and that's you. And he doesn't need to do that.

But of course, since the South African government is facing all this difficulty, someone has to get the blame, you see. And this time it is the turn of the United Democratic Front. Mr Le Grange made a speech a while ago, and as usual that speech was full of threats, and intimidation, and promises of more intimidation. And he singled out again, the United Democratic Front as an organization that is creating a climate of revolution in South Africa. I want to say to Mr Le Grange: "Mr Le Grange, I am actually getting a little sick and tired of all these threats. And the people of South Africa are getting a little tired of these threats. We are engaged in a struggle for liberation, not because we want to die, but because we want our people to be free. We are engaged in a struggle for liberation not because we wish to die, but because you oppress us, and as long as you continue to oppress us we will have to resist. We are people, and we are people who belong in this land. The climate of revolution, Mr Minister, is not created by those who struggle for justice and peace, but the climate of revolution in this country is created by those who make policies that despise and undermine the human dignity of people. The climate of revolution is created by those who make policies that exploit our people, that take away the necessities of the many to give luxuries to the few. The climate of revolution is created by those who make policies that create hunger and starvation in the homelands while the tables of the rich in white South Africa are sagging with food that will be thrown into the dustbin. The climate of revolution is not created by the United Democratic Front, but by those people like Mr Le Grange, who refuse to listen to the voice of reason, who refuse to listen to our people when they say, we want our rights, and we want them here, and we want them now, because they are our rights. The climate of revolution is not created by the United Democratic Front but by those people like Mr Le Grange who detain without trial, by those who allow our people to be tortured in their jails, it is created by those who allow the wanton killing of our people on the streets of our nation. These are the things that are creating a climate of revolution in our nation, and Mr Le Grange must not blame the United Democratic Front — he must put the blame where it belongs, right in front of the door of the South African government, of which he is a part."

Now the government has charged some of our brothers and sisters with treason. As has been said over and over again, this is a serious charge. Treason is described as organizing, or taking part in, or instigating armed revolt in order to overthrow the government. Alternatively, they are charged with a section under the Internal Security Act in which any act of subversion which can include, speaking out against the South African government, or calling for pressure on the South African government — that is also treason. It is wide, it is irresponsible, but it is a law that is on the statute books of this country. So these people will be charged with treason. I want to say that I consider this a scandalous, dastardly and cowardly act. I have worked with the people who are being charged for a long time, I have not heard them call for violence. From its inception, the United Democratic Front has been an organization committed to non-violence. Under the most difficult circumstances, we did not ask people to take up arms, we said to our people, let us find ways and means, with all of the odds against us, even at this late hour, to try and express our legitimate political aspirations peacefully in this country.

We know that we have had a long battle behind us. We know that every single effort towards peaceful change in this country has been met by the government with violence, and ended in massacre. We know how our people marched peacefully on March 21st, now 25 years ago in Sharpeville, and their peaceful demonstration ended in bloodshed, most of them shot in the back. We know that in 1976 our children took to the streets with nothing in their hands except placards which said to the South African police, we do not want to fight, please release our comrades and our friends. And those children were shot down by the police by the hundreds. And we know that in 1980 in Cape Town our children took up the challenge and marched peacefully for a better future for themselves expressing that they do not want to grow up in a country where racism is rife, and where oppression is the order of the day, and where exploitation is around every corner, and where our people are being pushed into little holes in the homelands where they will die of hunger and despair. And the answer the South African government gave once again was guns, and dogs and tear gas and our children died. And you will remember when little Bernard Fortuin was shot dead on the streets of Elsies River, 10 years old, lying there bleeding to death, his mother wanted to talk to him, and they refused and they shoved her away with their gun butts and when she said to the policemen please, he's my son — he said the words that reverberated around the world, to the shame of South Africa — Let the bastard die! You know that.

And in 1984, after we had formed the United Democratic Front and said to people, let us not despair, let us not say that the only answer to the South African government's violence is violence, let us not seek to repay them with the same things that they are doing to us, let us not seek to be overcome with evil, but indeed to find a way to overcome evil with good by peacefully demonstrating what it is that we want, and we made this organization into a force that even the whole world will now have to reckon with. And we never picked up a single stone but they came again with their dogs and their guns and their bazookas and they killed our people even on the night of the election of August 22nd & 27th. And we said in the United Democratic Front let us try and find ways of telling our young people to commit themselves once again, even now, to a strategy of non-violence. And we did. And the world respects the United Democratic Front for it. It was the South African government who turned around and detained our people. It was the South African government who turned around and sent their police

to our demonstrations on the night of the election and it was they
who again started to shoot at our people. What is it that we have
done? We in the United Democratic Front, have created a unity
that this country has not seen for almost three decades. We
brought back the spirit of the struggle that we knew in the 1950s.
We were the people who were able to bring people together even
in this racist land where hatred is the order of the day. We have
been able to say to people do not look at the matter simply in
terms of the colour of a person's skin, but try to judge that person
in terms of that person's commitment to the struggle for justice
and liberation. And we have succeeded in doing that.

In one single year, in a short 12 month period, we have brought
together a mass movement now representing millions of people in
this land. We have challenged the South African government's
constitution, and what is more, we have won. We have made
people aware of their rights in South Africa. We thereby exposed
the violent, oppressive nature of this government. We have given
the people of this land back their self-respect, we have given them
a faith in the justness of our struggle, we have given them a belief
that we shall overcome. This is the United Democratic Front. We
stand for things that the South African government cannot understand. We stand for democracy. They don't know the meaning of
the word. We stand for non-racialism, they cannot stand it when
people of different races can live and work together. We stand for
an open democratic society, they cannot stand it, because then
they know that their violence will have come to an end.

But there is something more. We must ask the question, Is what
we have done treason? I, brothers and sisters, have called for the
foundation and the formation of the United Democratic Front. I
have spoken, more than anybody else over the last year. I have
said publicly, that apartheid is evil, that it is a blasphemy, that it is
a heresy. I have said that the South African government is unjust.
I have said that this government is undemocratic, it is unrepresen-
tative, it does not have the love nor the support of the people, it
has no right to exist, it is illegitimate, it should not be there. I
have said openly that the South African government is a violent
government, I have said and called for Christians and people of
other faiths to pray for the downfall of the South African government, that God should give us another government, that God
should remove them. I have, from the very beginning resisted this
government on the basis of my Christian commitment and of my
Christian faith. And I shall continue to do so as long as God gives
me breath in my body. If this is treason, then I am guilty of trea-

son, and I would say to the South African government: If I am guilty of treason then charge me with treason and put me in jail.

I say this, brothers and sisters, not out of a sense of bravado. I have no desire to be a martyr — God knows my life for the past months has been hell enough. I say this not out of defiance, because I know that the Minister to whom I am speaking now is a very powerful man, he is a man without a conscience, he can do whatever he likes and get away with it. But I say this, because in a perverted, unjust and cruel society such as ours, where those who fight for freedom and peace and human dignity are banned, detained and charged with treason, while criminals sit in Parliament and receive accolades from those who share in their power and privilege; this is the only decent thing to do. And so, if I have committed treason by resisting the South African government which is exactly what our brothers and sisters who are now in jail have done, the South African government must now put me in jail and charge me with treason.

But you must know, that we are indeed in the beginning of a decisive phase of our struggle in the history of our land. This is the beginning of the end of apartheid. Their days are numbered. And what you must do, Mr Le Grange, you must do quickly, for your day of judgement is near. And I want to say to you that you must remember that the struggle does not depend on one or two or three or four people, and that the strength of the United Democratic Front has always been that we do not simply depend on those people that we have put in positions of leadership. The strength of the United Democratic Front has always been the people, has always been your commitment, has always been your participation in the struggle. So in the end, it is not a question of whether the UDF will survive the onslaught because of a few of the leaders are in jail facing trial, but in the end it is a question of whether you in your own commitment will remain faithful. And so I must say to you my people, do not begin to fear the future, do not begin to give up faith in our struggle and in the justice of our cause. Again do not be overcome by the evil that this government represents, but overcome evil with good.

So in the midst of trial and tribulation I must exhort you to remain a faithful people. In the midst of hopelessness and despair that sometimes overcome us because we think that the powers opposing us are so invincible, remain a hopeful people. In the midst of fear and uncertainties that come up in our own hearts because we do not know what tomorrow will bring, and we do not exactly know what will happen to us inside those jails where we may not

even come out alive, be a strong people. In the midst of unfaithful-
ness of so many, where they turn around and for a mess of pottage
sell the birthright of our people just to sit in a bogus parliament
and be given power and be given honour by people who do not
even know the meaning of the words, be a committed people. And
in the midst of the violence of this South African government
which shall continue and which shall be more because they have
created the monster that in the end is destined to devour even
themselves. In the midst of the destruction that may come, remain
a peace-loving people. In the midst of the madness of racism and
hatred that still reign in this country, be a compassionate people.
And in the end, if we remain faithful, if we take the risks that are
necessary and if we remain committed to what we believe in, we
will be also a victorious people.

CECIL MZINGISI NGCOKOVANE

The Church and Politics of Our Time

In 1938, Karl Barth delivered an address under the title of "The Church and the Political Question of Today" which elaborated the new understanding of Nazi totalitariarism and the responsibility of the Church in eight brilliantly argued theses.[1] Barth contended that National-Socialism was not merely a political regime, but was basically an "anti-Christian counter-church."[2] He argued that such a form of state or total dictatorship confronted Christians with the question of God, and was therefore, a question of faith.[3]

He said:

> Between the witness of Jesus Christ and the domination of National-Socialism, there can be no peace; Nazism may indeed be a judgement of God upon the world and upon the Church, but does not mean that we must stand helpless before it.[4]

Karl Barth was disturbed by the fact that proponents of Nazism perpetuated such an evil system in the name of God. Moreover, the church was taking directions from the German Führer instead of the other way round. This same issue disturbs me with regard to the Church and apartheid in South Africa. I contend that the characteristics of Nazism as observed by Barth are similar to those of apartheid. When I read Barth's letter to French Protestants after the fall of France, I found it to be relevant for Christians in South Africa today. Barth indicted Nazism as follows:

> With its lies and cruelties, with its arbitrary justice, with its persecution of the Jews and its concentration camps, with its

attacks upon, and poisoning of, the Christian Church, with its fundamental denial of freedom of, and consequently of responsibility for, thought and speech, with its conscious and wicked repudiation of spiritual values — Nationalism-Socialism ... has not changed.[5]

I decided to use Barth's concern about the church in relation to Nazism as a paradigm for three basic reasons. First, the situation of blacks (all South Africans who are not white) in apartheid South Africa resembles that of the Jews in Nazi Germany. Second, the role that the church plays in apartheid South Africa is similar to that played by the church in Nazi Germany.[6] Third, Barth is the author of the Barmen Declaration and, therefore, he is important for South Africa since there is great need for a Confessing Church in our troubled land.

I would like to analyze the role that the church plays both in fomenting and in attempting to resolve South Africa's persistent racial-political conflict. Suffice it to say, therefore, that the Nazis persecuted and discriminated against the Jews on the grounds that the Jews were *untermenschen* ("subhuman beings"). In the same way, the Nationalists in South Africa dehumanize and discriminate against blacks on the basis of a false assumption that blacks are the *onderworpe* (subjugated) people.

During the Nazi era, the Church in Nazi Germany was divided into two camps. The *Deutsch Christen* (German Christians) supported Nazism in the name of God. But a Confessing Church emerged. This Confessing Church culminated in the publication of the Barmen Declaration. The Confessing Church strongly opposed Nazism and the actions of the *Deutsch Christen*.

The church in South Africa today, is faced with a similar situation. The Kairos Document summarizes the South African problem as follows:

> The time has come. The moment of truth has arrived. South Africa has been plunged into a crisis that is shaking the foundations and there is every indication that the crisis has only just begun and that it will deepen and become even more threatening in the months to come. It is the KAIROS or moment of truth not only for apartheid but also for the church.[7]

I would like to examine the significance of this moment in our history. However, I am not interested in what this moment of truth is all about, but in why it exists in the first place. The issue under consideration, is a touchy one. The debate over politics and religion in South Africa has a long history. One of the reasons for such a long history is the fact that in South Africa, politics and the church have been, and remain, "bound together in one historical drama," to use J. de Gruchy's terms, "one persistent struggle".[8]

The history of the church in South Africa shows that religion is directly and intimately related to the socio-political and economic history of our land. The question as to whether or not the church in South Africa should have been involved in politics in the manner it has been and still is, does not change the fact that the church in South Africa has played a crucial role in supporting the racial ideology of the maintance of the *status quo* of white supremacy on the one hand, and in challenging it on the other. Nonetheless, one of the major controversies in South Africa is the question of mixing religion with politics. But South African churches are highly politicized in that they have been a power for and against political change.

The *Nederduitse Gereformeerde Kerk* (Dutch Reformed Church) leaders and those of its sister churches are clearly linked with the ruling Afrikaner Nationalist Party. Ironically, the *Nederduitse Gereformeerde Kerk* (NGK) leaders frequently counsel leaders of the "English-speaking" or "multiracial" churches especially those that are member churches of the South African Council of Churches (SACC) not to "meddle in politics".

However, the discussion of mixing religion with politics remains at the level of principles. Hence the gulf between the NGK and SACC member churches, especially before 1968 has been very narrow. A close examination of the NGK's justification of apartheid on the one hand, and the SACC member churches' criticism of it on the other, will help us understand this narrow gap between these churches. Such an understanding will help us further understand why the moment of truth has arrived in South Africa. Thus I will analyze three categories relative to politics and the church in South Africa. These categories are: "theology of differentiation", "theology of racial unity" and "theology of the voiceless".

Theology of Differentiation
The Afrikaner theological justifications of the ideology of apartheid can be divided into two eras. First, its 19th century era is characterized by notions of "chosenness" and "Ham theology". The second one is the 20th century theological justification emphasizing the biblical grounds for racial and ethnic differences.

In the 19th century the Afrikaner theological justification for racial segregation rested on the idea that the Afrikaners as a people filled a role similar to that of the people of Israel in Old Testament times. It was very much alive during the Great Trek to the interior and also among those who "founded" the two republics (Transvaal and Orange Free State).[9] These theologians also defended the so-called "Ham theology" which was used to put down blacks as being a cursed people. But in the 20th century, the Afrikaner theologians sought other ways to defend apartheid. They constructed a theological bulwark to sanctify the ideology of apartheid.

In 1947, for example, E.P. Groenewald, a New Testament scholar of the *Nederduitse Gereformeerde Kerk* (NGK) developed a biblical basis for *apartheid*. His conclusions would represent the common view of the NGK up to this day. He concluded for example, that:

"Scripture teaches the unity of mankind. The history of the Tower of Babel in Genesis II teaches us, however, that when people came together to preserve the unity of mankind, it was God himself, according to his own sovereign will who created the separateness of people, establishing not only separate people (nations), but separate geographical areas and boundaries for each. The event in Babel is underlined by Pentecost, Acts 2. *God het aparte volke gewil* (God willed that there be separate peoples). If a nation guards its separateness (i.e. purity of blood/holiness) it will enjoy the blessings of God. Galatians 4 teaches us that the strong (whites) have a responsibility to the weak (blacks). In order to organize this relationship two things are necessary — (1) Responsibility in love of whites towards blacks. (2) The exercise of piety".[10]

For Groenewald, love meant authority and piety meant obedience. In other words, according to him, whites have a duty to exercise love toward blacks (i.e. exercise of authority) because blacks are the subjugated people *(onderworpe)*. Blacks, in turn, must obey that exercise of authority on them (i.e. piety on their part). "The immature people (blacks)," said Groenewald, "shall subject itself willingly to authority placed over them."[11]

These positions have been subjected to serious criticisms over the years. J. Verkuyl offers three points to criticize some of these positions. On the position which emphasizes differences between races, for example, Verkuyl argues that this theory is a serious form of pseudo-theology. The concept of "race", he says, "in the modern sense occurs nowhere in the Bible." Racial and ethnic differences are not "creation ordinances". Verkuyl contends that they are phenomena which come into being, develop, change and shift in the course of history; in no way whatever do they destroy the unity of the human race. He concludes this point by arguing that one who takes one's departure from the position that differences between the "races" are "just as important" as human unity and the restoration of that unity, will end up with a race-ideology which leads to a separate cult and a racist ethnic creed.[12]

In his criticism of the interpretation of the story of the Tower of Babel in Genesis II, Verkuyl contends that the interpretation of this story by NGK theologians such as Groenewald is complete nonsense. "Moreover, it overlooks," says Verkuyl, "the fact that the Babel episode does not contain the last word concerning God's intentions for men and [women]." For Verkuyl, "God's real intention appears in the vision of the oecumenopolis, the New Jerusalem of Revelation 21, and in His command to begin here and now along the lines of this new world-city."[13]

On the question of boundaries, Verkuyl uses the Apostle Paul's Areopagus speech which is a powerful attack on the racial rites, myths, and ethos of the Greeks. To use it as a foundation of a new racial myth (as NGK theologians do) is certainly one of the crassest specimens of pseudo-theology.

Afrikaners' justification of apartheid ideology in the name of Jesus Christ has been increasingly criticized by many religious leaders. The assault on the integrity of He who came to break down the walls between the races and reintegrated humanity into one body, is viewed by many theologians as a pseudo-theology which profanes the name of Christ. The protest has come from within the NGK as well as from without.

NGK theologians such as Beyers Naudé have been ostracised by white society, harassed by the regime and declared heretics by the NGK for protesting against the theological defence of apartheid. Naudé spent seven years under a banning order served on him by the regime. He re-emerged as committed as ever. When asked why he experienced an almost spiritual conversion as a result of the violence in South Africa of some 25 years ago (on the *ABC News' Nightline* television show on March 21, 1985,) he said: "... I came to the conclusion on the basis of my theological study, on the basis of my personal contacts with 'blacks' and 'coloureds' and 'Indians' that the policy of apartheid was unchristian, it was immoral, and it was unfeasible. And the events since 1960 have more than proved that fact."

The South African Council of Churches (SACC) in 1968 called the theological justification of apartheid a "novel gospel". In August 1982 the World Alliance of Reformed Church (WARC) in Ottawa called apartheid a "sin" and that "anyone who justifies it on biblical and theological grounds is practising heresy". All these charges or criticisms demonstrate that there is an identity crisis in the NGK.

The WARC General Council argued that the NGK, is not only accepting, but actively justifying the apartheid ideology by misusing the Gospel and the Reformed faith, contradicts in doctrine and in action the promise it professes to believe. Thus the WARC declared that such a situation constitutes a *status confessionis* which means that it is not possible to differ in our opinion without seriously jeopardising the integrity of our common confession.

Indeed, the NGK faces the same dilemma with which the German churches were confronted in 1933: the dilemma of obedience to God or to certain influential men; the dilemma of the loss of its members, support and money or the "loss of its identity as church". The NGK must not only denounce racial discrimination (as the Cape Synod did in 1983), but also the rigid racial ideology of apartheid. It ought to do this because apartheid as a political policy as well as a pseudo-religious ideology, is rooted in racial prejudice. Indeed apartheid involves both the *Glaubensvragens* (questions of faith) and the *Emessensvragens* (questions of calculation).

Theology of Racial Unity
Historically, theology of racial unity in South Africa, is associated with the theological position of the "English-speaking churches" (ESC). When the Nationalists won the election in 1948, the election victory meant one thing to the NGK and something else to the ESC. For the NGK and its sister churches, the 1948 election victory of the Nationalists meant monitoring the implementation of a racial policy that the Afrikaans-speaking churches had advocated since 1857.[14]

For the ESC, the election victory of the Nationalists meant advocacy of the general principle of unity of the races. But the problem with ESC was that these churches never shifted from their advocacy of the general principle of unity of the races to concrete challenging of specific legislations. These churches' theological position with regard to race relations can be best understood against the backdrop of the role of the Christian Council of South Africa (CCSA) in South African politics. The CCSA was later known as the South African Council of Churches (SACC) of which most mainline ESC were members.

In 1949 the CCSA held a conference at Rosettenville near Johannesburg. This was the first ecumenical conference since the Nationalist Party (NP) had come to power. The CCSA conference drew resolutions that high-lighted its differences with the Afrikaans-speaking churches. One of the things that the CCSA stressed was unity. It emphasized that "beyond all differences remains the essential unity" and that "the real need for South Africa is not apartheid [or "separate development"] but unity through teamwork". The CCSA's affirmations at Rosettenville represented a meaningless attack on the unfolding policy of apartheid. Indeed, the CCSA's desire to maintain unity between Afrikaans and English speaking churches hampered its opposition to the apartheid policy.

Although the CCSA represented an official view opposed to apartheid, there was in fact little to distinguish it from the NGK. Historically, the CCSA had not been an unflinching champion of equality for blacks before 1948. That position was unlikely to change in the apartheid period. Racial segregation continued to be a part of both the CCSA member churches and the Dutch Reformed churches alike.

The opposition of CCSA member churches to the gradual entrenchment of apartheid was theologically rooted, but its effectiveness was hampered on several counts. Members of the CCSA member churches, for example, were considerably less enthusiastic about racial integration. Hence the majority of blacks in the CCSA were overwhelmed by white leadership. Consequently, the CCSA was not a genuine vehicle of black thought and expression prior to 1968. This white "counter-revolution" continued within the CCSA until 1968. There are reasons why this continued to be the case.

First, the CCSA could not speak convincingly because, as a body that advocated the general principle of unity of all races, it could not maintain credibility with the NGK.

Second, the CCSA's witness in matters of race relations was undermined by the fact that it was not made sufficiently clear that black members of the CCSA member churches were welcome at any altar. In other words, the CCSA member churches had not eliminated from within their own ranks what they were asking the apartheid regime to remove from the nation. This is still true of the ESC today.

Third, the majority of members in the CCSA member churches were black. However, these blacks were under white control. Thus the impact of blacks on church policy, especially with regard to racial policies was minor in relation to their members. On the other hand, the CCSA's positions against apartheid policy were ineffectively expressed by whites. Influenced by the existence of a large majority of black members within the structure of the CCSA member churches, these whites felt obligated to make meaningless positions against the prevailing racial policies.[15] Blacks within the CCSA could not effectively challenge racial policies of the time because of two basic reasons.

One reason was that the majority of blacks were poorly educated and often not comfortable with English which was used in church judiciaries. Beyond local black congregations, meetings were held in white urban areas and English was always used as the means of communication. Thus white delegates outnumbered blacks, and few blacks had the confidence or the training to express themselves effectively in English on a conference floor dominated by whites. A second reason for the lack of black influence in the CCSA was the existence of a "prominent strain of conservatism in the black community and in the black church in particular". This soon became noticeable at two levels.

First, the majority of blacks were more inclined to establish their own small organizations within the existing order rather than set out to reform that order. These organizations in which blacks held leadership positions, were revivalist and evangelical (i.e. pious or fundamentalist) in orientation. They concerned themselves mainly with saving souls and were thus apolitical. Thus Christianity in the black community became notably pietistic and other-worldly, promising later salvation in return for present social and political inequalities.

The church did not discourage such development both because whites wanted it to be so, and also because such religion provided a protection for blacks from the problems of having to make choices about action in this world. Furthermore, black clergymen who had attained positions of respect in the black community (by virtue of being ordained) were not inclined to jeopardize those positions by speaking openly about political issues. Thus the existence of conservatism in the black church made the CCSA's opposition to the rigid racial ideology of apartheid more weak and ineffective.

These trends continue to this day. Today, anti-apartheid churches (ESC) who are members of the SACC give in to the political policies of the apartheid regime despite the fact that they are unanimous in denouncing most government policies. The failure of churches which advocate a theology of racial unity is due to their inability to act in unison. Consequently, ESC find themselves making choices that are rarely between good and evil, but ones that are between evil and evil. Thus they are forced to decide which of the two is the lesser. But such a choice is deplorable and unchristian. The church much choose justice over injustice. However, such a choice is costly because it means laying one's life on the line "for the sake of Christ", to use D. Bonhoffer's terminology.

Today, Christians are faced with political repression and national crisis in South Africa. This is the time when many black political and religious leaders, together with their white allies, are detained without charge or trial. Indeed, it is an opportune time for the church to stand by the victims of the unjust and immoral laws of the country. The church also needs to seriously challenge the NGK's position with regard to apartheid. But the church is unable to assume the responsibilities that are required of it in the struggle for justice, freedom, equality, respect for human dignity, peace and reconciliation in our troubled land. In fact, the church in South Africa today, has become an ineffectual body. However, signs of a Confessing/Prophetic Church are emerging. This emerging church consists of men and women who advocate a theology of the voiceless even though they do not get support from their denominations.

Theology of the Voiceless

A theology of the voiceless is a representative theology. It is put forth on behalf of the victims of injustice and oppression who cannot speak out for themselves. Proponents of such a theology vehemently criticize South African church leaders for being hypocritical in their responses to the present crisis in South Africa. Church leaders are charged by this theology of pretending not to know that apartheid is, in fact, violent. But the same church leaders criticize counter-violence which is carried out by the victims of apartheid.

Furthermore, this theology indicts members of white churches in South Africa who pays taxes to the apartheid government, thus contributing directly to the Defence Budget of South Africa. It is an indisputable fact that a great deal of tax money is used to buy arms.

This money also provides military training for white youth and many of them are members of the South African churches. But the anti-violence church leaders in this country have not made press statements supporting the UN arms embargo on South Africa. Moreover, church leaders have not objected to white Christians' consistent funding of South Africa's form of institutionalized violence.

Such a silence of church leaders when one side of the shooting line (i.e. side of the white regime) is given support, is a clear indication that the real issue is not violence, but a commitment of the majority of white South Africans to apartheid even if it causes a lot of social injury to black South Africans.

Proponents of theology of the voiceless have reconciled the meaning of death and their ministry. They are prepared to lay their lives on on the line "for the sake of Christ", to use D. Bonhoffer's words. These men and women are not prepared to be silent when pastors in rural areas are conducting more funeral services than baptism services because of a high rate of infant mortality caused by malnutrition in a country that even exports food. They cannot keep silent in the face of mass funerals almost every weekend in urban centres as a result of police shootings. Pastoral visitation in urban areas is a dead concept because South Africa is increasingly becoming, if not already, a police state. Hence the following words of D. Bonhoffer are relevant here:

> The church [must confess] that she has witnessed the lawless application of brutal force, the physical and spiritual suffering of countless innocent people, oppression, hatred and murder, and that she has not raised her voice on behalf of the victims and has not found ways to hasten to their aid. She is guilty of the death of the weakest and most defenceless brothers [and sisters] of Jesus Christ... (*Ethics,* S.C.M. Press, London, 1971:91).

Conclusion
The church in South Africa needs to do three things with regard to the politics of our time. First, the church needs to develop a deeper understanding for the concern of the liberation movements, which, the South African political propaganda regards as "terrorist movements". Such an understanding will enable the church to stand on the side of the victims of political repression and national crisis in South Africa. By taking such a stand, the church will make its members aware of the necessary confrontation between the South African churches and the state. Moreover, the church will also enhance the credibility of its Christian and biblical concern for justice in the eyes of the liberation movements.

Second, the church must seriously raise one of the crucial questions namely, Christian integrity and consistency in opposing the use of violence. If the violence of freedom fighters (i.e. the so-called terrorists) is to be condemned, can Christians defend institutionalized violence? Moreover, if any person says that Afrikaners were justified in the use of violence in their struggle against "British imperialism", or that the British were justified in the use of violence to further their aims, "it is hypocritical to deny that the same applies to the black people in their struggle today".[18]

Third, the church as a confessing or covenant community, needs to raise its voice and to stand by the oppressed. John Calvin's words are relevant here when he said:

> None of the brethren can be injured, despised, rejected, abused or in any way offended by us without at the same time injuring, despising, rejecting and abusing Christ [by the wrongs we inflict on others] .... We cannot love Christ without loving Him in the brethren.[19]

Hence the church as a confessing community; as a community of the faithful; as a transcendent community must raise its voice against injustice and inequalities. Furthermore, the church "ought" to stand by the oppressed and take counsel from people like Calvin in statements such as the one quoted above.

In proposing a three-pronged strategy, I hope that the church will achieve three things. First, the church leaders will become honest with themselves. In other words, church leaders will use the same measuring rod in their condemnation of violence with regard to both the state and the liberation movements. Thus they will no longer be indicted with hypocrisy. Second, the church will regain and increase its credibility and Christian integrity among the masses who yearn for freedom from the chains of an evil and oppressive system. Third, the church will truly be serving God through its ministry to victims of apartheid or "separate development". But the church can achieve these objectives only if it is faithful to its calling.

Because its going to be difficult for the church to serve God and His people in South Africa today and in the months ahead, it will be worthwhile to remember the words of George Kennan when he said: "There comes a time in our lives when we have no choice but to listen to the dictates of our conscience, throw ourselves to the mercy of God, and stop asking questions."[20] Indeed, such a time or Kairos has come to South Africa. The time has come when our confession as Christians needs to be translated into concrete action so that we can effectively transform South Africa's unjust social and political order. I am taking such a position with full awareness of being a Christian and of being only responsible to God for my actions. All this flows from the love and lordship of the grace of our Lord Jesus Christ.

REFERENCE NOTES

1. c.f. W. Herberg's "Introduction" to Karl Barth's *Community, State and Church*, Peter Smith, Gloucester, 1968, p46
2. K. Barth, "Die Kirche und Politiesche Frage von Heute" in *Eine Schweizer Stimme*, 1938–1945, p87

3.   K. Barth, op cit, p46
4.   Quoted in Ibid, p46
5.   Ibid, p48
6.   c.f. S. Mzimela, *Apartheid: South African Nazism,* Vantage Press Inc., 1982. This study compares the church under Nazi Germany and the Dutch Reformed Church in apartheid South Africa.
7.   SACC, "The Kairos Document: Challenge to the Church" in *Journal of Theology for Southern Africa,* No 53, December 1985, p62.
8.   J.W. de Gruchy, *The Church Struggle in South Africa,* Wm. B. Eerdmans Publishing Co., Grand Rapids, 1979, p 218.
9.   The Great Trek was an exodus of Afrikaner farmers in about 1836 from the Cape to the interior and the north of South Africa. They were leaving in protest against the British government which, among other things, tended to require whites to treat blacks as human beings.
10.   E.P. Groenewald in G. Cronje, *Regverdige Rasse-apartheid (Just Racial Apartheid),* Stellenbosch, 1947, p 62
11.   Ibid
12.   J. Verkuyl, "The Dutch Reformed Church in South Africa and the Ideology and Practice of Apartheid" in the *United Nations,* Notes and Documents of the Unit Against Apartheid, Department of Political and Security Affairs, No. 2/71 February 1971, pp 6-7
13.   Ibid, p7
14.   In 1857, the Dutch Reformed Church Synod decided that due to the weakness of some, it was permissible to hold separate services for blacks and whites.
15.   E. Regehr, *Perceptions of Apartheid,* Herald Press, Scottdale, 1979, p158
16.   Ibid, p157
17.   Ibid
18.   J.W. de Gruchy, op cit, pp 140-141
19.   c.f. The preparatory paper on the question of racism with regard to South Africa for the General Council of the World Alliance of Reformed Churches, which met, August 17–27, 1982, Ottawa, Canada.
20.   c.f. P. Ramsey, *War and the Christian Conscience,* Duke University Press, Durham, N.C. 1961, pp161-2